Stanley Marcus

The Relentless Reign of a Merchant Prince

Thomas E. Alexander

State House Press
1 McMurry University, #637
Abilene, Texas 79697-0001
325-793-4682
www.mcwhiney.org

Cataloging-in-Publication Data

Names: Alexander, Thomas E., author., 1931- author
Title: Stanley Marcus: the relentless reign of a merchant prince |Thomas E. Alexander
Description: Trade paperback edition. |Abilene, TX: State House Press, 2018. | Includes bibliographical
references and index.
Identifiers: ISBN 9781933337746 (softcover)
Subjects: LCSH: Marcus, Stanley, 1905-2002. | Neiman-Marcus.
Classification: LLC HF5429.5.D2M37352018 (print) | DDC 381/.141092; B

This paper meets the requirements of ANSI/NISO, Z39.48-1992 (Permanence of Paper).
Binding materials have been chosen for durability.

Second edition 2018

Cover Design by Rosenbohm Graphic Design

Printed in the United States of America
Distributed by Texas A&M University Press Consortium
800-826-8911
www.tamupress.com

Contents

Acknowledgments

Unlike my four previous books that were built upon a framework forged by countless resources, colleagues, advisors and well-intentioned critics-in-advance, this work required just a handful of wonderful people to bring it to fruition.

First, of course, the obvious inspiration for it all was the inimitable Stanley Marcus himself. Although I was never in any way his protégé, he did abide my frequent missteps while constantly pushing me toward becoming far more than I could have otherwise been. The counsel he provided frequently came hard. His bite was sometimes worse than his mellifluous bark, but after my many miscues were sternly made clear to me, he was quick to praise what little he found to be praiseworthy in our early years together.

In time, urged on by his hundreds of daily memos and countless phone calls at all hours, I finally began to figure it all out. More important, however, he somehow seemed to sense that I was going to figure it all out. Eventually, he began to trust me to follow the marketing trail he had so boldly blazed and relentlessly maintained at Neiman Marcus for so many years.

To be frank about it, there were many times when his insistence on perfection, fueled by his mercurial genius, caused me far more than a little grief, but what I cherish most among my many memories of Stanley Marcus are the words he inscribed in my copy of his 1974 autobiography. "For Tom Alexander," he wrote, "who has brought satisfaction to me personally through his ability to learn from me and improve on my favorite job in the store."

It has taken me much too long to write this book but I have been encouraged to keep at it by many people. Richard Marcus and Jerrie Marcus Smith, Stanley's son and daughter, have been most helpful and supportive. I thank them both.

Dr. Russell L. Martin III, Director and Librarian of the DeGolyer Library which houses the Stanley Marcus Collection at Southern Methodist University, has been of immense assistance. He has put up with me for nearly six years while my wife and I have pawed our way through the three hundred cubic feet of Marcus archival material to be found in his library. Dr. Martin's staff, Cynthia Franco and Anne Peterson in particular, always proved to be both highly efficient and warmly courteous in the clearly tedious if not downright maddening work of finding and transporting heaps upon heaps of archival files to the table of an often impatient researcher. Thanks to them all.

Carol Roark and Brian Collins at the downtown Dallas Public Library helped us find many precious items that I knew had once existed but feared might have disappeared altogether. Where else could one hope to find a 1984 photograph of the Queen of Thailand dancing the "Texas Two-Step" with a cowboy on the 6666 Ranch? Their tireless detective work among the hidden and restricted stacks of the library produced much that not only stirred a flood of memories but also proved to be highly useful as well.

My daughter Ann Alexander Leggett, who has heard some of my "Stanley Stories" for years, often got me back to work recording them in print by simply asking the loaded question, "When?" My step-daughter Michelle Cummings was another equally effective motivator when my interest in pursuing this labor of love temporarily faded in favor of some exciting new military history writing project. My thanks to them both.

Finally but foremost, there is my wife Capy. She has never flagged in her dogged determination that someday I must write this book. Fellow researcher, computer whiz, and the most severe of any editor anywhere, she simply would not allow me to abandon the idea of writing about the remarkable man we both knew and admired so greatly.

I first met Capy more than thirty years ago when we both worked at Neiman Marcus in downtown Dallas. I guess in some totally unintentional way, Stanley Marcus brought us together. For that, I cannot ever give him thanks enough. If he were alive today, I would buy him a beer.

Meeting a Prince

The newspapers had dubbed Stanley Marcus "America's Merchant Prince" by the time he turned twenty-one and kept at it even after his death three quarters of a century later. Although he claimed that he disliked the colorful journalistic title, saying that it made him uncomfortable, it is easy for those of us who knew him to speculate that the hint of royalty, albeit a reign in a retailing empire, did not truly make him uncomfortable at all.

At a chamber of commerce banquet in St. Louis in 1972, he was introduced to his fellow diners as "The world's most famous Merchant Prince." Standing to acknowledge the applause that followed, he muttered almost inaudibly, "I always wonder how you get to be a Merchant King."

Prince or king, Stanley Marcus was undeniably a merchant. Biographers who cling to the "great man theory" rather than embrace the "great event philosophy" seem to take pleasure in pondering if heredity or environment made their subject truly great. In Stanley's case, it was a rare combination of the two.

1

From the Marcus gene pool that he shared with his father, Herbert, and his aunt, Carrie, he acquired an innate sense of fashion, an appreciation for the highest quality, and an absolutely relentless urge to make a sale. The fortuitous fact that Herbert and Carrie had co-founded a store called Neiman Marcus in Dallas just two years after he was born gave him direct access to the retail environment within which he was destined to excel.

Along the way, and strictly on his own, he somehow also developed a world-class knack for showmanship and how to generate often outrageous publicity. These two acquired traits, uncommon among twentieth century retailers, combined with both his natural born gifts and a brick and mortar store to showcase his talents, served to propel the Neiman Marcus he inherited in 1950 into an international institution unlike any other. It became, under his soft but firm touch of genius, a retailing empire more worthy of king than a mere prince.

In the process, the names "Stanley Marcus" and "Neiman Marcus" became virtually synonymous and would remain so for the better part of the twentieth century. Both born in Dallas, the store and the man grew to epitomize all that was elegant, sophisticated, and fashionable in a town that only a few years before had been little more than a dusty rough-and-tumble cotton market center that boasted far more saloons than it could claim churches. The coming of the exciting era of big oil in the early 1900s quickly changed the face of Dallas. Under the gifted leadership of Herbert and his sister Carrie, Neiman Marcus gave that new face an enduring look of beauty unlike that of any other Texas city at the time.

It was, however, for the son and nephew to robustly capitalize on that which good genes and an equally good fortune had bestowed upon him. The little Neiman Marcus store grew in lock step with the seemingly endless rivers of sweet crude oil that gushed forth from the hard baked soil of Texas, both east and west. As a direct result, its future seemed secure by the time the brash young Harvard graduate, heir apparent to it all, came back to Dallas to try his wings at the shop his family had founded not quite twenty years earlier. It was he who would soon enough transform it from a respectable if conservative ladies-ready-to-wear salon into an unparalleled jewel among all retail stores. At the same time, he would make of himself an internationally known Renaissance Man, a nearly infallible arbiter of all that was impeccably correct and fashionable. Like it or not, Stanley Marcus had indeed become America's Merchant Prince.

When I first met Stanley in the fall of 1965, he had already enjoyed a nearly forty year reign. As a relative newcomer to the heady world of luxury retailing at the time, my somewhat fearful apprehension at the prospect of coming face to face with the colossus who continued to dominate the very top echelon of all retailing, I reasoned, was understandable but as it developed on that memorable day, unfortunately far too accurate.

My meeting with him had been arranged by a retailing placement agency in response to both Stanley's request that their specialists find a new sales promotion director for his store and by my far more urgent request to find a better job. The plan called for us to meet for breakfast at the Sherry Netherland Hotel located on New York City's Fifth Avenue. Having been repeatedly instructed by my agency contact that Mr. Marcus placed great value on promptness, I arrived at the hotel's coffee shop a full ten minutes ahead of schedule, only to find that the great man was already finished with his breakfast and was halfway through smoking a particularly pungent if likely illegal Havana cigar.

At sixty years of age, Stanley Marcus, sitting that morning in his blue cloud of Cuban tobacco smoke, had an unusual but nevertheless striking appearance. To a reporter for the *Washington Post*, he had seemed to be only an inch taller than short. Though somewhat heavy set, he never became truly portly despite a prodigious appetite for a limitless palette of food that ranged from the most exotic of international cuisine to the hottest and greasiest bowl of rough hewn Texas style chili imaginable.

His complexion was the color of an almost albino olive, accented by a beard that became his virtual trademark even as it changed over the years from a flecked grey to Santa Claus white. The bald dome that went from his brow to well past the crown of his head was noble in the sense that any Roman emperor would have taken pride in it. An artist once rather infamously borrowed, without its owner's permission, the image of Stanley's head and face to adorn the body of one of the Pharisees depicted in a Biblical mural.

Curiously, from the moment he first affected the beard until his death nearly a half century later, Stanley's appearance never seemed to drastically change. To be sure, advancing age inevitably served to diminish him in size but never in stature. His gait, always confident and purposeful, faltered in time and eventually came to rely on walking sticks and such for support, but somehow he seemed, at least to me, to remain more or less the same as he had appeared in the smoky half light of a hotel restaurant on that cold and rainy big city morning.

His face that usually seemed an inscrutable mask could also burst into a light every bit as bright as a desert sun when something or someone triggered what I later discovered to be a slapstick and often ribald sense of humor. His eyes, some said, were avian. When the brilliant but often fickle focus of his attention ran its course and grew dim, almost invisible translucent shutters not unlike those of an emu appeared to move across his eyes, signaling to those who knew him at least moderately well that their allotted time in his presence had expired.

At that first New York meeting, one of a series of job interviews that did not bear fruit until some five years later, the bird's-eye shutters must have come down early on, but I was not yet adept at reading that telltale signal. After inquiring about my views on the artwork of Paul Klee, how I felt about the prospects for the desalinization of sea water on a grand commercial level, and other curious topics totally alien to me, I can now only assume that my responses were unsatisfactory or at least not satisfactory enough to delay him from far more promising activities in Manhattan.

Perhaps annoyed that I could not read his eyes, or just plain bored, he promptly ground out the partially smoked cigar in the yellow core of a half-eaten egg and quickly rose to his feet. Clearly, neither the breakfast, nor the Havana, nor the interview with the job applicant had been to his liking and after an unenthusiastic handshake that yielded little promise of ever being repeated, he strode off, giving me the distinct impression that the interview had not gone well at all. I doubted I would ever see him again, and indeed I did not for almost two years.

Being the sales promotion director at Neiman Marcus at the time meant holding the somewhat impressive and enviable title of senior vice president of a retailing institution that had no peers in Dallas or indeed, by 1965, anywhere in the world. It also carried with it the daunting challenge of being judged on an almost hourly basis by the man whose family name was on the store's front door. In time, the job description became modernized to director of marketing in order to more adequately reflect the expanded scope of the office's responsibilities. While the title changed over the years, the hovering presence of Stanley Marcus, the master of marketing, remained a very real and constant companion as well as an equally very real and constant threat to long term employment.

Because of this, sales promotion directors by whatever title came and went from Neiman Marcus headquarters with an almost predictable regularity. During the mid-1960s, the average tenure of the job was a short twelve months, giving the New York headhunters fertile ground upon which to ply their trade.

From time to time, I would receive a call telling me that Stanley was once again on the prowl because the latest sales promotion/

marketing man at the store had failed to live up to his lofty initial expectations. About every other year, I would make what became a routine and familiar trek to Dallas to go through the time tested interview ordeal, but now in Stanley's often smoke-filled lion's den rather than a New York hotel coffee shop.

That lion's den was almost as unique as the man who occupied it. One entire wall was all but plastered with certificates reflecting the recognition and appreciation of countless nations, states, and organizations both large and small. The teak furniture was as cold and impersonal as the Scandinavian countries whose craftsmen had created the various pieces. Artwork was almost starkly contemporary while the few glass shelves held a cross-grain representation of whatever collectible curiosity currently held the attention of the occupant of the office.

As new fascinations came onto his limitless collecting scope, items ranging from first edition Italian books to fertility symbols from New Guinea's Sepik River would come and go, only to be replaced by some other often priceless knickknack that his endless travels and insatiable curiosity had yielded.

The man's desk itself was a lovely Danish creation, likely hand crafted from a single slab of the rarest of teakwood. Not that this mattered, however, because except for the gracefully turned legs, the piece was without fail buried beneath unkempt teetering mounds of paper. Newspaper clippings, sales reports, as well as page upon page of personal and business correspondence often overflowed the broad surface of the desk to cascade to the floor where they would remain untouched until a bustling secretary policed the office between appointments, making sure that each errant sheet was placed back in its proper stack on his desk.

The same mountains of paper provided Stanley with another exit device should his visitors somehow miss the trick of the dropping emu eyelids. As soon as he had harvested all that he wanted from the person seated across the desk and thus perhaps too far away to catch the eye signal, Stanley would abruptly stop talking, or listening, and begin to slowly forage around in the towering stacks much as a squirrel might casually rummage through mounds of dry leaves in search of a misplaced acorn. As the often bewildered visitor looked on in amazement, the search would go on interminably, until such time as it became painfully obvious that no more words were going to be either spoken or heard. Thus dismissed and in essence discarded, the hapless visitor could only rise and silently make for the doorway without the benefit of anything that sounded like either thank you or goodbye.

It was during my third interview that the routine was changed to some degree. Leaving the cordial and by now well-acquainted group of other would-be sales promotion directors convened in the outer lobby awaiting their interviews, I entered the familiar office. For the first time in our long series of fruitless visits, Stanley arose from behind his desk with its towers of paper and, after motioning me to a hard-as-a-rock Danish chair, took a seat across from me. There were no pleasantries exchanged and no inquiries about how my trip, this time all the way from Seattle, had gone thus far. Allowing that he had but five minutes to spare, Stanley instantly asked my views on the architectural work of Louis Sullivan. Fortunately, I knew a little something of Sullivan's work in Chicago, but before I could fully expound on the subject even to the tiny limit of my knowledge, he looked at his watch and then announced that I had two minutes to present my definition of the term "marketing."

As I really did not at the time have the slightest idea about marketing, at least in the academic sense, I mumbled something about Colonel Sanders and the success of his Kentucky Fried Chicken marketing scheme and was just warming up to Ray Kroc and what he had done for the lowly McDonald's ten-cent hamburger when somewhere between my ramblings about cheeseburgers and the famous French fries, Stanley abruptly stood, thus announcing that my time was up.

With no handy papers behind which to secret himself, he had no option but to shake my hand and walk me to the door. As I turned to leave, he smiled and, of all things, winked. On the plane flying home, it suddenly occurred to me that maybe he hadn't winked at all. Maybe it was just one of those emu-lids coming slowly downward over his left eye to tell me he had been only half-bored this time. As things developed, that must have been the case.

Two weeks later, I was on my way back to Dallas to begin a nearly twenty year stint as the executive vice president for marketing at Neiman Marcus, courtesy, I suppose, of architect Sullivan, Ray Kroc, the inexpensive hamburger king, and old Colonel Sanders himself.

Laying the Foundation

The little store that grew to become the internationally known Neiman Marcus had a humble beginning. It opened in 1907 on the corner of Elm and Murphy Street in what was then the heart of the retail district of a Dallas that was still years away from becoming the "Big D" of fact and fiction.

While the building was small, measuring only fifty by one hundred feet, the rent was unusually large at a then exorbitant rate of $9,000 per year. Upon signing the lease, Herbert Marcus, his sister Carrie, and her husband, Abraham Lincoln Neiman, gave their new firm the grand if not particularly imaginative name, "The Neiman Marcus Company." After paying the first year's rent in advance, the partners had less than $17,000 to purchase the merchandise needed to fill the rented racks and shelves.

Under-capitalized, under-stocked, and seriously over-extended by the terms of their lease, the founding trio surely must have recognized the urgent need to formulate a business plan that would enable their enterprise to stay long afloat. It is a wonder that the three young people, whose average age was less than twenty-seven, arrived at, or even agreed upon, a sustainable marketing strategy that might give them enough of a competitive edge to at least break even for the first few years. However, their ultimate strategy would not only bring them instant success but also provide a firm foundation for a prosperous multi-store national retailing institution that would endure and flourish for the next hundred years.

A transplant from Louisville, Kentucky, Herbert was twenty-seven when his son Stanley was born in Dallas in 1905. Having never finished high school, he made up for his lack of formal schooling by constantly reading, with a special emphasis on the classics. Tall and handsome, the new father had begun his retailing career as a janitor for the Sanger Brothers store in Dallas and then moved up the ladder of responsibility by becoming first a traveling salesman, then a ladies' shoe clerk, and eventually a buyer of boys' apparel. With just enough money in his pocket to give him confidence, he soon asked the diminutive Miss Minnie Lichtenstein to become his wife, despite the strong disapproval of him openly voiced by her parents. Being immigrants and conservative in the European tradition, the Lichtensteins viewed Herbert's tendency to be what they considered a flashy dresser as an indication that he was untrustworthy. Based on what proved to be a grossly inaccurate assumption, they obviously were incorrect in perceiving him to be a man with limited prospects for success.

The nattily attired Herbert had a natural talent as a salesman, and his early success fueled an ambition that drove him rapidly upward. Working for other stores but being denied what he felt to be his well-earned reward soon prompted him to strike out on his own. When Sanger Brothers failed to promote him rapidly enough to satisfy his increasingly restless ambition, he left the company in 1905 to join his sister Carrie and her husband, known to the family as Al, in a retail venture in Atlanta, Georgia.

Referred to only as a "sales-promotion business" in most accounts,

the retail undertaking involved helping small rural Georgia stores re-
duce their inventories through sidewalk sales and similar events. It
proved successful enough in just under two years to be sold for a then
respectable amount of $25,000. In later years, Stanley Marcus would
delight in telling the story of what became of that nest egg. Family tradition had it that Herbert, Carrie, and Al were offered the franchise in
either Missouri or Kansas for a new taste sensation called "Coca-Cola"
in exchange for their sales promotion enterprise. To walk away from a
statewide franchise for such a potentially successful new beverage in
favor of returning to Texas to open a store of their own seemed far-
fetched and risky to many of the Marcus clan. The younger Marcus
often regaled business page editors years later with the observation
that his retailing empire was founded on his father's bad business
judgment.

Early in 1907, the trio of ex-Atlantans, Herbert, Carrie, and husband Al, brought their money back to Dallas and began looking for a
site from which to enter the retailing fray in direct competition with
their former employers. These stores included Sanger Brothers, Titche-
Goettinger, and A. Harris, where Carrie had once worked as a buyer
of ladies' blouses.

In the years to come, many questions were asked about what led
to the new store's nearly instantaneous success. Were the young and
relatively inexperienced founders of Neiman Marcus truly gifted and
natural marketing geniuses, as some have suggested? Or were they
simply smart enough to understand the Dallas retailing scene for what
it was in 1907, and clever enough to quickly and perceptively move
to offer something totally different?

According to the written words of Herbert Marcus, who was the
store's only advertising copywriter in addition to being one of its
founders, he and his two partners had studied the Dallas retail market
carefully. He and his sister had come to know much about the city's
shoppers firsthand during their years as salespeople in other stores in

town. They had heard complaints about the sameness of the merchandise and about the absence of quality ready-made dresses on the racks. They had seen the crowded aisles and the gloomy darkness that hung over the cluttered countertops at Sanger and A. Harris. In their new store, Herbert and Carrie deliberately set out to meet the clearly expressed needs of the shoppers they had once served. This unstructured but apparently intentional early form of a marketing research focus group proved invaluable in identifying the store's prime target market.

In the company's first newspaper advertisement that Herbert wrote for the September 8, 1907, edition of *The Dallas Morning News*, the founding trio's marketing strategy was clearly set forth:

> Our decision to conduct a store in Dallas was not reached on impulse. We studied the field thoroughly and saw there was a real necessity for a shopping place such as ours. Our preparations have not been hasty.

The ad went on to invite the confidence of all those who had shopped at stores elsewhere in town. One line in the ad copy established a tenet that ran through the store's marketing philosophy for more than seventy years until an epidemic of nationwide expansion saw once strictly local retailing giants crossing state lines to bring, for example, New York's Bloomingdale's to Dallas, Chicago's Marshall Field's to Houston, and even a Neiman Marcus to many cities far away from Texas. That tenet was exclusivity.

> We have secured exclusive lines that have never been shown in Texas before . . . garments that stand in a class alone as to character and fit . . . only the finest productions of the best are good enough for us.

The first ad, eagerly read by Dallas society women grown weary of waiting for dressmakers at local tailor shops to create something for them to wear to the next cotillion, was written with a colorful hyperbole that was in vogue during the first part of the twentieth century. The store was described by Herbert, its copywriting founder, as a "store of quality, a specialty store" with "wider varieties and more exclusive lines than any other store in the South." If those claims were a bit exaggerated, no one in Dallas was likely to care. What the shoppers at the new store did know for certain was that they were finding exciting apparel unlike any they had ever seen at other stores in town. Herbert and Carrie had learned through experience what the women of Dallas desired and then cleverly edited their merchandise offerings to satisfy those desires.

When it came to store layout and design, the founders of Neiman Marcus believed it was essential to give their high-quality merchandise more than enough room to be seen and appreciated. The aisles were broader than those in the competitors' stores, the counters neater, and the lighting a bit softer and more flattering to both clientele and merchandise alike. The paneling was of red mahogany while the carpet was a billiard table green. This expensive dedication to a pleasant ambiance was to prevail for a century. In making certain that customers felt good about themselves from the moment they walked into his store, Herbert perhaps instinctively knew that the first hurtle to successful merchandising and strong sales production had been cleared.

To ensure the loyalty of each and every customer that he lured away from the longer established Dallas stores by his eloquent advertising copy, Herbert set forth another enduring cornerstone of the company philosophy. "We want to sell satisfaction, not just merchandise," he wrote in another ad. That guarantee of satisfaction worked both ways, as Herbert frequently pointed out to his son over the years. By not irritating a dissatisfied customer with rigid rules and regulations about merchandise return policies, store management was, and continues to be, pleasantly willing to refund any disputed amount to keep every valued customer in the fold. The loss of a few dollars on a single transaction paled in comparison to the hundreds of thousands of dollars potentially to be lost in future sales should the spurned and unhappy shopper storm out of the building never to return.

Stanley Marcus often told his senior lieutenants and other key employees that it was far better to lose an immediate battle with an unhappy customer in order to win the war of keeping her as a longtime client. It was a lesson he had been taught by his father, and finding it to be both valid and timeless, he passed it along to us. When I eventually came to the store, my office was the first to be found by an irate customer hotly steaming toward Stanley's den next door. I often experienced the initial attack wave of a battle we were already committed to lose, by virtue of a chief executive decree, in order to ensure her eternal patronage.

This devout dedication to customer service set Neiman Marcus apart from its competitors, who still stubbornly adhered to the self-serving adage, "let the buyer beware." In the time honored tradition of frontier horse trading, anyone who fell for a slick and spurious sales pitch had no one to blame but himself and no hope for recovery of his funds. In turn-of-the-century Texas retailing, once money had changed hands, there was no getting it back short of brandishing a six-shooter.

By adhering to a well-planned but simple marketing philosophy, the team of Marcus and the two Neimans had found the path to an almost instant success. Through the offering of a well-edited selection of mostly exclusive lines of merchandise of indisputable quality in an attractive environment staffed by knowledgeable salespeople devoted to satisfying each customer, a winning template was formed that would endure for generations.

Herbert realized early on that good news about a euphoric and memorable shopping experience had a way of spreading. Through their almost uncanny ability to offer the then largely provincial women of Dallas the exciting fashions of the world coupled with impeccable service, Herbert and Carrie quickly established the Neiman Marcus reputation for being the ultimate place to shop. Gone, or at least going, was the nineteenth century ordeal of trudging through store after dreary store in search of just the right dress, gown, or shoe. It soon became apparent to Dallas society that if Neiman Marcus did not have it, no store in town would. On the off chance that the dress that had seemed so very right in the fitting room at the store did not fare as well in the mirror at home, Neiman Marcus would gladly take it back and refund the money with absolutely no questions asked. What dedicated upscale shopper could possibly resist such a pleasant win-win experience? As history would prove, very few indeed.

A few years later, looking back on the store's bold and, for the time, revolutionary philosophies, Herbert Marcus seemed to breathe a sigh of relief when he wrote in another advertisement:

> [The store's] impetus . . . led by spare means but unlimited ambitions succeeded by all peradventures of doubt [and] the clouds soon gave way to sunshine.

There was always an appealing earnestness in the writings of the elder Marcus. Although a largely uneducated reader of Plutarch's *Lives* and Gibbons' *The Decline and Fall of the Roman Empire*, he was naturally gifted when it came to writing candidly about what he believed. His obvious sincerity won him the trust of his readers. Of the many assets of character and talent he passed on to his first son, this ability to write with a conviction that seemed to flow straight from the heart was among the more important.

If the elder Marcus harbored any sibling rivalry with his sister and co-founder Carrie Neiman there is no record of it to be found. To the contrary, the brother seemed to take every opportunity to publicly praise his sister who was five years younger than he. Described by those who knew her, Carrie was said to be beautiful, sloe-eyed, elegant, and quiet but forceful, yet most commonly she was seen to have been a natural-born selector of high fashion apparel. Her clientele apparently worshipped both her and the seasonal wardrobes she personally picked for them on buying trips to New York and eventually other fashion markets around the world. Her professional credo, somewhat different than the more structured and traditional views of her brother, stated that "There are no rules in the fashion business." In her own right, Carrie established Neiman Marcus as a national leader by sensing what was right in any fashion season and what was likely to wither and die on the racks, unsold in other stores.

In the absence of any firm rules, Carrie surveyed what the fashion markets had to offer with a practical eye toward specific customers in her market. She selected apparel that made more sense in Dallas than in New York City. For example, when the cut of one season's popular high fashion designs seemed too slim for the sometimes more fully proportioned Texas women, she asked designers to modify the lines to suit her clientele. Knowing that the big brimmed hats favored by the ladies who strolled down New York's Fifth Avenue in the early 1900s would not fare well in the gusty winds of Texas, she demanded and received more aerodynamic and at least somewhat gale resistant adaptations. That Carrie Marcus Neiman could at the age of twenty-four so quickly earn the respect of the big city fashion houses is an indication of her common sense disdain for the "rules" in buying merchandise, and her ability to persuade the suppliers to yield to the demands of their clientele.

Perhaps as a protective bulwark against the constant ebbing and flowing of the fashion palette, she nearly always wore black with a single strand of pure white pearls at her throat as the only touch of contrast. Photographs and oil portraits of Mrs. Neiman depict a strong willed but somewhat sad individual. Her stormy and ultimately doomed marriage to Al no doubt contributed to this apparent unhappiness, but her eyes, still magnetic today as she peers out from aging film or fading canvas, tell of the decisive no-nonsense soul that dwelled within. If indeed there are no rules in the world of fashion, there can be little doubt that Carrie Marcus Neiman had any number of rules of her own when it came to being the mistress of merchandise at the store she had helped establish.

She never had an office in the building and usually took her lunch in the form of a quick sandwich in one of the fitting rooms. If she saw a client walking toward a store exit empty handed, Carrie would all but block her path, insisting that some new item had just come in and must be seen immediately. Her nephew, once old enough to watch his aunt in action, learned from her the art of aggressively pursuing a potential sale until it became a reality and entered in the day's accounting. He later became a master at the technique his aunt had taught him frequently pursuing reluctant customers to unbelievable lengths, doing whatever was necessary to make the sale.

There are many students of the Neiman Marcus mystique who believe that it was Carrie Neiman's impeccable fashion selections that lent visible credence to the overstated and often overblown advertising copy of her brother. The $17,000 worth of dresses and gowns that she bought for the soon-to-be-opened store sold out to the piece within one month's time. Her first foray into the potentially hazardous New York City fashion arena was a rousing success. When asked about it years later, Carrie smiled wanly and said, "I have not been a success. The Store is a success." In emphasizing the word "store," Carrie might have created what was to become a Lone Star custom. In Texas, other stores were referred to by their proper name. Neiman Marcus was, and remains, simply "The Store."

Her husband Al was the exact opposite of both his shy and quiet wife and her serious minded brother. Flamboyant and darkly handsome, he had a violent temper and was given to venting his rage on hapless employees in public as shocked customers looked on. When not on one of his frequent rampages, however, Al Neiman could be smooth and charming.

Stanley considered his Uncle Al to be a volatile man, too full of himself and too fond of his own opinions to be the sort of team player the fledgling store required. He overheard enough conversations at home to know that his father, the quiet dreamer and master salesman, had little use for his sarcastic and overbearing brother-in-law. In his autobiography, *Minding the Store*, Stanley recalled that the two male founders of the store clashed frequently about how the business should be run and that as success came, the arguments grew increasingly contentious.

Herbert, as president, wanted the fledgling business to become firmly established on the basis of outstanding relations with its new customers regardless of the initial expense involved. Al, the money man, was more interested in extracting every possible penny in profit from the dollars generated from the merchandise that was sold. Too, friction arose early on when Al was suspected of working with certain vendors to cut back on quality to lower the wholesale price of the goods. By buying for less and selling at a high price, the profit margin was to Al's satisfaction but not at all in keeping with Herbert's often repeated pledge of quality assurance.

Despite the tensions that existed between the male founders, Neiman Marcus experienced a rapidly escalating level of acceptance by the public and increasing sales volumes. With Carrie selecting the goods, at least initially with the support of her husband, and Herbert leading the selling and customer relations aspects of the business, the original $25,000 investment soon began to pay dividends. Unlike most newly born retail stores, Neiman Marcus realized a profit in one year and repeated that feat for each of the next six years in a row. In its first year, the store's profit was just over $9,000. In 1913, its last full year of doing business before it was leveled by fire, the Elm Street store posted a profit of nearly $20,000.

The city of Dallas, the rough cotton market town of the early 1900s, began to grow and prosper just as did Neiman Marcus. During a banquet speech in 1982, newspaper humorist Art Buchwald pondered the relationship between the town and the store. "There are some people who say there wouldn't have been a Neiman Marcus if there hadn't been a Dallas," he chuckled, "and there are others who say there wouldn't have been a Dallas if there hadn't been a Neiman Marcus."

Stanley himself was frequently asked why Neiman Marcus had been founded in Dallas rather than Atlanta or some other city in which the Marcus family or Al Neiman had connections. His responses varied from time to time, depending on the enthusiasm of his audience, but the most consistent and logical motive he offered was the obvious fact that Dallas was home to the closely knit Marcus and Lichtenstein clans. If his in-laws had as yet grown fond of Herbert as early as 1907 is not known, but it is clear from letters sent from his wife in Atlanta to her parents, that Minnie Lichtenstein Marcus was very eager to come home to Dallas. It is easy to speculate that she played a major role in the decision to return to Texas. Too, Herbert and Carrie had a large extended Marcus family living in the city.

This strong family factor, enhanced by their keen knowledge of the local retail scene likely made the decision to open the new store in their hometown an easy one for the founders to make. Later, Stanley would claim that his father and his aunt did not come back to Dallas with any intention of creating a legend, but rather to be close to their relatives and to make a suitable living in the process,

A good number of those relatives were given jobs at the store over the years. His nephew, for example, became Herbert's chauffeur when the growing profits made such a luxury possible, and an aged uncle was given a stipend to sit in a rocking chair near the front door just to welcome incoming shoppers.

Neiman Marcus benefited directly from its association with Dallas. The two entities grew up together and prospered together and some of the store's fabled mystique indeed stemmed directly from its historic link with the Texas city. It is doubtful that even Herbert's heart and intellect, Carrie's intuitive fashion expertise, and Al's talent for handling financial matters would have led to as much success in Chicago, St. Louis, or Atlanta in 1907. Dallas was a relatively unsophisticated city when Neiman Marcus appeared on the corner of Elm Street in September of that year. While the ladies in most other cities of any respectable size had plenty of fashion-wise emporiums to guide their steps, Dallas did not. Fortunately for the new store, Texans hungered for its advice.

Later, when the store's reputation as the arbiter of taste began to emerge on a national level, it was the perceived incongruity of the sophisticated elegance of Neiman Marcus flourishing in the still rustic, provincial Dallas that gave the store's mystique its earliest wings. As many Americans perceived it, Dallas was the rough from which the diamond-like Neiman Marcus so brightly shone.

Just two years after the store opened, the newly chartered Dallas Chamber of Commerce set about launching one of the most aggressive city building campaigns in the nation's history. Lacking any traditional growth magnets such as seaports or navigable waterways, Dallas simply created itself on a barren plain without any particularly redeeming geological features. However, using a burgeoning railway system as a catalyst, it soon became a major center for business and banking.

The city built new parks and public buildings, all the while luring large financial institutions and major insurance companies to open headquarters along its newly paved streets. An elegant union station was opened and railway tracks were relocated away from the downtown area. Southern Methodist University, one of the Southwest's most prestigious private schools, came into being in part because Herbert Marcus led the efforts to open a "Harvard of the Southwest." As certain more ardent boosters saw it, Harvard was actually the "SMU of the Northeast."

As the new banks and other businesses opened, more potential customers arrived to be wooed by the siren song of Neiman Marcus advertising. Most store advertising in the early twentieth century placed the emphasis solely on price. Products were occasionally acclaimed as being "new" or "improved" but in Dallas, few stores used expensive newspaper space to tout such intangible benefits as customer satisfaction or quality. Neiman Marcus was the first store to articulate a retail philosophy while promoting its merchandise. Perhaps dazzled by the quick success of his store, Herbert began to include compelling superlatives to describe Neiman Marcus. Such soaring phrases as "The world's most luxurious furs" and "the South's finest store" began to appear in the newspaper ads. Even if success had given his muse a touch of swagger, it is clear that the clientele flocking into the little shop on Elm Street accepted what he wrote as gospel.

When a fire destroyed the Elm Street shop in 1914, the often squabbling partners at least temporarily put an end to what had become heated disagreements about who should be in charge, how to more profitably expand the business, what new lines to carry, and just how liberal the merchandise return policy should actually be. A united team once again, the partnership promptly opened a much larger store in a lavish new building constructed for them uptown at Main and Ervay Streets. Often expanded but forever elegant, this became and remains the flagship Neiman Marcus store. To many, the classic old original is still the best of the more contemporary company stores that now stand in cities across America.

Herbert wrote about the Elm Street fire both eloquently and, as always, from his heart. "A disastrous fire drove the ship from its moorings and nearly set it adrift," he wrote to his customers. His knack for hyperbole still well intact, he assured everyone that the new store, "anchored deep enough in North Texas bedrock to allow for future growth skyward," would carry "the best merchandise lines in the world." What Neiman Marcus was now able to offer its customers was as Herbert so proudly put it, an even larger "stock of merchandise that would reflect credit on the largest city in the land."

At a time when people's access to high fashion depended on the limited availability of locally made garments, Neiman Marcus's stock of ready-made quality merchandise was the foundation of its growing legend. Exclusivity would also continue to be a basis for the store's appeal. In working with the best manufacturers to gain an exclusive line or label, Neiman Marcus offered prime selling floor locations within the store for the goods to be displayed. Advertising agreements were also negotiated that gave the exclusive brand a clear priority over any other even remotely similar items. Sales people received slightly higher commissions by selling those garments that were available only at the store.

Although the new building was nearly eight times larger than the first one, it still featured the concept of specially edited selections of merchandise. Everything that had initially spelled success downtown on Elm Street was magnified uptown on Main. The aisles were even wider and always highly-polished, the lighting still soft and flattering. A well dressed and courteous sales staff that exuded a combination of knowledge and sincere willingness to be of service was always on hand to assist the growing legions of well-to-do shoppers who glided through its doors.

The newly opened store not only weathered the national economic and social chaos that came with America's entry into World War I in 1917, but in fact benefited from it. Although the discontinuation of imports from Europe at the beginning of the conflict did hurt the fashion apparel business, the all-out push to discover and develop new sources of oil to fuel the machines of war quickly translated into a booming economy for the petroleum-rich state of Texas.

Oil, Texas, and Neiman Marcus thus became forever intertwined in the public consciousness. Although Stanley Marcus later would bristle slightly at any hint that it was solely, or even principally, oil that had early on propelled the store's profits to almost stratospheric heights, there can be little doubt that the massive flow of spendable income generated by the crude oil flowing from deep beneath the plains of Texas did do wonders for the profit ledger of the firm.

A large number of Neiman Marcus customers at that time became latter-day Cinderellas, uneducated wives of poor cotton sharecroppers made fabulously wealthy literally overnight by gushing wells that spewed riches from their hardscrabble land. By turning to Neiman Marcus, they entered a world of instant cachet, social mobility, and self-assurance that first set the tone for the emergence of Dallas as a fashion capital. Neiman Marcus helped the *nouveau riche* confidently change their station in the world, and in return, the new customers gave the store their everlasting loyalty and many of their dollars.

Colorful if apocryphal stories of barefoot, oil-splattered country women rushing into the Dallas store with the plaintive demand, "Dress me!" were something of a tribute to the marketing and fashion acumen of Herbert Marcus and his sister. No such tales circulated with any other Texas store as the subject. Only in Neiman Marcus, it seems, could such confidence, fictional or otherwise, be so blindly placed.

A nationally syndicated magazine cartoon depicted a tattered, work-weary woman standing on the porch of a dilapidated shack that is apparently her family's home. Everything around the building is in disarray. All bespeaks poverty and despair. Across the field runs her husband, his arms raised in exultation and behind him, a gushing spout of black crude oil shoots upward through a derrick and skyward, up and out of the cartoon panel. The careworn farmer's wife takes it all in with wide-eyed surprise and then gives voice to the cartoon's caption which reads, "It's wonderful news, Harry!" she exclaims to her onrushing husband and then asks, "How late does Neiman-Marcus stay open?"

By establishing the store as the ultimate purveyor of luxury and an arbiter of taste, Herbert and Carrie had made their store the twenty-four-carat gold ring in the merry-go-round ride of Texas retailing by the time the riches of the World War I oil boom were created. As a result, why would any self-respecting newly minted Texan millionaire buy from a store that was other than the very best? By swapping cotton flour sack frocks for elegant gowns created by Lanvin of Paris and available only at Neiman Marcus, the wife of the new oil baron not so subtly announced to her less fortunate sisters that she had climbed to enviable heights.

The founders of Neiman Marcus outdistanced their competitors by creating a store that became, at just the right time and at just the right place, the very hallmark of luxury. It was exactly what once poor dirt farmers craved after wildcat wells brought forth barrel after barrel of sweet Texas crude. As one Lone Star wag put it, "The two best smelling things in the world are perfume on a pretty woman and crude oil if it's yours." More often than not, that perfume and much more came from Neiman Marcus.

In 1913, the final full year at the Elm Street store, the profit reported to those members of the extended Marcus family who had invested in the firm was more than they expected. By the end of the first year in the Main and Ervay store with Texas oil just beginning to flow, however, the profits had more than doubled despite the cost of constructing the new building. Two years later, the family-owned business generated a profit of nearly $130,000, more than six times the highest amount ever realized on Elm Street before it burned.

When World War I ended, it had become increasingly clear that the Neiman Marcus venture, though wildly successful, was at risk when the long-festering relationship between Al Neiman and the Marcus brother and sister team worsened. Surrounded by what must have seemed to be a large sized regiment of Marcuses working in the store or at least living close enough to it to cause him daily grief, Neiman grew even more volatile and difficult.

An eyewitness to both the store's progress and the internal feuding over the years was the fourth but unofficial member of the Neiman Marcus founding group, Minnie Marcus, the small but forceful wife of Herbert. Until her son Stanley was old enough to go to school, she devoted herself to the home and to his upbringing. The family dinner table was Stanley Marcus's first valuable education in the retailing business. Minnie always had a delightful evening meal ready when Herbert, often weary from confrontations with Al Neiman, came home to their house on South Boulevard.

As Stanley would recall many years later, Herbert and Minnie always discussed the events of the day during supper. Her words of solace and advice were apparently very important to her husband, particularly when the store and its bitter inner strife began to take on a life of its own. Stanley would recall that somehow his mother had an intuitive way of knowing if the day's sales volume at the store had met expectations or had been a disappointment. "If it had been a bad day," he wrote, "Mother would always serve roast chicken which was one of Dad's favorite dishes and this cheered him immensely." Stanley confessed that he, too, was fond of his mother's roast chicken, so much so that in his naïve youth he often felt disappointment that good business days far outnumbered the bad, making the cherished chicken dinners few and far between.

Only two years old when the first Neiman Marcus opened in Dallas, Stanley regularly accompanied his father downtown on business. Initially unable to afford either a maid or babysitter, his parents entrusted the younger Marcus to the care of the store tailor, who no doubt eager to both pacify the child and get on with his sewing, often gave the tot empty spools to play with on the floor of the alterations shop. In later years Stanley would delight in telling journalists that he had learned the retail business literally "from the ground floor up."

By the time World War I ended in 1918, the family around the Marcus dinner table had grown to six. Stanley now had three younger brothers, Edward, Herbert, Jr., and Lawrence, who was born in 1917.

The Neiman family, Al and Carrie, however, was never to grow beyond its original two in number, a fact that would eventually spell trouble for Al Neiman's ambition to control the company.

In the early years in Dallas, Neiman Marcus-watching was already a popular pastime. It was obvious to curious onlookers that if there were an heir apparent within the family structure, it had to be Stanley Marcus simply because there were no junior Neimans waiting in the wings. It is possible that had Carrie Neiman not suffered a miscarriage just days before the Elm Street store opened and had instead produced an heir, Dallas might, at least for a time, have had a Neiman store on one corner of Main and Ervay and a competing Marcus store on the other.

As it was, the only viable heir apparent to the family business was not at first certain he wanted to succeed his father as store president. Whether Stanley really wanted to be a titled member of the retailing royal family or not, by the early 1920s Neiman Marcus was moving forward nicely without him. New departments were created within the Main Street store and lines of merchandise other than fashion apparel were added into the mix.

The core of the business, however, remained fashion merchandise including such accessories as shoes and handbags. The high profit margins to be realized in selling expensive furs became apparent as the years went by and the addition of a home decorative and gift department expanded the appeal of the store beyond what were known as soft lines. In time, such big ticket and highly profitable goods as precious jewelry appeared in the store, much to the delight of the doyennes who felt the need for some obviously expensive glitter to add some showy sparkle to their designer gowns purchased at the store. Menswear, added later, gave the gentlemen something to occupy their attention while their wives pursued the latest fashions elsewhere throughout the store.

It was easy to be overwhelmed by the experience of walking into the new building on Main Street. "This is not a store," a newspaper reporter declared, "it is too spacious and colorful." Neiman Marcus was, as another publication saw it, "The most beautiful store in America."

Of course, it was not all just marketing and merchandising and having a beautiful store. There was the financial side of the business as well, and the key to that was the unsung fiscal wizardry of Abraham Lincoln Neiman. His vital role as the principal money man among the founders has been all but obscured by a well-orchestrated Marcus-dominated subtle public relations campaign that has prevailed for decades. History is, after all, written by the victors, and even though Al Neiman's family name is still written large across the facades of many beautiful store buildings, his contribution to the triumphant rise of the glittering retail empire is all but forgotten. There are some hard-core Marcus loyalists who even contend that the Neiman in the company name only refers to Carrie and not poor Uncle Al.

By the early 1920s, it was probably clear to most interested parties that the partnership between the Neimans and Marcus was not likely to succeed in the long run. Domestic difficulties were soon to surface that would jeopardize the marriage of Herbert's sister and Neiman but before that, the question of survivorship was evident. Al and Carrie could not produce any heirs but Herbert and Minnie already had several at home. Stanley, the eldest, seemed to be the most likely to claim the title of merchant prince in the Dallas retailing dynasty. Willing or not, his future had already been cast by his doting father.

Becoming Mr. Stanley

Few could ever successfully claim that the heir apparent, young or old, was particularly handsome. When his classmates at Dallas' Forest Avenue High School bestowed upon Stanley the dubious title of "Ugliest Boy" in 1920, his mother quite understandably took umbrage and in her quiet but forceful manner quickly got the title changed to "Most Natural Boy." While distinctive in appearance, the newly named "Most Natural Boy" was nevertheless simply just not handsome. Throughout his long life, however, he more than compensated for any lack of superficial beauty by the sheer force and charm of his intellect and personality. Even as a younger man, he exuded an undeniable aura of authority and sagacity which blended with a sense of humor that was usually more slapstick than wry.

Photographs of him as a boy depict a dark-skinned, liquid-eyed, and rather large-eared youth, small in stature. Fully grown, he claimed to be five feet eight inches tall, more or less, but it was likely more less than more.

Stanley's once thick crown of coal black hair rapidly receded even during his youth and by the time he was in his late twenties, his balding but noble brow had nearly reached the top of his head. His skin, always a bit darker than white throughout his long life, took on an unusual hue that became even darker after brief exposure to the sun. His trademark beard acquired in the 1960s served to emphasize the unusual color of his skin.

By the time he entered the family business at age twenty-one in 1926, Stanley had assumed the brisk, no nonsense public persona that would be his for life. He was, after all, a Harvard graduate by this time with an additional year of graduate school to his credit. His path to higher education, however, had not been an easy one.

Despite the high expectations of his father, Stanley had been neither a brilliant student nor a winning athlete as a youth. He had tried his luck at baseball without success and a graceful game of tennis was never to be his. Golf, that insatiable siphon of time, was never to lure him away from his office at the store or his vast nearly ten thousand volume library at home.

He was, however, president of his high school freshman class and he rose to the exalted rank of private in the school's Junior ROTC program. A photograph of the smallish uniformed private soldier in formation with his fellow cadets of Forest Avenue High's Company A depicts an unwilling warrior who appears to be wishing desperately to be anywhere else but on the drill field. It is highly possible that being in any library anywhere would have been much more to his liking.

Stanley made it through high school without either any spectacular achievements or embarrassing failures. His grades, while acceptable and above average, were not sufficiently enough above average to gain him admission to Harvard College, the school his father had chosen for him. With Herbert urging him ever onward, he enrolled at Amherst College in an effort to improve his grades in order to meet Harvard's stringent entrance requirements.

According to the many letters he sent home to his adoring mother, his time at Amherst was both pleasant and scholastically rewarding. Perhaps relieved to be forever out of his high school ROTC olive drab military uniform, Stanley immersed himself in his studies and was soon found himself on the road to Cambridge, Massachusetts, and the ivy covered walls of the very prestigious Harvard College. To show that he was part of his new academic environment, he even acquired a full length raccoon coat that upon reflection in later years he pronounced to have been somewhat ridiculous.

It was during his years at Harvard that his lifelong love affair with books and the printed page began in earnest. Encouraged by his bibliophile father, Stanley had been an avid reader throughout his childhood, but his time spent in the vast libraries of Harvard prompted him to seriously consider foregoing a career in retailing in favor of becoming either a publisher or perhaps a seller of books.

The printed page appears to have been an elixir to the nonathletic Harvard freshman. He formed a book club and operated a one man rare book mail-order service from his room in the dorm, displaying an early knack for catalogue selling that would crystallize as the "Neiman Marcus Christmas Book" many years later. He became so completely immersed in books that he dared to share with his father his dream of becoming a publisher. There can be little doubt that Herbert Marcus, who had other plans for his son, agonized over this announced possibility, but at least at first he wisely let Stanley amuse himself with bookish dreams, but not for a moment did Herbert waver in his intent for his son to succeed him at the store. "My father had no doubts at all that I was going to enter Neiman Marcus," Stanley recalled many years later. "This was a foregone conclusion with him and he told me very frankly he expected me and my brothers to follow in his footsteps." Despite his muted protests to the contrary, there can be little doubt that the young prince always fully intended to come back to the kingdom when his college days were over.

Many personal letters to and from Stanley at Harvard are housed in the remarkable Stanley Marcus Collection at Southern Methodist University's DeGolyer Library. In addition to the correspondence, the archives contain box after box of sometimes seemingly inconsequential documents such as receipts for dry cleaning, eyeglass prescriptions, and even grocery shopping lists dated in the 1930s. In the three hundred fifty cubic foot collection, of course, there are also all manner of other far more important and significant papers with the personal correspondence being the most natural and insightful. The letters speak volumes about the family over the years, their inner relationships, and their total focus on the store virtually day and night.

Among this assortment are letters from Minnie Marcus to her Harvard student son. Miss Minnie, as store personnel affectionately knew her, did not mince any words with the young man who, by all indications, was no stranger to the spirited extracurricular activities that take place at all universities, even the mighty Harvard. In one letter, written in a scrawl not unlike the handwriting style exhibited by her son later in his life, his mother asks him directly how much money he had spent on liquor the previous week. Since Stanley's answer to her pointed query is curiously not in the file, it is easy to imagine he might have preferred not to disclose such an accounting to her. "I am not telling you never to drink alcohol," she wrote, and then contradicted herself with a closing line printed in a bold script that strongly commanded, "I forbid it!" Her message was clear and the enlarged block printing of it meant that she was forbidding his drinking in a very loud way.

The forceful message apparently was received. While not a teetotaler in his adult life, his taste ran to the milder side of the beverage spectrum to include beer, wine, and the occasional aperitif. Not for him was the bourbon and branch water liquid diet of so many of his fellow prototypical Texans of the time.

Miss Minnie's letter writing activities continued until she could no longer firmly hold a pen in her over ninety year old fingers. Her letters provide an interesting glimpse into her recorded dreams and ambitions for her son. It is clear from her writings and his responses that her admonitions about the importance of honesty and good character made an impression upon the young man that he carried into adulthood.

Kept informed and reasonably well disciplined by his mother, Stanley did well at Harvard. A great many of his college examination books have survived with his already notorious scribble in their margin. Graded, the books demonstrate that his excellent performance in English literature provided him with a high enough grade average buffer to permit him to navigate successfully around his lesser achievements in certain foreign language courses. Understanding French, the language of fashion, was clearly not among his academic strengths.

In due time, acceding to his father's fervent desires and likely to his own true ambitions, he agreed to come home to Dallas to become an executive of the store. His father, perhaps sensing a bit of hesitation, treated the graduate to his first trip to Europe and to the magnificent city of Paris which he grew to love. Further, Herbert curiously insisted that his son continue his Harvard education a bit longer to include the obtaining of a then relatively rare Masters Degree in Business Administration.

Perhaps it was the recent memory of his riotously good times in Paris, enjoyed only after his unsuspecting father, cum chaperone, had gone to bed, or an itch to get on with his newly chosen career path that compelled him to leave Harvard prematurely for good and to join Neiman Marcus after only a short time in the graduate school.

Down in Texas, the skirmishes between Herbert Marcus and his partner Al Neiman had become often out-and-out and sometimes public battles. Carrie, sister of one combatant and wife of the other, was obviously caught in the middle of what was essentially a tug-of-war between two forceful men struggling to determine who would control the prospering business.

The issue came to a head in 1926, the very year that young Stanley, abandoning his one time dream of becoming a book publisher, left the Harvard Business School before getting his post-graduate degree. It is easy to assume that Herbert's suddenly urgent commands to his son to abandon any other thoughts except those involving coming into the family business immediately had much to do with the escalating problems with his partner.

Herbert was approaching fifty years of age when Stanley left Harvard. Life expectancy figures in that era did not offer too much long-range optimism to men who were nearing the half-century milestone. Al Neiman was three years older than his brother-in-law and caught up in the same actuarial statistics as the slightly younger man, he likely realized that the issue of the future leadership of the store needed to be resolved before Stanley had a chance to prove himself, or perhaps even fail and ruin the business in the process. As it would develop, Al outlived Herbert by twenty years but of course no one could have foreseen that in 1926. Even with any such impossible foreknowledge, it would likely not have made any difference whatever in the ultimate outcome of the store's leadership.

With no heir of his own to bring in from the wings to be groomed for the store's top job, Al keenly felt that he should very quickly assume command. Herbert, on the other hand, with his Harvard-educated son having been back in the family fold for a short time and performing at least reasonably well enough, understandably thought just the opposite. The leadership issue quite naturally might have continued to fester for a few more years had not Al's still handsome face and his roving eyes served to decide the matter swiftly and decisively in 1928.

Al had already informed his partners that if he were denied the president's job he wanted out of the partnership, but Carrie, torn between two strong forces, at first refused even to consider breaking up the founding team that had done so remarkably well. It was about then that Al's personal charm led him into a not-so-private fitting room tryst with a female employee of the store. Upon hearing accounts of this sordid episode, the wronged wife and the outraged brother-in-law quickly accepted Al's request to terminate the partnership and bought his interest in the firm for $250,000 borrowed from a bank.

Carrie immediately sued for divorce from her wayward husband who was ordered in the decree to stay out of the Dallas retail scene for a period of ten years. Al almost immediately violated the court order, was successfully sued by Herbert, and finally left Dallas in disgrace.

Stanley's recorded dislike of his one time uncle by marriage is uncharacteristically volatile. In his writings, he virtually accuses Neiman of being just short of criminal in his arrangements with various suppliers to the store. The erstwhile nephew's verbal assaults on the personality and overall character of Uncle Al leaves no question about Stanley's deep antipathy toward the man. To be sure, Neiman did fan the flames by orchestrating a negative campaign within the store to discredit the younger Marcus, very likely in an effort to create trouble between the son and his father and thereby block Stanley's ascension.

It is entirely possible, too, that Al Neiman, a veteran of many retailing wars, truly felt that the young Harvard trained scion, just two years out of college and with no real executive experience, might have been better off selling books somewhere preferably far away from Dallas. If that could be arranged, Al likely speculated, he might well seize the reins of leadership.

Whatever had stoked the heated emotions on both sides of the issue, Neiman was now gone for good and only blooded Marcuses remained at the store. The former Uncle Al never really recovered from his divorce from Carrie even though it was he alone who had caused it. In comments about his former wife made soon after she had died, Neiman often took oblique aim at the Harvard upstart who was getting all the credit for making Neiman Marcus a famous store. He once commented that Carrie had contributed more than anyone else to making the store the success that it was. In the same breath, he then named himself as the second most important factor in that success indicating more than a touch of subjectivity in his evaluation. It was clear that he still held his former wife in high regard.

In a handwritten letter to Stanley dated March 10, 1953, Neiman sadly noted the very recent death of Carrie Marcus. "She was a grand and noble woman," he wrote, "and I am much afraid I caused her much unhappiness." He went on to praise Carrie for her "great inspiration" and "tremendous ability" that made "NM the great institution it now is." He told his ex-nephew, "Deep down in my heart, believe me, I say a prayer for her."

The letter, now much the worse for wear, was written on a sheet of paper bearing the imprint "Neiman—New York," the wholesale garment business founded by Al after he was ordered by the court to leave the Dallas retailing scene forever. He married again and lived in relative luxury for a time until his business failed. However, when he died in 1970 at age ninety-five, a distant relative noted, "He lived high on memories. This is the tragedy of it—being many times wealthy, he ended up poor."

The long enduring ill will between Neiman and Stanley Marcus never fully abated. When a much older Stanley recruited a Broadway team to script a musical play based on his book *Minding the Store*, the lyricist member of the team insisted that even the frothiest of musicals required a darkly villainous figure as a contrast to the traditional light, bright, and happy, if usually mindless, plot. Without hesitation, Stanley named Abraham Lincoln Neiman as the most villainous character in the history of the store, even though his book does begrudgingly suggest that the uncle did have a certain amount of personal charm, but not enough to offset his flawed character.

Incidentally, the prospects for bringing Stanley's book to Broadway quickly faded when only a small number of financial backers could be found. One potential investor walked away unimpressed from a music and lyric run-through staged at Stanley's house to raise money. He declined a request to put any money in a show that he saw as promising to be nothing more than "Fiddler on the Escalator."

After Al Neiman died penniless, with only a single cufflink tucked away in a cigar box to his name in the Dallas suburb of Arlington in 1970, Stanley and two of his brothers went to the funeral in a limousine. When a reporter asked what role the deceased founder had played in the great Neiman Marcus success story, Stanley was all but mute on the subject, turning abruptly on his heel to walk away. He did, however, contribute toward Neiman's burial expenses on "humanitarian grounds," he said, "and not that I had any lingering feelings for the man."

Al Neiman was buried in Fort Worth's Emmanuel Hebrew Rest Cemetery, a final resting place for indigent Jews. A few years later, an unknown donor arranged for a relatively expensive marker to be placed on the grave. Its inscription could not be less informative. It reads, simply, "Abraham Lincoln Neiman—July 4, 1875—October 21, 1970." The famous store he co-founded is not mentioned on the tombstone.

The departure of the disgraced Al Neiman from Neiman Marcus, as events were quickly to prove, was without doubt one of the more important turning points in the company's long and successful history. Herbert, no longer challenged by his adversarial partner, turned his full attention to making the already successful store even more so. Carrie, by then apparently all but permanently saddened by her childless and now ruined marriage, nevertheless continued to work her fashion magic in the leading apparel markets throughout the world to the delight of her clientele.

While Neiman's leaving provided the opportunity for his two former partners to get on with their jobs without distraction, his departure was vital in clearing the upward path for his erstwhile nephew. Stanley Marcus, by his own admission too aggressive and often brash in his overheated desire to bring an unheard of new dimension to his father's store, blazed with great intensity up the career path suddenly made passable by the absence of his former Uncle Al.

It is hard to imagine that anyone else but Stanley Marcus, born of Herbert and Minnie, could ever have attained the charismatic presence that became the mythic and legendary merchant prince. His years at Harvard had given him a liberal slant on social and political issues while both his father and his aunt had imbued him with a special insightful knowledge of profound retailing skills and philosophies that no Harvard training could possibly impart. It was, indeed, a classic combination of heredity and environment.

He had risen, literally, from the floor of the store's tailor shop to begin his march toward the office of company president. Cocooned by unquestionable job security, he was free to experiment and probe as no one else could have possibly done. Any hint that it would be nearly twenty-five years before the death of his father would give him the reins would have likely come as a shock to the young man, but blissfully unaware of this unwelcome twist of fate, he wasted no time and absolutely no energy in beginning to shape what someday he knew would be his company into the superior world-class institution he believed it could and should become.

Usually with his father's blessing and concurrence but sometimes not, Stanley early on brought about dazzling changes that would serve the store well until he could take full command, whenever that time might come. Until then, at a time much more distant than he could have possibly imagined, there was the exciting era when the elegant and traditional Neiman Marcus created by Herbert and Carrie first began to dance to the modern retailing tune of the upstart they all called "Mr. Stanley."

Taking Command

In his autobiography, Stanley Marcus makes a sly note of the fact that his entry into the family business just might have been at least a factor in the ultimate departure of his uncle, Al Neiman. Al's admitted philandering and the understandable distress it caused Carrie Neiman was indeed the final breaking point, but the aggressive pushing of Stanley into a top executive position by his father very likely set the stage for Al's increasingly virulent temper tantrums.

By his own admission promoted long before his experience warranted it, Stanley often alienated veteran store personnel who would then take their grievances to Al, the only partner without a direct blood-tie to the young man from Harvard. "In my innocence of the business world," Stanley contritely wrote many years later, "I was almost destroyed by zealousness, aggressiveness, and my associates."

Uncle Al, out to protect what he more or less rightly viewed as at least partly his turf, apparently was without mercy in his critical attacks against his wife's nephew. In one week alone, he accused Stanley of no less than sixteen misadventures that would likely have caused anyone with another family name to be summarily dismissed. Stanley made a list of these misdeeds as "a matter of record," later admitting that "there was an element of truth in some of the charges."

At any rate, the charges amounted to little in the much larger scene being played out in the store's executive offices. With Al out of the business, young Stanley to no one's real surprise was given the responsibility for the all important better merchandise part of the retail operation with the secondary challenge to repair the damages that Al had wreaked among the store's fashion vendors.

It was in this first truly executive position, bestowed upon him by his doting father, that Stanley gained the business fundamentals that would quickly transform him from a zealous and aggressive upstart into a knowledgeable and progressive merchandising genius. It clearly was his father, steeped in the tradition of eventually passing the torch to the eldest son, who provided the golden opportunity for Stanley to succeed.

It was his Aunt Carrie, however, who gave him the tools to make the most of that opportunity. She apparently awakened his nascent talent best described as having an unerring eye for fashion. Under her daily tutelage, Stanley gained the appreciation for minute detail and color, the knack of reading trends long before any computer-driven predictors existed, and the ability to convince all others, customers and co-workers alike, that what he said was without any equivocation, absolutely fashion right.

The indisputable value of quality in all things was principal among the key lessons learned from Carrie. With his father in full command of the business and serving as a staunch defender of his often headstrong son, and with his Aunt Carrie teaching him the rarefied ABC's of the fashion business, Stanley began to come into full bloom, overshadowed only by the presence of his imposing father, the founder and intellectual master salesman. Few young men have enjoyed such a

heady team of mentors as did Stanley Marcus, but even fewer succeeded in making the most of stellar opportunity and inherited qualities to such an unparalleled degree.

None of these positive gifts would have likely proved of any significant value whatever had Neiman Marcus foundered in the Great
Depression of 1929 as so many businesses and stores did. Although
the bleak waves of the national economic depression did not wash
across Texas until the early 1930s, the effect was still devastating to
many. Neiman Marcus, catering then as now to a more affluent clientele, was not affected as immediately as were the general merchandise
stores who served cotton farmers whose crops went unsold and cattle
ranchers whose beef could find no market in the Depression-ravaged
eastern part of the nation.

As the Marcuses viewed with growing apprehension the advancing
tide of bank closings and foreclosures that preceded the full tidal wave
of the Depression as it rolled westward, a single perennial big time
loser in the oilfields stemmed the tide of disaster with one last desper-
ate push of his oil drill bit into the soil of Deep East Texas.

Although oil had been flowing from deep pools under the Lone Star
State since the Spindletop Field literally blew in with 75,000 barrels
on one day in the early 1900s, it was Columbus M. (Dad) Joiner who
made the words "Texas" and "crude oil" virtually synonymous beginning on October 6, 1930. After countless futile efforts and on the
verge of abandoning all hope of finding any profitable oil play in East
Texas, Joiner, the quintessential oilman, brought in the Daisy Bradford
Number 3 in a field that eventually proved to be almost fifty miles long
and over twelve miles wide.

Although the price of a barrel of oil was only a tiny fraction of
twenty-first century prices, the sheer volume of crude flowing from the
East Texas field began to provide cash enough to slow and eventually
halt the forceful surge of the Depression. In the process, the new
wealth stemming from the field, and countless others that soon came

on line, the name Neiman Marcus joined the synonymous phrase of Texas and oil.

When the petroleum production of the Permian Basin to the west of Dallas eventually proved to be even more enduring than the East Texas fields, Dallas found itself literally in the geographical and professional midway point between the greatest oil fields then known to exist in the United States. As large oil companies moved to the city with relatively highly paid employees, and as former cotton farmers and ranchers found themselves transformed overnight into oil barons, the fortunes of Neiman Marcus soared by virtue of its already established position as a purveyor of only the best that money could buy.

Not for these suddenly well-off status seekers were the run-of-the-mill garments and accessories to be found on the racks of Dallas' plebian and relatively shabby department stores. New money in vast quantities created a hunger and a need for self assurance and guidance as to how to dress for the high society role that fortuitous geology and a kind fate had instantly thrust upon them.

It almost seems that Neiman Marcus had been created just for the oil boom that served to shape the fashion consciousness of the newly emerging society in Dallas. Not quite a quarter of a century old when the Daisy Bradford well proved Dad Joiner to be a wildcatting genius after all, the store was, philosophically and geographically, in just the right place at exactly the right time. If money could not, in and of itself, buy good taste, it could certainly open the doors to Neiman Marcus and its brief, but well-earned, reputation as the ultimate purveyor of good taste and the confidence building assurance that came with its label.

Neiman Marcus, devoid of the brilliant but trouble-making Neiman, rose to the occasion with gusto. As the pensive Herbert, often with fingertips pressed together in an almost gesture of prayer, guided his firm with strict adherence to the customer relations dictums he had created, his sister visited the fashion capitals of the world to bring silks and satins to those who but yesterday had worn shapeless cotton frocks.

Still as zealous and aggressive as he would always prove to be, the son and nephew of the two remaining partners discovered deep within himself a characteristic, indeed a rare talent, that neither his father nor his aunt had ever exhibited. Stanley was, he found apparently to his own dismay, a showman. To forever affirm and cast in stone the sheer storekeeping sense of Herbert and to amplify if not glorify the innate but brilliant fashion acuity of Carrie, Stanley introduced the dazzling concept of the store as theater.

Haltingly at first, but with growing enthusiasm as his weekly fashion shows and spectacular Broadway-type national ads proved overwhelmingly successful, he set about proving to himself, and then showing to the store's clientele that the company's logotype, its distinctive signature trademark, was the viable symbol of all of its many facets. Through models strutting their stuff in the latest designer apparel selected by the impeccable Carrie, and telling the world through colorful advertising that Neiman Marcus was a fashion leader, he began to create that intangible, indefinable something called image. Because the image that this showman/merchant was able to fashion for his father's store was built upon the rock solid and uncompromising foundations of customer service announced on the company's very first day of business, the modern vision of Neiman Marcus and its world famous mystique was established and destined to endure.

If Herbert wholeheartedly approved of what his headstrong and daring oldest son, still in his twenties, was doing to transform the traditionally staid Neiman Marcus can, of course, never be known. Stanley suggests, however, that the senior Marcus never interfered with or suggested alterations to any of his schemes. While Herbert was to remain president of the company until his death in 1950, total blindness overtook him some years earlier and, by default, the reins of management slowly found their way into Stanley's eager hands.

It is apparent from his own words, both written and spoken, that his ambition to assume full control of Neiman Marcus was held in check by his father. Having graduated from high school at the age of sixteen and from Harvard by the time he was twenty, Stanley had somehow come to the conclusion that he should become president of Neiman Marcus in 1945 when he turned forty. His father, though blind and nearly seventy years of age when his eldest son became forty years old, doggedly refused to relinquish the role of chief executive officer. This denial of Stanley's self-designed career path was even thirty years later considered by him to be the greatest disappointment of his long and otherwise stellar career in retailing.

There can be little doubt that Stanley idolized his father. Throughout the many pages he put on paper during his lifetime, the recurring reverential message about Herbert, his philosophy and his wisdom resounds from nearly every chapter. The father's words became gospel to the ears of the son who in turn built them into a sermon that became the guiding light to the multitudes of Neiman Marcus employees who were expected to cling to every word.

Some of those who heard the sermon often enough over long periods of employment might have held out at least a bit of suspicion that some of the gospel according to the Herbert/Stanley team of retail evangelists might have been apocryphal. Even though Stanley often claimed, perhaps only half in jest, to being blessed with total recall, it seems almost too good to be true that Herbert's word for word sage observations about sales techniques and how to keep customers coming back could have remembered verbatim by Stanley after a half century had passed. That he fully believed his father had mouthed such perfectly well remembered pontifications cannot be denied, but if the senior Marcus was truly every bit as gifted and infallible an oracle as his son later imagined him to have been will always remain a mystery.

By the time he reached his fortieth year, Stanley was nevertheless already hard at work in blazing new trails into the heretofore dark and musty world of traditional retailing. His personally commentated weekly fashion shows, the first such in the nation, featuring the most beautiful of models wearing the most exquisite of gowns, became the talk of the city.

The success of the shows and the attention showered upon them by the local newspapers led to Stanley's brilliant 1938 concept of an annual spectacular fashion event that would focus on the work of the most truly significant designers. Thus was born the Neiman Marcus Award for Distinguished Service in the Field of Fashion extravaganza that was to continue for over fifty years. The motive behind the award idea might have been more than a little transparent to some, particularly certain competitors, but to Stanley, the concept completed what to his mind was a perfect circuit. By anointing key designers with an annual award, widely known as the "Oscars of the Fashion Industry," Neiman Marcus further enhanced its position as the ultimate arbiter of great fashion taste.

Among those who were honored by the award were Coco Chanel, Yves Saint Laurent, Salvatore Ferragamo, Christian Dior, James Galanos, and Ralph Lauren. Over the years, individuals other than designers were given the award, as always with great fanfare and publicity. Actresses Grace Kelly, Greer Garson, and Dolores Del Rio were among those named.

In the process, future business relationships with those fashion houses and fashionable individuals so grandly anointed were likely to remain cooperative and enthusiastic vendors. Further, designers and other resources eager to receive this annual accolade from the prestigious Dallas store became more pliant about granting exclusivity and accommodating in making shipping dates, all in hopes of being contenders for the award next time around.

It was this uncanny ability to dream and, in truth to connive, in a circuitous way that made Stanley the marketing expert he was to become. Blessed with a limitless vision that enabled him to see far beyond the city limits of Dallas and even the far reaching borders of Texas, Stanley managed to put the store his father had so firmly founded well on the way to national retail stardom by the time the store was barely thirty years old.

Despite some mild misgivings of Herbert, Stanley moved to put the store directly into the national spotlight. Devoid of any real competition in Texas for the headline creating haute couture high-end business, Carrie Marcus had persuaded many top name designers to sell their creations exclusively to the Dallas store. So diligent and so talented was Aunt Carrie that New York and Paris designers soon made it possible for Neiman Marcus to boast with considerable accuracy but always in its refined manner, that more famous designer labels were to be found at Neiman Marcus than at any other store in the United States. By the mid-thirties, Carrie's ability to impress the big players in the world of fashion combined with Stanley's talent for showcasing the dazzling fashions his aunt had assembled pushed the Dallas specialty store into the forefront of American retailing.

To take full advantage of this brighter spotlight, Stanley approached the influential and trend setting New York City fashion magazines with offers to purchase very expensive full page advertisements. By touting the scope and brilliance of the fashion assortments available at Neiman Marcus, Stanley hoped to accomplish several things. First, he would let the whole world of potential fashion-loving clientele know that his store, down in the Texas sticks though it might be, was now in the big leagues and able to satisfy the status-seeking, or perhaps status-reaffirming desires of the most discriminating shopper.

Second, by becoming the first advertiser outside of New York City in the national magazines, readers scanning the pages would quickly note that those garments chosen by *Vogue*'s editors to appear in elaborate settings were now available at Neiman Marcus, Dallas, Texas. The rule adhered to by the fashion magazines was a simple one. Without a full page ad, fully paid by the advertiser, there would be no editorial credit in the colorful spreads that created conversations in the finer homes and beauty salons all across the country.

A third good thing that might come about through spending thousands of dollars on national advertising was the rather remote possibility that the featured garment might actually be sold to some big-spending fashion maven. Over the years, it became apparent that such expensive ads could not be evaluated by the sales resulting directly from them. They were only rarely successful as specific merchandise sales generators, but as messengers of the newly-crafted image, the ads were superlative. Who dared question the fashion authority of the editors of *Vogue* or *Harper's Bazaar*? By association, then, who could successfully challenge the premise that any of its advertisers, even a little store in Texas, were indisputable arbiters of fashion correctness?

In the mid-1930s, as the ad campaigns began to hint at the remote elegance apparently abiding within the walls of far-off Neiman Marcus, an anachronism developed that was to serve the store extremely well for over a century. The public perception of Texas in general and Dallas in particular was of a rough and ready, oil-bespattered, dusty back country sort of place as frequently seen in the countless horse opera movies then streaming out of Hollywood. How any store could pretend to fashion elegance in such a forsaken environment triggered the curiosity of those who lived beyond the borders of the Lone Star State.

Stanley gleefully seized upon this anomaly when he came to realize its diamond-in-the-rough potential. When the state of Texas gained national recognition in 1936 on its hundredth anniversary, Neiman Marcus had already carved a highly visible and publicity-rich niche for itself. Through elaborate fashion extravaganzas, and the importation of East Coast and European visitors who left the big Dallas birthday centennial celebrations with their heads spinning, the store ensured that henceforth, Texas and Dallas and Neiman Marcus, and oil, of course, should rightfully be considered as one entity and mentioned in one breathless phrase.

As his importance grew, Stanley decided that he should have as his residence a palace worthy of a prince. In an effort to ensure that the end design of the home he envisioned would be nothing but first rate, he retained the services of the world famous architect, Mr. Frank Lloyd Wright.

The relationship between the two headstrong and highly creative individuals was perhaps predictably stormy and eventually completely futile. After several rancorous meetings and disagreements over Wright's all but total disregard for any budgetary restraints, the association was terminated in favor of a local architect who appreciated the fact that even rising young retailing stars did not have totally unlimited funds to put into a new house.

Mr. Wright took his dismissal just as sarcastically as might be expected. "Dear Stan," he wrote in late 1935 upon seeing the newly hired architect's drawings, "Why in the Hell you should show me your lousy bastard [design] is more than I can appreciate." His spleen not fully vented, the colorful if spurned architect raged on. "If this mongrel is your idea of the ideal home for the Southwest you have neither seen the Southwest nor any real home. When Texans go out into the sun bald headed, then they may build 'homes' like yours. Poor Stan, so this is what I was working for all the time. Well, you paid your money and you took your choice." Signing off at last, the famously eccentric Wright wrote "My best to you all, for what it is worth." Beneath his flamboyant signature, he could not resist a final shot. "Looks to me like you dropped big money to pick up small change."

The house finally built for Stanley and his wife Billie was a contemporary architectural delight that remained vital and exciting throughout the rest of the century. Boasting leather floors in some rooms, the building served as both a home for the Marcus family of three children and a museum for Stanley's always changing and expanding collections of art and artifacts. His tastes in collecting were every bit as wideranging and probing as was his management style. Including rare fertility idols to Native American artifacts, Stanley's collections famously contained fine art that any museum would, and did in fact, envy and court. The list of masterworks in his home gallery at one time or another contained pieces by Dali, Picasso, Matisse, El Greco, Toulouse-Lautrec, Giacometti, Rodin, and Miro. Other artists represented included his friend, Georgia O'Keeffe and Mexican artists Rivera, Tamayo, and Orozco. Clearly, such a collection deserved a worthy setting and the house, even without the creative skills of Frank Lloyd Wright, served Stanley's tastes well for nearly half a century.

As the years passed quickly by and the dark clouds of war unmistakably gathered abroad, Stanley pushed even more forcefully to guarantee the unique qualities of the store that would someday be his alone. To make certain that the nation's newspapers, magazines, and radio stations were fed well-crafted tidbits to fuel the perceptions about the shining gem of a store hunkered down on a mesquite covered Texas prairie, Stanley surprised the store family by hiring a public relations manager to work full time in spreading the news. Although he was without question a natural born public relations wizard, he clearly felt the need to formalize the store's publicity seeking efforts. In a speech delivered late in his life, an 85-year-old Stanley Marcus claimed that "the best public relations stems from good intentions." While that has a noble ring of truth to it, it is easy to speculate that his challenge to the store's first publicity person was to further the good intention of enhancing the already shimmering image of Neiman Marcus through whatever public relations techniques could be legally and ethically brought into play.

As the war clouds grew ever darker in the late 1930s, the store's publicity machine sent forth endless but always exciting messages reaffirming the growing stature of the company and its enviable position in the likely soon-to-be war-challenged world of retailing. When an expansion and vast remodeling of the store was commenced in anticipation of likely wartime construction constraints, press releases spread the news and then used the opportunity to reiterate the company's high standards of quality and superb assortments of only the finest in merchandise. A larger store, claimed the press releases, meant even more opportunities to buy only the best.

The expansion and remodeling of the store was completed on September 7, 1941, almost thirty-four years to the day since the first Neiman Marcus store had opened its doors. In that relatively short period of time, the company's success as a fashion leader had done much to change the nation's perception of Dallas itself.

A writer for *Atlantic Monthly* dared venture westward to see for himself why the New York fashion wholesale houses were abuzz over this upstart store in the heart of the Wild West. His article clearly indicates that he was all but overwhelmed by what he discovered:

> "Dallas is famous for its well-dressed women and the store which leads the way in dressing them well. Beginning thirty years ago when Dallas was a small town in an area where the voice of the cow was loud in the land, Neiman-Marcus has taught Southwestern women to dress well without self-consciousness. [It] has contrived to sell more fine clothes than any similar store in Chicago and almost as much as the largest in New York."

While it is doubtful that the voices of many cows were that loud in downtown Dallas when Neiman Marcus opened its doors in 1907, the writer's allusion is an accurate one. The city of Dallas and its best known store had matured together in a remarkably short time, with Neiman Marcus establishing the city's image as a brash, but refined community filled with, as the writer put it, "youthful, energetic people who were unafraid and had never tasted the bitterness of disillusion."

Elizabeth Penrose, the editor of *British Vogue*, accepted the invitation of Stanley to come to Dallas to see the newly expanded store and to see for herself if the *Atlantic Monthly* writer had perhaps been a bit overly enthusiastic, at least to perhaps more refined English tastes. She, too, was soon caught up in what she perceived to be "A leisured gentle existence combined with a progressive spirit." After her visit to the store, she added, "I was particularly impressed by Neiman Marcus. I have seen many stores in many countries, but nowhere, I think, have I ever encountered a more charming atmosphere...and as lovely, luxurious merchandise as I think exists here."

The time just before America's entrance into World War II saw new sales records being set that underscored the fulsome praise being heaped upon the company by visiting journalists. In the year 1940, the store realized its highest sales volume in its history, and 1941, which ended just as the war started, even surpassed the prior year's record.

Meanwhile, the apparently heartfelt advertising copy kept flowing from the town's newspapers. One ad that appeared on the day the re-modeled store was announced sought to reiterate what had given the store its unique position in the world of fashion. "What is Neiman Marcus?" the copy asked, only to answer its own question in glowing words of self-appreciation. "It's a crystallization of ideas and ideals. It's high adventure in store keeping, carried forward...a business founded on determination to buy and sell not just good merchandise but the finest. It's an eye for what's new and smart and choice, wher-ever it originates."

This almost breathless broadside of self-confidence would likely not be taken too seriously by more world-wise twenty-first century read-ers, but in the half-light of the still emerging era of store imagery, it apparently captured and held the attention of Texans over six decades ago. The Dallas that had "not yet tasted the bitterness of dissolution" as described in that long ago issue of *Atlantic Monthly* wanted to believe what the copywriters at Neiman Marcus insisted on telling them. Even though the city and its environs were growing rapidly and reaching skyward even faster, it still needed to have its collective self-confidence massaged by the store that had led it from homemade dresses to haute couture gowns in just over thirty years time.

On December 7, 1941, when the United States was finally plunged into the war already engulfing Asia and all of Europe, the world reeled. Shocked momentarily to a standstill, it then rushed into a future that would render all that had gone before outdated and sentimentally old fashioned and quaint.

Neiman Marcus, or at least that visible part of Neiman Marcus that surfaced in the store's advertising copy, seemed aware that an irreversible threshold had been crossed the moment the first Japanese bomb shattered the Sunday morning calm in far-off Pearl Harbor, Hawaii. The store's traditional New Year's Day editorial copy displayed more than a shade of self-absorption when it stated, "And now we come to 1942—and a world engulfed in war. Doubtless many of you are asking the question, 'What about a store like Neiman-Marcus in war time?'" Doubtless, very few in fact were likely terribly concerned about Neiman-Marcus in the three weeks after Pearl Harbor, but apparently believing otherwise, the copywriter, carried on philosophically. "We have thought about this a great deal too," the ad proclaimed. "We believe that as distributors of fine merchandise, we have a special function to perform—now perhaps more than ever before. It is only the article of quality that endures and that is why Neiman Marcus has always said 'buy quality,' and we say it again now and think it is more important than ever."

In a sense, the copy is a tribute to the lofty mantra of the company whose founding principals included quality along with service. With a war at that time without any visible end seen as its challenge, the company could rightly point out that buying on the cheap meant sacrificing durability, and with production of all civilian goods certain to diminish, buying better goods easily translated into having a dress or a suit or a coat to wear as the war dragged on and on, for who knew how long.

Although Stanley was called to an important civilian war-related position in the nation's capital and his three younger brothers each went into military service, the store flourished as the city rapidly became a major center of wartime activity. Officers and airmen from Dallas' Love Field and their families made Neiman Marcus their favorite shopping destination. The store's reputation had spread far beyond the borders of Texas and many military men, some with more disposable income than ever before chose to buy tailor made uniforms as well as gifts to send home from the already famous store. The city's average military payroll during the war was estimated to be over $60 million per year.

Even though Stanley was away in Washington and busy with his dollar-a-year duties with the powerful War Production Board, he found time to send countless letters and telegrams to Dallas containing specific orders about how the business should be run. His father was still serving as president of the firm, but already suffering from the debilitating illness that would first take his eyesight, and in 1950, his life.

Under Stanley's long distance instructions, even in wartime the store continued its pre-war climb toward ever-increasing sales and profits. Spectacular in-store fashion shows were gamely staged throughout the darkest days of the war. Despite the difficulties encountered in transporting apparel and models out of the country, the store managed to present a major fashion show in Mexico City in early 1945, even as the war on two fronts raged on.

Fabric shortages and the closure of all European designer houses apparently had little overall impact on the ability of Neiman Marcus to remain dominant in the fashion world during the war. As Stanley had foreseen, his use of national advertising, effective professional public relations campaigns, and the wooing of America's top designers had solidified and enhanced the store's climb toward permanent national prominence.

In the September 3, 1945, issue of *Life* magazine, the editors paid tribute to the store and its success during the war that had ended just one day earlier. The magazine article pointed out that Neiman Marcus sold "more dresses of more exclusive designers" than any other single store in the country. This was heady praise for the Dallas company, particularly since this recognition came at the very end of a war that had made doing business difficult for most retailers.

When Stanley returned to the store after his tenure as a public servant in wartime Washington, he naturally turned his full attention toward making the company even more successful, both in terms of profit and national and international image. As executive vice president and de facto chief executive of the store, he continued his relentless pursuit of the lofty ideals as originally set forth by his father who was still the nominal company president. The two men, as well as their tightly knit cadre of dedicated lieutenants, no doubt actually believed in the fundamental elements of the business. To be sure, any broad history of American retailing will include a list of countless other merchants who espoused many of the same ideals, but at Neiman Marcus, the incessant stating and restating of the mantra was more than adequate to make it into a reality.

If there is any one word to sum it all, it is consistency. Once in place, the philosophy, the credo, never changed and the basic premise was in every advertisement, every speech, and every press release consistently and unwaveringly put forth to an ever increasing army of dedicated clientele. If, in the parlance of building baseball stadiums, the message is "build it and they will come," in retailing, the challenge is "say it often enough and prove it, and they will believe it and they, too, will come and buy and buy until they can buy no more."

When Herbert Marcus, philosopher, dreamer, and master salesman died on December 11, 1950, at age seventy-two, the company he had co-founded was already in capable hands. Although Stanley had revered his father, it is clear he had long chafed at the bit, restlessly eager to put his indelible print on all things Neiman Marcus. With his father gone, there were no roadblocks to his taking stands on issues, often controversial, but always heartfelt.

In later years, Stanley would still note with at least some bitterness that it was very difficult to please his father completely. There was always something that could have been done better, or a line chosen that should have been ignored, or a person hired who should not have even been interviewed. "He was almost impossible to satisfy," wrote Stanley some twenty-five years after his father's death.

The irony in that statement is abundantly clear to anyone who worked closely with him throughout his long career in retailing and beyond. He professed, sometimes with eyes twinkling, to embrace the ancient Greek adage about pacing off half the distance to the wall and then half of what was left and so on until no space apparently remained. The secret was that some miniscule microscopic space would always remain. That proved, at least to him and probably to his father before him, that pure perfection, getting all the way to the proverbial wall, was impossible. On a scale of one to ten, with ten being perfection, the digit closest to that highest score was probably a nine, or in Stanley's personal scheme of things, maybe a nine and a half only when it came to his favorite ice cream or licorice candy, but seldom to store operations. Sometimes, an eight might be scored and anything below a five sent suddenly ex-employees swiftly out the door.

When he assumed the full mantle of company leadership at the age of forty-five, he instantly set about enhancing the remarkable legend he had helped create. Free from any parental constraints, except perhaps an occasional cautionary word from his mother, Stanley set his own course.

His personal influence on the merchandising of the store was clearly evident. He had benefited mightily from the fashion teachings of his Aunt Carrie who was still close at hand to guide him even further, but most significantly his innate showmanship now had no fetters. He had quickly ascertained that the unique geographical location of Neiman Marcus in the perceived wasteland of Texas provided just the right setting for his gemstone of a store.

Stanley also had long before recognized that the greater the stature of his store became on a national scale, the more successful it would become at its home in Dallas. Under his direction, Neiman Marcus acquired an increased sense of pride in itself and that pride was readily transferable to any and all who would or could shop there. Self-confidence and self-assurance came part and parcel with the pride and for the next quarter century he would without pause push his store to a level of proud success only dreamed of by his father. His goal was excellence in all things, and his pursuit of it gave new meaning to the word "relentless."

Fashioning the Fortnights

Although Stanley Marcus was known throughout the retail industry as being an innovator even before his father died, it was during his years as chief executive of the company that his marketing prowess reached its zenith. His extravagant fashion shows, publicity campaigns, and colorful national advertising had set his store apart from most others by the time he took sole command of Neiman Marcus in 1950. As he saw it, however, there were two exceptional marketing creations that were truly the capstones of his entire retail career.

The first of these were the Neiman Marcus Christmas Books. Although the company began mailing Christmas brochures to its clientele as early as 1911, it was Stanley who transformed them into international news through his clever use of public relations and imaginative if often outlandish extraordinary gift ideas.

As well-known as the Christmas Books are today, in Stanley's personal view the most famous of all his original creations were the Neiman Marcus Fortnights, annual events that captivated and dominated the Dallas marketplace for thirty years. Though discontinued in 1986, memories of the events remain strong among the thousands of customers who still vividly recall the unique mix of whimsy and circus-like excitement that each of the Fortnights brought to the city.

"The Fortnights," wrote Stanley Marcus "were probably the most talked about and most widely copied retail events of all time." Never one to shy away from the spotlight, Marcus might nevertheless have been a bit overly lavish with his praise for the events he produced, but few can deny that the Fortnights were spectacular and frequently imitated by other stores across the nation and around the world.

It is interesting to note that the idea for the Fortnights was not of Stanley's origin at all, but rather a concept he deftly purloined from the Nordica Department Store in Stockholm, Sweden. During a trip to that Scandinavian city in 1955, he happened upon a French promotion that was attracting many shoppers into the store which had been decorated with Parisian themes and filled with merchandise imported from France. Special events including musical concerts and wine tastings were being featured throughout the store, and Stanley's fertile imagination quickly envisioned a similar event but produced, of course, on a much grander scale in his store back in Texas.

His conversations with Nordica executives indicated that while the event had been expensive to mount, much of the cost had been borne by the French government and by vendors in that country eager to find new markets for their goods. After watching the crowds that for several days flocked into the store to buy those imported goods, Stanley convinced himself that what was successful in Stockholm could easily be even more successful in Dallas.

He hastily changed his travel schedule and returned to Paris where he had been just before journeying to Sweden. In hastily arranged meetings with the appropriate government officials, Stanley told them of his desire to emulate if not markedly improve upon the Nordica promotion he had just observed. Always persuasive, he convinced the authorities that despite its relatively remote location in the northern part of Texas, the city of Dallas held great potential for the staging of a French themed event far more grandiose than the one in Stockholm.

To ensure the success of the proposed promotion, Stanley promised the trade officials that he would encourage the presentation of all manner of French cultural events throughout the city to coincide with the in-store event, unlike the Swedes who had focused solely on merchandise in the store itself. That he made good on that initial promise was the key to the thirty-year spectacular run of the Neiman Marcus Fortnights.

With a pledge of generous financial support from France in hand, Stanley hurried back to Dallas to make sure that all the cultural organizations he had so blithely committed to participate in the French event would indeed do so. Without difficulty, the Dallas Symphony, the theaters, the museums, the library, Southern Methodist University, and even the public school system eagerly signed on to participate in what promised to be a citywide event unlike any other ever staged in Dallas or, in fact, anywhere else in the world.

One of the key elements in the initial success of what Stanley had christened the French Fortnight was the simple fact that it was staged in Dallas rather than a New York, Chicago, or San Francisco. In 1957, when the first Fortnight was launched, Dallas was still in many ways a relatively bucolic town, albeit one tinged with some delusions of grandeur.

Long established old-cotton-money citizens had grudgingly if half-heartedly accepted the claims to an elevated social status being clamorously made by the newly rich oil people. For the most part, though, only a few of the town's citizens were wealthy enough to frequently travel abroad to savor the storied excitement of such lands as France or England, and certainly not Japan or Australia.

The Fortnights, which ran from 1957 through 1986, provided to a broad spectrum of Dallasites and countless other Texans a brightly colored fairyland glimpse of erotic faraway places that for most people had previously only been available through travel films in the movie houses or *National Geographic* magazine. There was, during the first Fortnight years, of course, no "Travel Channel" to whisk armchair voyagers magically out of their Texas dens and onto the boulevards of Paris or to the charming side streets of London.

In their own simplistic way, the Fortnights were magic carpets that brought to Dallas at least a hint of the lure of many foreign lands. They were never, in truth, intended to present anything resembling an actual picture of any particular country. As the executive producer of over half of these events later on, it is easy for me to declare that the driving motivation behind them was to increase store traffic and thus hopefully expand the volume of sales during the normally listless pre-Christmas selling season that occurs in mid-October. If school children learned a little something about a particular land, so much the better, and if the many cultural entities located in the city were pleased to unite under one international theme for a few weeks each autumn that, too, was wonderful. The fundamental idea behind it all, however, to Neiman Marcus in Dallas as it had been to Nordica in Stockholm, was to provide customers with an intriguing and compelling reason to come into the store at a time when they traditionally did not do so.

To be sure, layered atop this basic retail motivation were eventually to be found some truly altruistic and public spirited aspects of cultural, educational, and social activities. The main thrust of the events in the store, however, was the introduction of newly discovered lines of merchandise from the country being featured. Many of the garments, accessories, wines, and foodstuffs presented throughout the store were being offered in the United States for the first time. This fact alone added directly to the already dazzling reputation of Neiman Marcus. How this still relatively small store in a middle size Texas city could discover and then get exclusive brand agreements with heretofore unknown but obviously high quality foreign vendors constantly vexed the competition.

The answer was simple enough. Under the watchful and strict editorial eye of Stanley Marcus, platoons of the store's highly experienced merchandising experts would descend upon the featured country for many months prior to the annual fall event. Their charge was to avoid the obvious clichés of merchandise and to use their established market contacts to seek out vendors of newly designed goods or remote craftsmen who might have the production capability of turning out only a hundred or so truly unique handmade items. The rarest of antiques, the wines from newly discovered vineyards, the wood carvings from some isolated village were found without fail as the merchants scoured the countryside to discover those items that they knew would satisfy Stanley, the master merchant who impatiently awaited news of their discoveries.

His was the final say about which merchandise should be purchased for the Fortnights, at least for those events staged from 1957 through 1975. When all samples from the featured country were assembled and presented to him at a meeting in Dallas, more items were usually rejected than accepted. Simply being made in France or Italy or wherever was by no means good enough reason for any merchandise to be offered during the Fortnight.

While the merchants were in the country, seeking new resources or encouraging longtime suppliers to create things both new and exciting, other store personnel were also combing the countryside seeking artwork to be displayed in the store or in cooperating galleries throughout the city. Artisans and craftsmen were put under contract to come to Dallas to demonstrate their skills. Musical groups and well-known musicians were signed to perform at the store or at concerts with the Dallas Symphony. Dignitaries including queens, princes, and ambassadors came in abundance to attend galas and opening ceremonies. Movie stars were invited to represent their country at a film festival at

Southern Methodist University and, of course, to appear in the store to the delight of the movie-loving Dallasites.

The discipline that absolutely mandated quality, originality, and excitement was the key element that made the Fortnights such memorable events. It was that discipline, that commitment to excellence demanded by Stanley Marcus in all things that also pushed the full concept of the Fortnights beyond the four walls of the store itself.

Had the events not been built upon the company's required foundation of quality, the involvement of nearly all major cultural facets of the city would not have been carried forward year after year following that very first French Fortnight in 1957. Further, had the events been anything but grand successes, the sponsoring countries would not have come frequently to Dallas asking to again be invited to be the underwriting featured country. Over the thirty year span of the Fortnights, there were four more French events after the first in 1957, five British, three Italian, four with a Far Eastern theme and one salute to a country that did not exist, but more on that later.

In addition to concerts and major art exhibits being presented throughout the city, all manner of other tie-in promotions occurred annually. Travel bureaus around town featured posters urging trips to the Fortnight land. A Texas version of a British pub once advertised a dart tournament with the winner to be dubbed "The Neiman Marcus King or Queen of Darts" and rewarded with a dinner for two at the store's famed Zodiac Room.

Schools were invited to arrange tours of the store during the event and every weekday morning saw fleets of squat yellow school busses parked next to the store where sleek black limousines would be seen later in the day. Some schools had essay assignments featuring an aspect of the Fortnight country.

During one of the Italian Fortnights, for example, most Dallas schools sponsored a "How to Straighten the Leaning Tower of Pisa" essay contest. This was motivated by a replica of that dangerously tilting landmark that had been created in the store. To give at least some idea of the scale of the actual building, the Neiman Marcus version began, in great detail, on the store's second floor and proceeded upward through the ceiling of each floor until it emerged, still atilt, on the fifth floor. In all, the replica was roughly fifty feet in height.

Out of the thousands of drawings and word pictures received from fourth and fifth grade students in nearly every Dallas-area school, several proved to be remarkably viable. One entry depicted an injection of water on a regular schedule to the base of the tower in order to slowly nudge it back to its original perpendicular position while another suggested the use of multiple bulldozers and an intricate web of strong cables to gently correct the slant. The water-injection idea was deemed the most likely to succeed by a panel of engineers and the ten-year old winner was given a dinner for herself and her proud parents in the store's restaurant. The winning drawing then was sent to the mayor of Pisa, a fact that was touted in a typical Neiman Marcus publicity campaign. Unfortunately, no reply has as yet been received from the mayor's office in the over twenty-five years since the design was sent.

It was the store's ability to compel an entire city to voluntarily participate in the Fortnights that paid homage to the marketing skills of Stanley Marcus and the powerfully influential store over which he presided. It is difficult to imagine any other store ever again accomplishing that level of community-wide endorsement. If it ever occurred to any member of the board of directors of any of the multitude of cultural entities that wholeheartedly participated in the Fortnights over the years that by doing so, a retail promotion was being overtly endorsed, no such complaint ever surfaced. Dallas and the Neiman Marcus Fortnights fit each other like the proverbial hand in the glove for exactly three decades.

Each of the events were heralded and promoted by large and colorful posters that were to be seen all around town for weeks in advance and during the Fortnight. They brightened supermarket windows, the elevators of the Dallas Public Library, and the bulletin boards of public and private schools. On one occasion, the principal design element of a poster was reproduced in the illuminated office windows of a downtown skyscraper.

Stanley was for many years the driving force behind the designing of the posters which have now become rare collectors' items. A complete set of all thirty of them has been known to change hands for several thousands of dollars, even though a quantity of the just created posters was once available from the store simply by asking.

To each artist chosen to create the design, Stanley would issue his customary challenge, "It must be a telegram and not an essay." As a result of that edict, each poster was simple but effective even from an appreciable distance with a minimal use of script but long on eye catching color.

Aside from the civic involvement and the vast array of exciting imported merchandise, it was the visual transformation of the store inside and out into a spectacular version of a foreign land that still resonates through the memories of longtime Neiman Marcus customers. A thumbnail recounting of some details of such a visual transformation is to follow, but words cannot describe the effect that such wizardry evoked. Customers leaving the store on the Friday before the Fortnight was to open on the following Monday would depart with the elegant first floor looking as it did during other weeks of the year. It was cool, refined, subtly illuminated and spacious. It was, in short, elegant.

In just two days, however, everything had changed. One year, for example, the sparkling tile floors had become a cobblestone roadway in a rural English village, the next, the shining metal elevator doors had changed into the doors of a German cuckoo clock, while animated cuckoos cheerfully announced the arrival of each elevator. The stately main floor columns, were from year to year, transformed into giant trees or perhaps the mirrored columns of an oriental palace. The cumulative effect was just short of electrifying and clearly reflected the thousands of man-hours and millions of dollars that it had taken to totally transform not only the main floor but the entire store with a dramatic suddenness not unlike the coming of a circus to a vacant lot, literally overnight and then, perhaps much too soon, vanish with equal abruptness.

The ultimate test of the effectiveness of the Fortnight décor was the compulsory tour of the entire building just prior to the public opening. Before the dignitaries and the movie stars arrived, and while merchants nervously fussed over their displays of imported goods, and as chefs began preparing the often exotic, unknown cuisine of Japan or perhaps Thailand, the obligatory and often dreaded tour with Stanley began.

Seemingly endless, particularly when I became the events' producer after 1972, the trip through the store included an inspection of individual items of merchandise, queries to buyers about the absence of one line or another that he had highly recommended and, above all, a constant flow of often pithy observations about the drape of the fabric in that display or the inaccurate color of paint used in yet another exhibit.

If the tour began even an hour and a half before the doors were to open, they were seldom completed before Stanley was needed at the microphone to introduce the stars who were present to officially open the event. Often, the slow trek upward through the building would be postponed while he performed his official opening day duties only to be resumed even as the hordes of shoppers began their daily assault upon the store.

He studied as many facets of the promotion as long as he possibly could until other issues needed his attention, but he was not yet finished. For the entire duration of the event, which in later years eventually grew from two weeks into three, memoranda containing minute observations or, more often, suggestions about how to improve something next time around flowed from his desk at the rate of twenty to perhaps forty a day.

He was without doubt a micromanager. It is well known that early in his career, the micromanaging aspect of his leadership style covered every time frame of every project and every product, from its inception to its conclusion and to its aftermath. As the years passed, he did not slow down but rather the products became more numerous, the projects more frequent, and the challenges of managing multiple stores too complex to such a degree that time did not permit his hands to be on everything. Earlier, when the number of stores was only three with downtown Dallas as the center ring, he had all the time in the world to peck away seeking his eternal quest for perfection in all things that carried the name Neiman Marcus.

If the fundamental strategy behind the Fortnight concept was the generation of surging crowds of shoppers eager to buy out-of-the-ordinary merchandise, then the Fortnights were undeniably highly successful. Further, if the ancillary value of a public endorsement of and participation in a retail promotion was worth the huge cost of the event itself, the answer must be resoundingly affirmative.

However, even as rosy as the memories of the long lost Fortnights have come to be, there were, along the way, some interesting sidebars that still serve to add a touch of humor to the still glowing tint of the recollections. For example, there was the Guinness incident. The designer on the Fortnight production team was a giant of a New Yorker named Alvin Colt. A costume and set designer of Broadway shows and the occasional movie, Alvin and I traveled the world together for nearly twenty years seeking Fortnight ideas as well as potential Fortnight countries with enough Fortnight-level cash to contribute to the production back in Dallas.

On one typically cold and damp Irish day, we made our way to the headquarters of the deservedly famous Guinness Brewing Corporation. After a strange luncheon consisting of huge quantities of "streaky bacon" and undercooked fish but with nary a drop of the flavorsome stout being brewed in the very same building, we proceeded to present our plans for a Guinness participation in an upcoming Irish Fortnight.

The executives with whom we met would have been very much at home at an attorneys' or bankers' luncheon with their Saville Row suits and Asbury neckwear. At any rate, we convinced them that their product, which I seriously doubt any of them had ever tasted, would benefit from the sort of introduction into the Texas market that only Neiman Marcus could give it. Because of our sales pitch, the brewery promised to give us a tidy sum of American dollars and an enormous quantity of Guinness Stout in massive refrigerated kegs to be shipped by sea to Texas at their company's expense.

This had clearly been a luncheon to remember as I recall us congratulating ourselves later in a Dublin pub over tall glasses of the incomparably rich yet potentially hammering "Liquid Bread," as the company called it. A few days later, on the plane bound for home, I suddenly realized that we might have created an interesting problem through our persuasiveness at the brewery. A check for many thousands of dollars to be sent from Dublin to Dallas was obviously one thing, but how to get one thousand gallons of refrigerated Guinness out of the hold of a ship at the Port of Houston and eventually into twenty ounce glasses at Neiman Marcus in Dallas was a different challenge altogether. As it developed, the logistics of transporting the generous gift to Houston by sea was the least of our stout problems. Not being fully versed on the rules and regulations set forth by the Texas Alcoholic Beverage Commission (TABC), as probably no one has ever been, I was blissfully unaware that, at least back in 1976, the size of the container being imported into the state was a serious issue.

By the time the kegs had been offloaded and stored in a cold wharfside facility at the Port, the Commission boys were on the move and headed in my direction. Stanley, who usually found such ironic distractions more amusing than irritating, gleefully suggested that since it was nominally my brew, it was clearly my problem to resolve.

When the two TABC field inspectors marched into my Dallas office, I knew that resolution of the serious problem of owning kegs that were a full gallon more commodious than state regulations would permit to be imported was not going to be simple. The two men looked as though they shared either the same father or mother. Each was short, balding, overweight, and possessed of what are sometime called gimlet eyes, possibly an important characteristic for TABC employees at the time. They wore seemingly identical black suits and the narrowest dark green neckties that I had ever seen.

After some impressive flashing of badges and credentials of one kind or another, we got around to discussing the matter at hand, namely a warehouse full of cold Guinness being held under state government impoundment because the kegs were just too large to satisfy the TABC. The resolution came about within an hour's worth of remarkably civil debate. The state of Texas, it was resolved, would release the Guinness to us in the large kegs only if we signed a pledge agreeing not to sell it. Having nothing to lose by signing such a pledge, I promptly agreed to this simple solution. After all, the gallons of Guinness had cost us nothing so giving it away, although doing so was something that Neiman Marcus rarely did, was not a problem, at least in the principles of Economics 101 sense.

By the time the Irish beverage finally made it to Dallas, about four months after it had left Dublin, we had developed a plan to put the free brew to good use. With Stanley's blessing, we had decided to replicate an Irish pub on one of our selling floors during the Fortnight. Traditional cold so-called pub grub would be served at a fee, of course, along with a single complimentary glass of imported Guinness Stout being drawn from the seriously illegal kegs well hidden from sight. The "complimentary" word somehow made it all legal despite the size of the kegs.

The Guinness Pub was without doubt the biggest hit of the Irish Fortnight. Perhaps it was the rare opportunity to get a "complimentary" anything within the four walls of a Neiman Marcus store, or maybe it was the tasty little sausages and meat pies that were consumed at a heady pace and at an equally heady price, or maybe it was the Guinness itself, so cold and soothing on a hot October day in Dallas.

It was that soothing aspect of the Guinness that very nearly got us into some difficulty. Those who have had the pleasure of consuming this time-honored beverage will likely attest to its potency. Sheathed within its dark creamy appearance is a subtle kick that makes itself known only after two or more servings have been consumed. As one Irish pub keeper once put it, "It's like a soft rubber mallet that slowly starts thumping at the back of your neck before slamming into the front of your skull."

Aficionados of Guinness know this from experience but to the uninitiated cadre of Texas beer drinkers during the Irish Fortnight, the experience was gained the hard way. Devoted consumers of such local favorite brands as Lone Star and Budweiser soon came to realize that one glass full of Guinness, particularly a free one, equaled somewhere between two or three good old Texas beers depending on the physical stature and stamina of the consumer.

Proof of this truism came to light during a two day time span toward the end of the Fortnight. One of the waiters in the pub had served the tasty but limited fare to a society lady widely known to be an excellent customer, and to his great delight, a generous tipper. When she had quickly downed her first imperial pint of Guinness, a substantial twenty ounces in volume, she rather forcefully asked for a second glass. This she also consumed in a matter of minutes before rising somewhat unsteadily to make her exit. The waiter, who had broken the one Guinness per customer ruling, was overjoyed to discover that his minor offense had garnered him a hefty gratuity.

There seems to be something about free and powerful booze that causes people to return to its source. As this compulsion seemingly knows no social stratification, it could have been expected that the two-glass high society Guinness guzzler would return, literally, to the scene of the crime on the very next day.

Once again, she went through the apparently well-intentioned act of devouring her little meat pies, washing them down with her one free glass of Dublin's finest product. As it was late afternoon on the last day of the Fortnight, and the pub was not crowded, the waiter was eager to get his hands on some additional old Dallas society money. Fortunately for him, the well-known representative of that society still had an enormous thirst to quench before the Guinness Pub closed its free-flowing taps forever.

According to witnesses, she signaled the avaricious young man by beckoning with one hand and extending two fingers on the other. Obligingly, he brought forty more ounces to her table and when the pub lights came up to indicate closing time an hour later, there she sat, still as properly bolt upright as she had been taught to sit while at Dallas' elite Hockaday School, but now totally incapable of movement. She still sat, staring smilingly straight ahead but fully immobile when two store security men approached her table. In complete silence, she reached into her purse, extracted a ten dollar bill which she handed to the by now distraught waiter, and her car keys which she gave to one of the security men. As she was very well known to store personnel and, as noted, an excellent customer, the ever discreet security detail waited until the floor was almost devoid of other visitors, before placing the still immobile but happily beaming lady in a wheelchair and transporting her to the private employee entrance.

One of the members of the detail brought the lady her vehicle, helped pile her into the back seat and drove her home without further incident. The moral to this story, if there is one, might be never quickly drink more than two giant glasses of Guinness, but if you must, do it in an understanding place like Neiman Marcus, where good customer relations knows no bounds.

Aside from the occasionally overly Guinnessed society matron, the Fortnight productions usually proceeded as planned. Long before the current year's event had run its course, plans were well underway for the next year's extravaganza. Although the cost of the annual production was enormous, the sales volume and good will generated made them too valuable to abandon, at least for thirty consecutive years. The company's aggressive expansion timetable as conceived by new corporate ownership eventually made the time commitment required of management more vital to opening stores in new markets than focusing on a foreign country and its merchandise in just one store. When there were just the Texas stores to oversee and the Dallas flagship store to virtually redecorate annually at Fortnight time, the extravaganzas made good business sense. After 1986, however, with multiple store openings scheduled every year, the Fortnight concept was deemed too localized and too time consuming to warrant continuation. There are those, however, who remembering the excitement the events created in a then not so cosmopolitan Dallas still question the wisdom of abandoning one of Stanley's few borrowed ideas.

There remains to this day, however, some curiosity about how these multi-million dollar annual productions were actually made possible. From 1957 through 1969, the selection of the country to be feted was the sole responsibility of Stanley Marcus. Using his impeccable contacts in almost every civilized and some not so civilized country in the world, he would explore the possibilities of governmental financial support for such an event. The next step involved studying the market to plumb the availability of suitable merchandise. With these two points as his foundation, Stanley would consider the level of acceptance of any given country to his Texas audience. Clearly, neither Germany nor Japan were likely subjects for early Fortnights, but as memories of World War II grew dimmer, both nations eventually became Fortnight honorees and proved to be great successes.

Once the identity of the next subject country had been made, a decision that was not announced until after the current event had closed, the store's merchants would begin visiting the next Fortnight country to begin the lengthy process of identifying potential quality resources, locating little known cottage industries and making sure that production and shipping promises made would evolve into promises kept a year later.

With two exceptions, namely Spain in 1970 and Australia in 1971, every Stanley Marcus chosen Fortnight honoree country proved to have been a reliable and worthy choice. It was my unfortunate lot to be faced with these two defaulting nations but the lessons learned from these relative misadventures were valuable ones.

Working with Stanley over the years on the creation of classic Fortnights afforded me the rare opportunity to observe the man in action. His knowledge of the world's marketplace was phenomenal and his ability to coax large sums of francs, pounds, lire, and yen out of frequently reluctant donors was without parallel.

One of my most memorable journeys with him was in 1973 when I met him in Tokyo to begin work on a long delayed Japan Fortnight. Each day was crowded with endless sessions of green tea-fueled meetings with governmental officials who, through interpreters, gave clear evidence that they were very much in awe of their famous visitor from Texas. At the end of every meeting, we all bowed endlessly as we left the conference room with signed contracts in hand for major contributions of Japanese money, gratis air travel, and free hotel accommodations for the waves of buyers who would soon be on their way across the Pacific.

For some reason, Stanley always seemed to consider the Japanese people as being a bit comical. The slightest missed nuance by a well-meaning interpreter would cause his eyes to lighten in barely contained merriment. Any mishap that arose from attempts to communicate with hotel doormen in guidebook Japanese stimulated the gloriously slapstick sense of humor that lurked just below the surface of the man who was perceived by some as being "the melancholy Plato of retailing." A retailing Plato he might have appeared to be, but being melancholy was not, at least as I knew him in those days, an element of his character.

On one foray out of Tokyo to the far distant home studio of one of Japan's famous "National Living Treasures," I handed the hotel doorman a carefully written note containing, in Japanese, the explicit directions to the home of Mr. Muriyamasan, located some ten miles from the Imperial Hotel. The summoned cab driver and the doorman studied the note with great interest and an animated discussion ensued. The cabbie would nod and then point in one direction, whereupon the doorman would shake his head with an almost theatrical dismay and, shouting all the while, point in entirely the opposite direction.

As Stanley and I looked on much as spectators might at a tennis match, another doorman and eventually a hotel concierge appeared to join in the debate. At last, a consensus was reached and as the cabbie slid into the driver's seat, the original doorman, apparently vindicated by his backup team, smiled broadly and opened the rear passenger door for Stanley. As I went around the back of the taxi to get in on the other side, Stanley hesitated for just long enough to pick up his briefcase. In that split second, the apparently overruled driver slammed his tiny vehicle into gear and roared out from under the porte-cochere, leaving me on one side of the spot where the taxi had stood idling during the five minute directional dispute and Stanley Marcus on the other, briefcase in one hand and an absolutely stunned look on his face.

The doorman, seemingly shell-shocked, looked from one of us to the other before breaking into very un-Japanese like snorts of laughter at the Yankee tableau that stood before him. His laughter was almost as infectious as the just completed scene was ridiculous and the two Americans could only join in laughing at what had been a Mack Sennett moment, Tokyo-style.

In my last conversation with Stanley, a year and a half before his death, we again chuckled over that frozen-in-time memory. "I would be willing to bet," said the ninety-five year old, "that the little doorman has told that story to his grandchildren a hundred times over."

Language barriers were always a potential trouble spot in the Fortnight process. On one rainy night in October 1974, I drove to the Dallas airport to welcome La Infanta, the sister of the King of Spain who had been named the guest of honor at the Fortnight saluting her country. The flight was late due to bad weather in New York where the Princess and her entourage had changed planes following their trip from Madrid. The various delays had given some of her fellow travelers good reason to participate freely in the kind offer of American Airlines to serve an unlimited number of in-flight beverages of varying alcoholic content by way of compensation for their delayed journey.

That it had been a long and lavishly lubricated day became quickly evident as the singing Spaniards loped down the jetway at Dallas en route to enjoying their first cocktail on solid earth after several festive hours aloft. Once contact and identification had been achieved with some difficulty, I finally managed to get the happy throng loaded into limousines and headed toward their downtown hotel. Before leaving, the senora-in-waiting to the Princess was thinking clearly enough to hand me a large envelope of baggage claim tickets that had been given the group in New York City during their transfer from Iberia's flight from Madrid to the American flight to Dallas.

It was obvious that personally taking possession of the vast quantity of luggage represented by this encyclopedia-sized assortment of baggage claim tickets was not high on our visitors' list of things to do in Dallas. An associate of mine who was slated to be on the scene to get the luggage out of the airport and to the downtown Fairmont Hotel had failed to materialize out of the Dallas gloom so with my huge volume of claim checks in hand, I arrived at the appropriate carrousel to claim what I assumed was going to be around forty pieces of luggage. How to get it all to the hotel would be an issue later to be addressed.

I waited. All baggage from the New York flight had soon been plucked by other passengers before I realized that not one single piece of the Spanish luggage had ever made it down the chute to the carrousel which by now had come to a complete stop. Fortunately, I knew a few of the American Airlines employees on duty that night and with their help and patience, it was finally determined that the bags, all thirty-eight of them, would not be coming to Dallas any time soon as they had been sent to Washington, D.C., instead. The reason for this as we learned the next day, was that the young Spaniard assigned to oversee the baggage transfer at JFK in New York had told the Brooklyn-born baggage master there that his party was catching a flight to Dallas. This appeared to be reasonable enough until it later came to light that to Brooklyn tuned ears, the name "Dallas," especially when uttered by a tired Spaniard, sounded enough like "Dulles" to get the luggage efficiently dispatched to that then relatively new airport near the nation's capital.

Fortunately, after some hurried visits to an all night downtown drugstore and an after-hours shopping spree at Neiman Marcus, at the visitors' expense, of course, to tide them over until their luggage arrived from Washington, our guests were content to wait for the big Spanish Fortnight party to commence the next day.

At first, the Fortnights ran for only two weeks, as their British phrase clearly implies, but the size of the attending crowds and the amount of money they seemed eager to spend eventually mandated the addition of a third week. This always seemed to provide a great source of amusement to our British visitors who could not quite grasp how the term Fortnight, the British shorthand for fourteen days, could possibly be used to refer to a twenty-one day period for which there was no convenient terminology. In fact, there were many who felt that the greatest language barrier existed not between Texans and Japanese, or Italians, or even Greeks, but between the British who had invented and honed an English language neither always successfully imported, nor clearly understood in all parts of the United States, particularly within the borders of the Lone Star State which has language barriers of its own.

When Stanley handed me the direct responsibility of producing the Fortnights in 1972 so that he could write his autobiography, I soon began to realize how time consuming the project proved to be in order to be successful.

Alvin Colt and I would ordinarily leave the United States the week before Thanksgiving to spend three to four weeks abroad developing our dreams and ambitions about how to upstage the Fortnight just completed. As taught by Stanley, I would spend several months prior to the annual trip studying the country soon to be visited to identify those elements that would lend themselves to our traditional Fortnight treatment. This treatment was once perhaps aptly, but certainly cynically, described as being "neo-cute." I don't believe that our end visual products were intentionally neo-cute, but they were indeed sanitized and stylized into a hint or an illusion of the real thing. For example, while most of our customers might expect to find how the Neiman Marcus version of Bangkok's famed Klong Marketplace might look, we reasoned they would not be amused by the filth and squalor that is an integral part of the actual site.

It was never the intent to patronize our clientele through our simplified version of a well-known foreign building or other popular tourist attraction. As the years went by, and Dallasites became increasingly more worldly, we knew that many Neiman Marcus customers had traveled Germany's Romance Road, for example, and in so doing had seen countless versions of the famous glockenspiels that adorn many clock towers throughout that part of Germany. These folks did not expect their favorite store to merely replicate what they had seen with their own eyes, but they did hope to see what a Neiman Marcus glockenspiel would look like, given the store's well-known penchant for whimsy.

When the glockenspiel constructed for the store's German Fortnight in 1983 featured the telling of "Hansel und Gretel" in miniature, the world-weary travelers might have been somewhat bored until, as the tiny tableau came to its close, a wee armadillo carrying a Texas flag appeared with the familiar "Eyes of Texas" theme overriding the music of Humperdinck. As hoped, those who knew this to be a traditional Neiman Marcus touch were amused and those many others who neither knew about nor cared little about glockenspiels at all found it to be delightful.

It was by no means an insult to the maturity of the good people of Dallas that the Fortnights were almost childlike in their design. The purpose was to amuse and entertain the clientele in keeping with Stanley's concept of making the store into a theater. He had launched it with his weekly fashion show idea, followed by the Fashion Award event, and then trumped it all with the Fortnight magic that endured for many years.

To maintain the momentum of the Fortnight tradition, Alvin and I sought the essence of excitement that we could interpret to titillate and enchant even that cadre who boasted of having never missed seeing a single Fortnight. Our journeys took us to the mines of Brazil, the summit of Australia's colorful Ayres Rock, the fishing villages of France, the remote jungles of Thailand, and Buddhist temples in rural Japan. With camera and notebook, we recorded our impressions and began to develop a vision of what next year's Fortnight might be like in order to be even better than the one just completed.

After each day's adventure, we would create outlines of what the main themes would be and by the time the trip was over, enough creative planning had been achieved to meet with our fabricators in

Dallas to rough out estimated costs and, in my early years at the store, discuss our vision with Stanley Marcus.

Although some elements of the projected Fortnight plans might well have given him good reason to employ his undeniable power of veto, I cannot recall that he ever used that power to alter or delete any aspect of the plans. He did, of course, offer valuable suggestions that as a master showman it was his natural inclination to do.

After he went into semi-retirement from the direct supervision of the store, it was still my somewhat apprehensive pleasure to continue the tradition of escorting him through the building on the opening day of the Fortnight. The tour usually took well over an hour, or longer depending on how many employees stopped us so that they could visit with him and shake his hand. As usual, his eye missed nothing even though he was by then in his eighties. If he saw what he termed a blank spot, he let me know. If something pleased him, a warm smile would spread across his face. Usually, the smiles outnumbered the pointed references to opportunities missed or even worse, opportunities recognized but squandered by ineffective execution.

Finally, it all came down to the moment of truth at our journey's end on the top selling floor. Stanley, I am sure, knew that I was awaiting either his benediction or his statement of displeasure as I had so many times before. I cannot say that, in the seventeen Fortnight tours that he and I made, every final critique was glowing. If he was disappointed, for example, in the coloration we had used to create the essence of a Brazilian village, he told me so. If the Zodiac Room restaurant, temporarily converted into an Irish Castle, lacked the proper lighting effect to live up to his expectations, I learned of that as well. Without fail, however, once his list of minor disappointments had been reviewed and offered as guidelines to future Fortnight productions, he would shake my hand, saying "Well, you've done it again." There could have been no greater, nor more welcome, benediction. He would turn and walk away to where a group of customers waited to have their hands shaken by Mr. Stanley himself. He was still very much a celebrity and he reveled in knowing that he was.

Since the abandonment of the Fortnight in the years since the Australian event in 1986, much has been written about how each contributed to add a temporary touch of show business glitz and glamour to a downtown Dallas that, until the beginning of the twenty-first century, had grown increasingly shabby and all but desolate. Though this unfortunate state of affairs is happily no longer the case, the Neiman Marcus Fortnights, symbols of another era are instead sadly gone but definitely not forgotten.

For those whose memories might benefit from refreshment, the following offers nostalgic highlights of some selected Fortnights.

ᔓ France ᔕ
1957

This was the original and to Stanley's mind until his final days, the best one ever. He produced it, had it financed, and sold the idea to the entire city of Dallas as only a master salesman possibly could. He had arranged for a special Air France flight to land at Dallas Love Field to disgorge its lovely cargo of French models, escorted by Parisian designers, a retinue of artists, writers, and perhaps more important, famous chefs. When the Air France plane, the first foreign carrier to touch down in Dallas had landed, as Stanley Marcus said not quite twenty years later, it was "the most exciting experience of my life." The initial foreign invasion of Dallas, courtesy of Neiman Marcus, had been benign but overwhelming, and created a store tradition that would continue for many years. The first Fortnight event received national coverage in *Time* magazine in a story entitled "Dallas in Wonderland."

As a reward for this groundbreaking success, which was as beneficial to France and Dallas as it was to Neiman Marcus, Stanley became one of the elite few Americans to receive the coveted French Legion of Honor medal.

✺ Demark ✺
1964

This was the first and only Danish Fortnight. It took place at a time when Danish design in fabric and wood seemed poised to establish a permanent new hallmark in the world of retailing. Unfortunately, the depth of quality goods proved to be inadequate to sustain the same levels of sales volume that had been generated by the British and Italian Fortnights that had preceded it.

By all accounts, however, Alvin Colt's use of the Tivoli Gardens theme for the all important main floor décor was brilliant. Its success served to establish an annual fervent attempt to make each main floor's décor even better than that of the previous year. As time went by, it became fashionable for customers to judge the Fortnights primarily on what was even then termed "The Wow Effect," stimulated by the first glimpse of the main floor on opening day.

✺ East Meets West ✺
1969

To the eyes of many, this Stanley Marcus/Alvin Colt creation was among the very best of all the Fortnights. Perhaps this perception is because this was the last one to be staged while the company was owned exclusively by the Marcus family and a handful of shareholders. In reality, the new owners did not interfere with Fortnights or any other sales promotion effort, but some customers preferred to imagine otherwise. The generous use of fresh flowers in many exhibits and displays gave the event a quality not previously enjoyed. Demonstrations of Asian crafts and artisans helped fuel the foreign "difference" that Stanley viewed as being one key to Fortnight success.

Each floor received greater visual attention than before and, as a result, the focus shifted at least to some degree to other floors rather than just the main floor. For its sheer beauty and dramatic demonstration of the fact that other cultures, though totally different than our own, can be highly impressive, "East Meets West" must be considered a trailblazing success.

✒ Fete des Fleurs ✒
1971

Following an embarrassing default of Australia as a subject country, to be discussed later, the substituted "Fete des Fleurs" effort was a rare second choice that proved to be a winner. Literally thousands of flowers and living plants adorned every niche and corner of the store. Because of the need for extensive air conditioning in Dallas in October, the store's atmosphere was nothing like a greenhouse. As a result, a rigorous inspection was conducted each morning to identify and remove any flower or plant that was even beginning to show signs of withering in the cool dry interior of the store. A famous San Francisco florist design firm helped create the imaginative and colorful displays, while a local greenhouse kept the blooms alive and well.

The greatest aspect of the entire event, of course, was the presence of one-time actress Grace Kelly in her new real life role as Princess Grace of Monaco. The crowds that blocked almost every aisle during her visit to the store soon required control by officers of the Dallas Police Department. Front page photos of a radiant princess and a beaming Stanley Marcus being protected by "Dallas' Finest" immediately told of the success of the event.

✒ Japan ✒
1974

Hours of debate served as a prologue to this ultimately successful event. For the first time, concerns were expressed about Americans', or at least Texans', attitudes toward what was widely regarded as having been a particularly bitter enemy during World War II. By combining an equal emphasis on traditional Japanese ceremonial beauty and the nation's leadership in the production of electronic products, the store managed to thwart any displeasure by veterans' groups or others.

The event was funded in large measure by such big firms as Sony, Panasonic, and Toshiba. In an effort to stimulate the interest of these and other companies, exhibit space on one of the store's selling floors was "sold" by the square foot. On a large plan of the floor, the amount of space already acquired by Sony, for example, was subtly indicated to competing firms. In just one day in Chicago, in a hotel suite located next to that city's annual electronics show, over $350,000 worth of space was snapped up by Japanese firms which were eager to share the limelight with such industry leaders as Sony.

✒ Brazil ✑
1978

While neither a great artistic nor commercial success, the Brazilian Fortnight introduced Dallas to a then little known culture. From the "Savior of the Andes" in Rio Janerio to the black voodoo magic of the Amazon basin, facets of this huge and brooding nation were represented in the store. The stark but striking modern architecture of the city of Brasilia was contrasted with the ancient facades of colorful Bahia, while hints of the still violent jungles were offered.

Of special interest to Dallas was an appearance of the internationally famous soccer star, Pele. Not content with simply handing out autographed pieces of paper, the gracious athlete often surprised his large crowd of fans by producing autographed soccer balls from a large bag concealed beneath a table. As word of his generosity spread throughout the store, the size of his new fan club soon grew to almost unmanageable proportions.

The only downside of this event came when the name of a famous Brazilian race car driver was mispronounced by the store manager during opening ceremonies. Even though his name did contain about

five distinct and unusually pronounced syllables, the driver took umbrage and stalked off the stage.

❧ Germany ❧
1983

Stanley was always hesitant to present a German Fortnight to his
clientele in Dallas. Even though he had retired from the store some
years earlier, we still sought his blessing before approaching the
German government in Bonn for support and endorsement. He re-
minded us that Germany had been considered several times before but
because of the possibility of negative public reaction, no approach had
been made. By 1982, however, Germany had become both a staunch
ally of the United States as well as a strong trade partner. We were
convinced that memories of World War II had faded at least enough to
proceed with the negotiations.

The end result was one of the most colorful and free-spirited events
in Fortnight history. Dancing, singing, and oceans of strong German
beer combined to provide a gala atmosphere for the unique merchandise never before seen anywhere in the United States.

The only hint of war-tainted memories came from the German government itself. When I suggested the son of Field Marshal Erwin
Rommel be permitted to attend the Fortnight as an honored guest, the
request was denied by the Bonn government even though Herr
Rommel himself was quite eager to visit Dallas. No reason was ever
given for turning down the request, but since Rommel was a government employee, the matter was not pursued.

Summary

People living in other cities may find it difficult to understand why
the Fortnights still occupy such a warm spot in the memories of the
thousands of Texans who experienced the events for so many years.

They were exciting productions, to be sure, and totally unusual events to be presented in a high fashion and somewhat haughty specialty store. Perhaps it was that out of context, lighthearted aspect that made them so popular and consequently even now so dearly missed after over twenty years.

In large part, however, the lingering memories might well stem from the citywide scope of the Fortnights that literally reached into every corner of the town's cultural and social life. That, in turn, brilliantly demonstrated the sheer magnetic power which Neiman Marcus enjoys.

With no intention whatever of disparaging the modern retailing behemoth from Bentonville, Arkansas, it is difficult nonetheless to even imagine a Walmart event on the scale of the Fortnights. Perhaps symphonies and school systems would join museums and theaters in participating in a city-wide extravaganza saluting a merchandising event being staged at their local Walmart, but somehow, with all due respect to Sam Walton's successors, it just doesn't seem too likely to happen anytime soon. It took Stanley Marcus to bring events of this magnitude to Dallas and his creative genius to enshrine them in the memories of countless longtime Texans.

Joining the Ranks

All that I knew with certainty as I walked into the Neiman Marcus flagship store in downtown Dallas back on January 2, 1970, was that my future was not bright. Four previously hired sales promotion directors had all too recently come and gone through what some store executives were now laughingly calling "Stanley's revolving door."

The "doorkeeper's" secretary met me at the employee entrance at the appointed hour and led me past what seemed to be a gauntlet of pitying eyes to the office of the great man himself. There he sat, sipping his special brand of espresso surrounded by his senior executive staff. It was fairly obvious that most of the assembled vice presidents had become somewhat bored with the now almost annual ritual of meeting the new sales promotion man but for the most part, the welcome was warm enough to lead me to believe I might at least last until lunchtime.

Stanley, in his lair after the executive phalanx had departed, could not have been more cordial. He gave me his views on every one of my department managers I was soon to meet and reiterated his confidence in my ability to do the job. I later learned that this optimistic opinion was not universally shared by my fellow vice presidents who had formed a betting pool to speculate about and place rather sizeable wagers on how long *this* one would last.

After presiding over an introductory coffee reception with my new staff, Stanley left me at my office door with an invitation to join him later for lunch at the store's famous Zodiac Room. When he failed to appear for our luncheon date, I called his office only to learn that he had been taken to the emergency room at Baylor Hospital just minutes after leaving me earlier in the day.

Nearly a week passed before any word came about the seriousness of, or even the nature of, his condition. Then came a message that I was to go at once to the hospital to see him. It was during that hospital visit that I learned that my professional life working for Stanley Marcus was going to be almost as much a mind game as it would be just an out-and-out job.

After hurriedly stuffing sheets of notes and correspondence into my briefcase, I rushed to Baylor Hospital with no idea what to expect. I found him propped up in bed in the largest and most elegant hospital suite I have ever seen. At his command inside his flower-filled domain was a bevy of attractive nurses and nurse's aides who scurried in and out seemingly catering to his every whim. Some brought him a fresh supply of books and newspapers while others re-arranged flowers and removed green plants that no longer pleased his artistic sensibilities.

The senior nurse in overall command of this busy platoon might have been sent from the central casting office if the call had been for a mean and tough old master sergeant of the nursing profession. Why Stanley had permitted her to remain at her post is a good question, as he was never one to long tolerate either mean or tough old female drill instructors. Yet, there she stood, arms folded across her starched white uniform sternly watching as her far more attractive charges fluttered adoringly around their obviously amused and pampered patient.

Perhaps she who was in charge of this medical chorus line had learned to read Stanley's eye signals or perhaps he merely nodded or raised a finger or whatever, but at any rate, the head nurse suddenly turned and moved quickly to the door, followed by her little army of candy stripers.

With just the two of us in the room, the clearly not suffering patient asked that I give him a full report on my first week on the job. About two minutes into this unrehearsed but likely whiney account of how I felt I had been cruelly mistreated by my fellow executives, Stanley opened a drawer in the stand next to his bed and pulled out what proved to be dozens of newspaper pages featuring Neiman Marcus advertisements. On each ad were numerous handwritten scrawls that over the years I came to know only too well as his daily critiques of every ad, its copy, its artwork, and often, its very reason for having been placed at all.

The verbal critique, delivered in his soft and beautifully modulated voice, went on for what seemed an eternity, but just as I was beginning to hope he might have a mild but not life threatening relapse of some sort, the infamous curmudgeon in hospital whites charged back into the room bearing his stack of daily mail, a few telegrams, and to my dismay, that day's editions of Dallas's two newspapers.

After silently reading the letters and other correspondence while blessedly leaving the consuming of the newspapers and his attack upon the ads until later, he settled back in his bed, giving me a look that for a moment seemed to question just who I might be and why was I sitting in his room. When this moment passed, he took me completely by surprise by asking if I would like a cigar. For some mysterious but time honored reason, the only known acceptable response to that question is, "I don't mind if I do." This answer seemed to be of great cheer to him and, beaming, he directed me to a cabinet across the room where I would find a box of fine Cubans, a snipper, and his favorite cigar lighter. As instructed, I took one of the Havanas to him, clipped the end of mine, a feat he watched closely, and fired the thing up. Stanley quickly repeated this routine, and we soon sat puffing away in as much luxury as any hospital room can possibly offer, chatting about the future of the Dallas Cowboys and other such manly subjects while gazing out at the skyline of the city he had so greatly influenced.

With no open windows to act as chimneys, the room was soon filled with the heady blue smoke that only fine cigars can produce. It was, in fact, becoming a bit difficult for me to clearly make out the hospital gown clad fellow smoker who was sitting up on the bed across the room. In obedience to the laws of physics, a sufficient quantity of the smoke had apparently found its way under the room's door and into the hospital corridor. This truth became acutely evident when the door literally exploded open and in charged the dragon in white, masquerading as a head nurse, who demanded to know, in a voice that could probably be heard in Fort Worth some thirty miles away, just who in the hell was smoking in this room. To deal with this seemingly unanticipated and unwelcome intrusion, Stanley deftly let his cigar-holding hand drop out of sight before pointing toward me, and in that mellow voice only partially made hoarse by all the smoke, he calmly said, "He is."

Without any respect for my rights either as a visitor or newly arrived Texan, she very strongly ordered me to grind out the burning end of my cigar in a Petrie dish she thrust in my face. I meekly obeyed this harsh command under her furious glare and then she turned on the flat heels of her crepe soled shoes and stormed out, nearly as forcefully as she had entered.

Stanley found all of this to be highly amusing. In the thirty years I was to know him, I never saw him laugh quite as heartily as he did that morning. As he chortled, giggled, and all but guffawed at my chagrin, he would pause long enough to take deep drags on the only cigar still burning in the room.

In time, of course, the accumulated smoke from even that sole Havana found an outlet under the door and once again, here came the fire warden. When she saw my now stone cold cigar still in its makeshift ashtray, she turned her steely gaze on the patient who looked back at her in all innocence with his left hand clutching his burning cheroot, cleverly hidden from sight.

When he assured her that cigar smoke always took a long time to dissipate in a closed room, she seemed mollified if not thoroughly convinced, but presumably not being a cigar smoker herself, she had neither the evidence nor the courage to question the famous Stanley Marcus.

Her departure from the smoky room bearing my dead cigar in its little dish touched off yet another round of glee in which this time I could not help but participate. I realized that I had been Stanley's enabler and from that early experience came a lesson that guided me throughout our long association, namely, that working with Stanley was not unlike playing pool with a true shark. His way of doing things involved a sly schematic that ran, "If I make this shot, then he'll take that shot, then I'll run the table, and win." Winning, suffice it to say, was of utmost importance to the man, and he seldom lost.

The final shot for that first round of gamesmanship came as I was leaving his room. "Tom," he said softly, handing me his still smoldering cigar, "would you mind taking this with you? That old gal has one hell of a temper."

Ending the Honeymoon

ollowing the cigar incident at Baylor Hospital, I did not see Stanley Marcus again for several weeks. The store's always fertile and active rumor machine had it that his illness had proved to be far more serious than originally believed and as a result, he had been transferred to some other, always unnamed, medical facility out of Texas. Another tale was built on the fact that he would soon turn sixty-five and as a result, he had abruptly retired and gone to live in the South of France without any departing fanfare. Not likely!

Stanley's favorite of the many rumors that swirled about as he quietly convalesced at home from minor surgery was that he had gone to a clinic in Switzerland to undergo a series of experimental youth-restoring treatments. When he and his elegant wife made a surprise visit to a company function a few weeks later, one longtime employee remarked to me that he had never seen Stanley look better, proving, at least to his satisfaction, that those "youth shots must really work."

Aside from a few battles over advertising issues that had arisen during my first month on the job, things seemed to be going fairly smoothly despite the absence of my mentor and protector. On his very first full day back in the office, however, a real crisis arose that sent the store into a tailspin. For the first time in the thirteen year history of the fabled Neiman Marcus Fortnight extravaganzas, Spain, the announced sponsoring country had withdrawn its support.

The previous chapter described in some detail the overall scope of the Fortnight concept that Stanley had initiated in 1957. Suffice it to say here, the social and cultural impact of these annual international salutes had grown to very impressive proportions over the years with virtually every major aspect of Dallas cultural activity being focused on the honored country during two weeks every October.

When the shock of Spain's politically inspired cancellation of its Fortnight commitment had subsided to some degree, it became imperative that a substitute promotion immediately be found to minimize the reduction in the enormous sales volume that the Fortnights had provided without fail. Further, steps had to be taken to notify the art museums, the Dallas Symphony, movie houses, and all matter of other entities that the events they had already planned to feature Spanish art and music ten months hence in October would need to be cancelled.

This was not the sort of introduction into the fabled world of Neiman Marcus promotion that I had envisioned. On several occasions over the preceding years, I had come to Dallas to see a Fortnight for myself and to learn why many retail trade publications devoted gallons of ink each year to praise these unique events. No country had ever defaulted and the shock of it all was staggering but particularly to me, the new kid on the block.

We met frequently to find an answer to this thorny challenge which now in retrospect seems almost trifling. Senior merchants cut short their buying trips abroad to hurry back to Dallas to meet with Stanley and his promotional staff in an effort to develop a strategy that would avoid the loss of the Fortnight's sales volume that was second only to

Christmas in scale. Volume is, as previously noted, the lifeblood of every retail store, and to realize in advance that the fall season was destined to be a catastrophe because of some behind-the-scenes political intrigue in Madrid spread a dark gloom through the executive offices of Neiman Marcus and particularly mine.

Planning for the Fortnights was a lengthy process, often involving many years as has been discussed. In the Spanish case, Stanley's time and effort had been wasted and it was clearly much too late to go knocking on any other foreign doors to solicit the kind of financial support required to stage such an elaborate event.

We called in outside experts to advise us. Long brainstorming sessions grew even longer as the time to find a solution grew shorter. There was talk of an American Fortnight, but the consensus was that Neiman Marcus *was* in itself an American Fortnight, every day of the year. Someone brought up the idea of a Cowboy Fortnight, another executive suggested a Mexican Fiesta, while still another wondered about doing a Native American promotion of some kind. It was clear that time was not in our favor and that a degree of panic was beginning to cloud our reason. After all, we were surrounded by Texas cowboys, Mexico was too close to be considered exotically foreign enough, and the Comanche and the Sioux tribes were not widely known for producing enough high dollar quality merchandise that would satisfy our demanding clientele.

Finally, we punted. The decision was reached, after truly heated debate and as it turned out, with justifiable reluctance, to create a country out of thin air and treat it as though it really existed. To be sure, merchandise imports were going to be difficult to locate in a land that never was and few, if any, visiting native musical groups were likely to be found for an appearance in Dallas, but the joke of the whole idea was far too appealing to Stanley to offset any of the terribly obvious drawbacks being voiced by the more pragmatic realists in the executive suite.

To create our invisible nation we first got permission from the publishers of the *World Book Almanac* to develop a descriptive account of our non-country in the distinctive style of their authoritative book. Choosing the name Ruritania, taken from a novel written by Anthony Hope and from the mythical kingdom depicted in the MGM movie, *The Prisoner of Zenda*, we began to write glowing description of a land soon to be inserted onto the *World Almanac*'s pages between Rumania and Rwanda.

The publishers obviously had a collective sense of humor as they permitted us to use the actual cover design of their almanac as a binder for the Ruritanian entry. Inside the cover, the location of the land was disclosed to be somewhere east of Brigadoon and north of Camelot, and so on, while the identity of its ruler was revealed to be King Rudolph, aided by his beautiful wife, Queen Flavia. The currency which was noted as being a chocolate covered coin called, appropriately enough, the "Rudy." On the open market, a "Rudy" was said to equal 165 calories to the American dollar.

It all seemed quite funny at the time, at least to some of us and to Stanley in particular who still chuckled over it thirty years later. A poster was designed that depicted a Walt Disney-sort of dream castle set in a pastoral Alpine setting, with sheep safely grazing outside its majestic walls. It was clearly a wonderful utopian land with absolutely no political or social problems whatever simply because it was nonexistent.

The local Dallas newspapers picked up on the ruse and announced in all seriousness that Ruritania was to be the next Fortnight country. The store's switchboard was then quickly overburdened by calls from people who were curious about the little known nation, where it was located, and how travel might be arranged to visit it.

The company's travel service got in the spirit of the thing and put up signs urging its clientele to book passage as soon as possible in order to avoid the traditional winter tourist rush. It is no fiction that this writer's own mother-in-law (at the time) fell for it all and asked with relative sobriety how long it would take her to get to Ruritania. The fact that I encouraged her to take the trip as soon as possible speaks volumes.

If the pro-Ruritanian promotional team, with Stanley at its helm, fooled more than a handful of such gullible folk, the store's merchants were neither fooled nor particularly amused. With no real goods to import from an unreal country, they had serious doubts about their ability to match the amount of goods that had been sold during the previous year's East Meets West Fortnight in which truly wonderful Asian imports had been featured and carried away by shoppers in great abundance.

Fortunately, the merchants' collective confidence in their leader, the master showman named Stanley Marcus, was enough to thwart any palace revolt. Several clever merchandising ideas soon came forth from those vendors who were willing to go along with us. A cosmetic company came up with Flavia's Favorite Fragrance, in honor of our mythical queen and the Godiva Chocolate people produced a mint's worth of very tasty "Rudy" coins that bore the imagined profile of the Ruritanian king himself. The fact that the "King" closely resembled Stanley Marcus was noticed by many Dallasites.

Since an elaborate in-store decoration scheme was an important part of each Fortnight, we needed real corporate sponsors to help offset the multi-million pesos we were obviously not going to receive from Spain, to say nothing of any spendable "Rudys" we would never be receiving from the national treasury of Ruritania.

To prove that the often cold and hard world of commerce does from time-to-time indeed show a soft underbelly of humor, it is a pleasure to recall that several hundred thousand very real United States dollars were raised to help underwrite the Neiman Marcus Ruritanian prank. American Airlines, flush with cash in those days, participated at an impressive level when we convinced their marketing people that even though Ruritania did not exist, only American Airlines would fly there if it did. I assume there was a bit of appealing if remote Zen to this logic.

We approached the American Wool Council and persuaded them to give us a very large amount of money to tell the public through our advertising that since all of the many sheep in Ruritania were bald, real American wool was being used in all Neiman Marcus woolen goods. The joke went on and on and, unbelievably, more and more sponsors asked to be part of it.

To add even more levity to the opening of this salute to a mythical land, comedian Victor Borge was asked to serve as the Ruritanian Ambassador to Texas. He carried it off with great style and characteristic humor. The mayor of Dallas actually issued a proclamation welcoming His Excellency to the city, and this appeared in the city's newspapers.

Many other social events were scheduled around town and one particularly important formal soiree seemed to call for royalty to be in attendance. After a bit of persuasion, no less a star than John Wayne, the Duke himself, came to Dallas to represent Ruritania at the black tie event.

In the store's widely acclaimed Zodiac Room, the menu featured what were said to be the favorite foods and wines of King Rudolph and Flavia, his Queen. Renamed "The Rose and Crown" for the two-week long event, the restaurant's menu noted that all Ruritanian food exports had been flown to Dallas via American Airlines.

The King's favorite food, Quaker Oats Grits, was offered with a straight face. It was the only time in its long and colorful history that lowly grits were to be served in a restaurant more famous for its elegant cuisine. The fact that the Quaker Company had given the store some $25,000 to enjoy having their name on a Neiman Marcus menu was not widely discussed.

At the very top of the menu was written the old traditional toast purported to be frequently used by Ruritanians in their own land. "Vod chompen, vod vinnen, und vod budden," read the brightly printed banner. To those not sufficiently versed in the language, an asterisk led the way to a translation at the bottom of the page. "Good food, good wine, and good friends" it read in English. Clearly, it was a toast worthy of any language.

After two hilarious weeks, the Ruritanian Fortnight, quietly but probably not quickly enough, faded into history. The best that can be said of it was that it was a critical success and great fun but the store's financial officers were not terribly overjoyed at the sales volume which somehow failed to come anywhere near matching the level of the 1969 Asian record breaker. It did prove, however, that Neiman Marcus could, if it wanted to do so, convince many people of almost anything.

Throughout what was also proving to be a Ruritanian minor financial misadventure, Stanley stood firmly alongside his newest sales promotion director. The partnership we formed during this one-joke event proved to be a long lasting one and formed a firm foundation for many far more successful future events.

Despite the frequent humorous episodes, working for Stanley Marcus was never a simple matter of coming to the office each day to perform routine duties. He always claimed that the sales promotion/marketing aspect was his favorite part of the business and as a result, he could not resist being fully involved in it on an hourly basis.

If, for some reason I failed to come to the store even on a rare scheduled day off, he seemed to delight in filling in for me. One Monday morning, I found a note on my desk that read, "I came by on Saturday only to find you not here." This guilt-laden preamble then led to notes about the need to have the advertising department cleaned. "It looks like it hasn't been touched by a broom since the first French Fortnight," he had claimed, before moving on to the results of an inspection he had made of the models' wardrobe area. "All the shoes look as tired and unhappy as your models did last week in the Zodiac Room," the note continued.

Even when I was at the store, as was usually the case, messages arrived from him almost continuously. One suggested hiring a leprechaun impersonator to roam the streets of downtown Dallas during the upcoming Irish Fortnight, while another voiced the opinion that the opening ads for a new store were "pretty cheesy for a multimillion dollar store."

Of the 265 messages that I received from Stanley during one of the French Fortnights, some were far fetched, such as the one suggesting that everybody with a French sounding family name be invited to come see the event. Others, more typically, asked why the store's phone number was missing from a certain newspaper ad.

Even at a time when the store placed many ads each day in the two newspapers then being published in Dallas, Stanley read each and every one. Although he had already studied advance proofs of the ads, he quite frequently had something to say about the advertising when it ran in the paper.

One example of his comments now to be found in the Marcus Collection most clearly defines the micro-managerial zeal with which he ran his company. The ad, announcing a semi-annual sale, was less than a half page in size and contained only a headline, an illustration of a sales tag, ten lines of almost boilerplate copy, and the store's logotype. The critique of this tiny rectangle was made up of twelve crudely scrawled observations offering such key phrases as "weak," "poor drafting," "too stiff," "very poor ink work," and the punch line, "looks like a preliminary sketch." I don't think he liked it. There were more words of criticism on the ad than there were words in the copy block.

On rare occasions, there were words of praise. For one single ad that ran during an Irish Fortnight, Stanley wrote, "At last, your sentence-makers and word-jugglers have departed from their usual fashion garbage!" Both the copywriter and I felt as though we had received the Croix de Guerre when the note came our way.

It is likely that such a constant barrage of criticism would have driven many who tried so valiantly to please him and perform to his standards out the door in a short time. The fact was, however, that Mr. Stanley was so respected by his employees and so admired for his principles that the critiques were taken in stride as being part and parcel of working for him. To be sure, there were times when many of us wished he would go on an extended year's long world-circling tour of some kind and be shipwrecked. Even had he done so, the endless stream of messages would have eventually found their way to the executive offices of Neiman Marcus even if they had come in a bottle that he had cast into the sea.

Herbert Marcus, Sr., the philosopher—co-founder of Neiman Marcus, n.d.
—DeGolyer Library, Southern Methodist University,
Dallas, Texas, A 1933.1869

Elm Street, Dallas, Texas, in 1910. The "Neiman" half of the first store's sign can be seen on the right.
—DeGolyer Library, Southern Methodist University, Dallas, Texas, A 1933.1869

Carrie Marcus Neiman, Herbert's sister, Al's wife, and a co-founder of the store, n.d.
—DeGolyer Library, Southern Methodist University,
Dallas, Texas, A 1933.1869

Abraham Lincoln Neiman (Al), co-Founder and the financial genius behind the store's early success, 1926.

—DeGolyer Library, Southern Methodist University,
Dallas, Texas, A 1933.1869

Breaking ground for the new uptown Neiman Marcus at Main and Ervay Streets, Dallas, 1913.

The Main Street store in the 1940's. Five more floors would be added over the years.

Mrs. Herbert Marcus, nee Minnie Lichtenstein, with sons Stanley on the right and Edward seated on the table, 1910.

Stanley, in uniform, with his brother Eddie, age 3, 1912.
—DeGolyer Library, Southern Methodist University, Dallas, Texas, A 1933.1869

"It's wonderful, Harry! How late does Neiman-Marcus stay open?"

© *The New Yorker*, 1956.
—DeGolyer Library, Southern Methodist University, Dallas, Texas, A 1933.1869

Stanley as a senior, at Forest Avenue High School in Dallas. Note the altered title "Most Natural Boy" and the line "Is this the face that launched a thousand votes?" 1921.

—DeGolyer Library, Southern Methodist University, Dallas, Texas, A 1933.1869

Stanley in his lilac-tweed plus-fours as a pre-Harvard student at Amherst, 1921.
—DeGolyer Library, Southern Methodist University, Dallas, Texas, A 1933.1869

"Miss Minnie," Mrs. Herbert Marcus, Sr., floral expert and the Neiman Marcus Vice President for Greenery, n.d.
—DeGolyer Library, Southern Methodist University, Dallas, Texas, A 1933.1869

Stanley as Harvard graduate and executive vice president of the store, 1935.
—DeGolyer Library, Southern Methodist University,
Dallas, Texas, A 1933.1869

Stanley at a fashion show rehearsal with his father shown at right in white suit, 1936.
—DeGolyer Library, Southern Methodist University,
Dallas, Texas, A 1933.1869

Stanley presents his innovation, the NM Fashion Award, to Grace Kelly, 1956.
—DeGolyer Library, Southern Methodist University,
Dallas, Texas, A 1933.1869

THE suit of the year, significant for the Persian feeling that is Paris. The dress of black Linton tweed with satin yoke and sleeves. The jacket furred with a minaret peplum of Persian . . . molded by a sloping, satin-draped waistline, the hallmark of its creator, **GERMAINE MONTEIL.**

NEIMAN-MARCUS
THE CENTER OF FASHION AUTHORITY IN THE SOUTHWEST DALLAS

One of Stanley's early national fashion magazine ads. © Harpers' Bazaar, September 1936.
—From the Collections of the Texas/Dallas History and Archives Division of the Dallas Public Library

The four Marcus brothers soon after the end of World War II. From the left, Herbert, Jr., Edward, Stanley, and Lawrence, n.d.

Stanley tries out either a new hairstyle or a new hairpiece, n.d.

The beaming new president of Neiman Marcus, age 46, 1951.
—DeGolyer Library, Southern Methodist University,
Dallas, Texas, A 1933.1869

111

The relentless communicator in his natural element. Note the partial view of his office wall covered with citations, degrees, etc., n.d.

A view of Stanley's notoriously cluttered desk. He often took refuge from boring visitors by rummaging about in the stacks of paper, n.d.
—DeGolyer Library, Southern Methodist University, Dallas, Texas, A 1933.1869

Stanley as many saw him, particularly his competitors, n.d.
—DeGolyer Library, Southern Methodist University, Dallas, Texas, A 1933.1869

The Merchant Prince returns from his first visit to China in appropriate finery, n.d.
—DeGolyer Library, Southern Methodist University,
Dallas, Texas, A 1933.1869

114

The proud author discusses his second book, Quest For The Best, *1979.*
—DeGolyer Library, Southern Methodist University,
Dallas, Texas, A 1933.1869

A cigar lover of great magni-tude, here Stanley reflects his new "twink-ling" persona, 1974.
—DeGolyer Library, Southern Methodist University, Dallas, Texas, A 1933.1869

Deplaning the hard way. Stanley's own caption for this photo was "Parachute-less jump from a helicopter in Atlanta, 1971."

—DeGolyer Library, Southern Methodist University,
Dallas, Texas, A 1933.1869

The Merchant Prince in his prime, announcing his plan to save the City of Paris dome in San Francisco, 1974.

—DeGolyer Library, Southern Methodist University, Dallas, Texas, A 1933.1869

Staying Afloat

By the time the store's accounting buzzards had finished pecking away at the carcass of the Ruritanian Fortnight, there was nothing left of it except a mildly humorous memory. As humorous memories do little to satisfy the shareholders of any corporation, my second full year at Neiman Marcus began with an obvious but never declared dark cloud hanging above it.

Batting somewhere below .150 in baseball-statistic terms, it seemed likely that I had best find a way to surge up to at least .250 or I would no doubt become an all too common statistic, passing quickly through Stanley's revolving door. While the annual retail success of Neiman Marcus did not by any means depend solely on the ebbing and flowing of Fortnightly tides, a home run in 1971 stemming from a record setting international event was clearly devoutly to be desired.

Stanley, perhaps only slightly chagrined at having been a co-conspirator in the Ruritanian misadventure, obviously shared in the desire to produce a winner next time around. When I suggested a country that never been saluted in the Fortnight manner, he enthusiastically agreed and, between us, it was determined that Australia would be our subject. The Australian ambassador to the United States warmly embraced the idea as that country's trade mission and within days of the Australian brainstorm, I was off to "the land down under."

Once there, things could not have gone better. All of the government agencies in Canberra with which I met were eager to be endorsed by the famous Texas store, and Qantas Airways generously offered to provide at no cost thousands of dollars worth of airline seats to Neiman Marcus merchants coming and going as well as to Australian celebrities and vendors headed to the United States when the big event took place.

After encountering nothing but great success for nearly a month in the Outback, I called Stanley to report the good news. He quickly promised to fly to Australia within weeks to finalize the deal and also to tour one of the few countries in the world that did not have its current official stamp on any of the nearly always full pages of his passport.

He did indeed get his passport stamped after Qantas made good on its promise to fly him from San Francisco to Sydney in its luxurious first class cabin. It was not until he disembarked in Australia that the whole thing began to unravel.

As an opening act, the government-provided limousine that was to be at the airport to whisk him to his hotel failed to materialize, its driver having become confused as to what time his distinguished visitor was to arrive. In fact, there was considerable confusion about what day of the week the flight was to be met. After waiting in the Qantas clubroom for a bit longer than much too long by his impatient estimation, Stanley, with the quiet fury of which he was a master, convinced the club hostess that it would be advisable to let someone in authority know that he was indeed in town.

It was never made clear why he simply did not put his vast array of luggage into a taxicab and be taken to his hotel, but, alas, he did not, and during his long wait for some kind of official transportation, the first ever Neiman Marcus Australian Fortnight in essence died a painful and premature death. It would be twenty-five years before such an event was staged at the Dallas store, and, perhaps ironically, it would be the last of the Neiman Marcus Fortnights.

At any rate, about an hour after the Qantas club girl swung into action, the government's substitute car pulled into the Sydney airport. From the dusty and dented Volkswagen stepped the sole member of the welcoming delegation, a lower level trade office employee who had been hastily pressed into service at the early morning hour even though he had just gotten home following a long evening's bacchanalian celebration at his neighborhood pub.

A tired and angry Stanley Marcus, accustomed to being greeted by ambassadors and on one occasion by a premier, found himself being bounced along on the road to downtown Sydney in a tiny Volkswagen being aimed, rather than driven, by a hardy lad who had only that evening apparently drained off several hours worth of Foster's famous Australian lager.

The next day was even worse. The official trade and tourism agencies of the government were apologetic enough, and proved suitably adept at producing an acceptable knot of Australian media folks to hear the famed merchant's words and learn about the forthcoming promotion. Before Stanley could say a word, through a heady combination of jet lag, flight fatigue, and still smoldering irritation at his less than low key greeting ceremony, a brash young television reporter thrust a camera in his face to ask why Dallas had killed John Kennedy. The quiet fury returned, instantly triggered by a question so often asked by foreign journalists in that decade. Rather than explain or even honor the query with an answer that would have likely gone unheard anyway, the man from Dallas stood up and walked to the door. The press conference was clearly over.

Although Australia had a great deal going for it in the early 1970s, its goods, scenery, and otherwise fine human beings could not overcome the sharp, double edged sword that keenly sliced through the first few hours of Stanley's visit to Australia. He did soldier on in an apparently sincere effort to overcome his initial displeasure with his first impression in favor of the positive bigger picture but apparently nothing could erase it. He went to the outstanding vineyards, visited the opal mines, favorably critiqued the country's fascinating fine art, exchanged philosophic folklore with Aborigine leaders, but it all came to naught, at least for another quarter century. Although he was grudgingly impressed by the struggling efforts of the Australian fashion industry to insert itself into the international scheme of things, he could not bring himself to endorse the commercial output of the country as yet being worthy of the potential Midas-touch of Neiman Marcus.

Through a 2:00 A.M. phone call that came to me in Dallas, I learned from him the news that a farewell media conference, just concluded, had not gone well. Stanley had not found it possible to be positive, although there were no more questions about the dreadful assassination day in 1962. As government trade and tourism officials waited with smiling faces and soaring hopes, the visiting merchandising authority declared quality goods to be too scarce to warrant any promotion at his Dallas store. His ride back to the airport was made in a sleek limousine, anyway, and the return flight to the United States was made possible by the generosity of Qantas, but the half-million dollar pledges in Australian support money for the Fortnight were left behind at the media conferences.

Not realizing the depth of the official Australian resentment at being so publicly denounced as being second rate, a diehard team in Dallas tried to salvage the situation. Even as Stanley was en route home, his brother Edward and I invited the Australian ambassador to come to Dallas for talks which we hoped would put the wheels back on the Fortnight cart. When he surprisingly accepted and flew to Texas the very next day, we employed the best food in town washed down with liberal glasses of excellent Scotch whiskey and superb bottles of wine to help state our case. It was a noble, but ultimately futile effort. When Stanley did return, after a week in Palm Springs to recover from his ordeal, he seemed at least mildly remorseful that he had single-handedly shattered months of effort and caused lots of money to remain in Australian bank accounts.

In an attempt to make matters right, he called Edward Clark, the former ambassador to Australia, to see if a personal intervention at the highest levels of the two governments might erase the tired and angry words of a frustrated merchant prince. In the end, that, too, came to naught. Someone in Australia did send Stanley a case of the country's best wine and someone else somehow arranged for him to receive an Australian terrier puppy. As I recall it, the wine made a far better impression and stayed at the Marcus home longer than did the little dog, cute though it definitely was.

In the hindsight of almost forty years, it is quite possible that Stanley's sinking of the first Australian Fortnight came about mainly because he truly didn't feel that the country's export potential was yet at the level the Neiman Marcus spotlight would require. As the originator of the international retail festival in the United States, no one was better qualified to make that call.

At any rate, the Australian default made it two in a row for me. I had joined the Fortnight production team just in time to participate in the Ruritanian fiasco, and now the very next year saw us again scrambling to come up with an idea to fill in the void created by the cancellation of the Australian event.

As planning time again grew ominously short, it was Stanley's mother who saved the day. As an avid horticulturist, co-founder of the Dallas Garden Club, and the store's vice president for greenery, Minnie Marcus suggested a storewide floral event. With or without an international theme, she reasoned, the appeal of flowers was universal. Floral motifs abounded in almost every kind of merchandise, so our buyers could not cry foul as some had when the admittedly rather vague Ruritanian concept was presented. The store's decorating theme was obvious and, it was correctly presumed, many of the flowers and plants used in the mammoth displays could be sold to the public when the event ended.

Miss Minnie took an active role in the planning of the event. Even though she was nearly ninety years old as the event was being planned, she proved to be every bit as resourceful, imaginative, and often as downright stubborn as her oldest son. Her demonstrated eye for color and attention to the slightest detail gave rise to considerable speculation in Dallas social circles that she had played a far more important role than usually mentioned in the early success of the store her husband and her sister-in-law had founded.

Dubbed the "Fete de Fleur" to give it at least a hint of an international flavor, the bright and wonderfully fragrant fall event was an artistic success and compared to the previous year, it was also a relatively effective sales volume producer.

Without doubt, the key to the refreshing success was the personal appearance in the city of Prince Albert and Princess Grace of Monaco. The serenely royal couple visited the store to the delight of sales people and throngs of customers alike. They also cut a very wide swath through the highest possible levels of Dallas society.

The most prestigious doors of Dallas swung open for them, permitting entry as well to the denizens of the upper echelons of both the old money and new money levels of social importance. At one memorable dinner event at the home of a prominent family, guests were unfortunately invited to arrive in waves, scheduled in descending order of perceived significance on the Dallas social scene. Even though the arbitrary pecking order was determined by the hostess herself, the store was caught in a social crossfire that continued for several years.

With the most elite of the prime assembled within the house and the lesser millionaires skulking about in the vast topiary gardens of the mansion, Rainier and his dazzling princess arrived. No stranger to Neiman Marcus fashions, Grace wore a simple green Givenchy floor length gown. She and the dress were almost startling to behold particularly since she wore not a scintilla of jewelry except for her engagement ring that was the size of a cantaloupe. There were no earrings, and no necklace swathed that swan-like throat. She was an un-bejeweled blond vision in muted green silk, radiant enough to outshine any of the diamonds or rubies said to rest back home in the vaults of Monaco.

The ladies of Dallas, regardless of their position in the two-tier platoon system of the invitations, had come prepared to show this former actress from Philadelphia that they could hold their own when it came to blinding lavalieres of diamonds, cascading emeralds and sapphires as big and blue as a West Texas sky. As they went through the self-conscious motions of a curtsy to the Princess, their jewels blinked and glinted from every facet with each carat being evaluated by the next doyenne in the receiving line. It was Grace alone who wore no such blinding gems. The waves of diners somehow managed to crash one upon the other without incident but the sun rose the next day on a Dallas society riven by the whim of a misguided hostess and motivated by the inspirational fashion statement to be made by not wearing all of those splashy, but still lovely, jewels.

The dinner event next scheduled to honor the Monacoan royalty was held in a much more egalitarian setting. As the large crowd of socialites awaited the royal entry, many had obviously reflected on the night before. The ladies who previously sought to outdo a princess had gotten the fashion message she had apparently signaled. "If less is better, then none is best." At this second event here was hardly a jewel to be seen. All the big rocks had gone back into the home safe and the brightly colored gowns of the night before had given way to beige, pale yellow, and, of course, muted green.

Just a few minutes later than the announced moment of entry into the hotel ballroom, the orchestra picked up its cue and launched into a rendition of "True Love," the main theme from the movie, "High Society" to signify the arrival of the one-time movie goddess who had starred in the film. The great doors swung open, the spotlights flared, and in glided Princess Grace swathed in brilliant red silk and absolutely dripping in diamonds and emeralds and jade, likely the most glittering display of such jewelry since the days of Marie Antoinette.

Without a word, Grace had trumped the best that Dallas fashion could offer, yet her beauty and her charm soon erased any vestige of resentment in the ladies elegantly clad in their most sober Neiman Marcus best, but not quite equal to the cool blond and glittering vision in her silken sheath crafted of the most vivid of reds.

The Princess had come to Dallas at the direct personal request of Stanley Marcus. He had known her for years, had presented her with the store's Fashion Award, supervised the creation of a portion of her trousseau for her marriage ceremony, and had attended her wedding to the Prince.

Over the years, I learned that if the store needed a superstar for any big event, a request for Stanley's direct involvement did the trick. His personal address book on file at the DeGolyer Library indicates how great was his reach. If you needed a big name, usually at no cost at all, he was the man to make headline news a possibility

Hitting the Road with Stanley

In early 1972, I set out for France with Stanley Marcus. It was my first of many trips abroad for the company and an exciting time. To him, it was a routine that had been repeated for decades. A trip to Paris was to Stanley much the same as a visit to nearby Fort Worth was to me. Everyone at his favorite hotel in the French capital seemed to know him by name and the heads of the country's trade and travel departments knew him by reputation. Their predecessors in office had clearly informed the new ministers that here was a man who delighted in asking for the moon.

On one memorable occasion, I watched all but spellbound, as Stanley reduced the imperious and haughty director of the Louvre to a virtually speechless wreck. It all began cordially enough with "Le Directoire" offering us a cup of typically harsh espresso which we both accepted as a cure against the cold fog of a Parisian morning in early February.

After a few exchanges of idle banter, the Frenchman lit up a tear-provoking Gauloise cigarette, leaned back in his leather chair and asked Monsieur Marcus how he might be of service. Stanley's response was instantaneous and as far as I ever knew totally extemporaneous. "I want," he said in his soft and melodious voice, "to borrow the Mona Lisa for three weeks." Had his visitor asked permission to provide a wardrobe of gloves for the armless Venus de Milo standing just outside the office, the director could not have been more shocked. He was in fact totally stunned, as Stanley looked on with all the amused detachment of a cat that had just flushed out a whole bevy of fat Parisian mice.

The Frenchman shot out of his chair, nearly tipping it over as he only partially exhaled a cloud of the bluest cigarette smoke I had ever seen. Most of the smoke that he had only seconds before inhaled deep into his lungs seemed to have found a temporary haven there. He coughed, and rolled his tear-filled eyes heavenward as if to seek permission from some deity to save him from this presumptuous Texan who was very likely dangerously insane. After downing a quick gulp of Perrier handed him by a concerned and ashen faced aide, the director recovered his composure just in time to see the mad Texan smile, shrug his shoulders, and extend his arms outward in the international sign language that signaled, "just kidding."

I never knew for certain if Stanley had any real hope of bringing Leonardo's priceless and well-beyond insurable masterpiece to Dallas for the Fortnight, but I seriously doubt it. One of his trademark tactics was a practice he claimed to have learned from the writings of Buddha. "It's not the fool who asks," he would declare, "but rather the fool who gives." If Buddha actually ever uttered this handy phrase is unclear, but the frequent application of it fit neatly into Stanley's scheme of things. If the museum director had granted this bizarre request out of hand, Stanley would have gladly accepted the treasure. As it turned out, however, he reached into his coat pocket to produce a list of works by several of the better known French Impressionists that he really had hoped to borrow for the two week event.

The director, no doubt inwardly congratulating himself for having parried the astonishing and lunatic "Mona Lisa" thrust, quickly agreed to send a Matisse, a Monet, and a Degas to Dallas for the October event. If he hated himself later in the day for that rash decision will never be known. When we left his office that morning, he had returned to his haughty demeanor but only after signing a binding letter of consent regarding the loan of the Impressionists. Stanley had politely insisted on this and apparently still convinced that he had won the morning skirmish, the director had signed with his pen locked in the grip of his tobacco-stained thumb tip and forefinger. That unique Parisian technique of holding cigarettes had left an indelible mark on his fingers, a clue that would have probably identified him as a Frenchman anywhere in the world.

The weekend after the Louvre experience found us in Paris' fabled Flea Market. Here, too, Stanley was widely known and probably more respected than he was at the Lourve. He told me as we walked abut this eclectic if not totally chaotic collection of shops and stalls that he had been coming to the market for almost fifty years. An amazing number of the vendors recognized him, often crying out his name to capture his attention in order to show and hopefully sell him a newly acquired treasure. His interests were every bit as eclectic and chaotic as the flea market itself. An avid collector of all manner of objects and with an endless portfolio of priceless art, his trained eye led him to a quick evaluation of the goods proffered him by hawkers who obviously knew the man by sight and what he might possibly take off their hands in return for a tidy bundle of francs.

It was cold that particular morning in Paris, and Stanley introduced me to his curious habit of buying handfuls of roasted chestnuts to be thrust into coat pockets to ward off the chill air. Thus warmed and perfumed, we set about seeking whatever it was that might strike his fancy. I am sure there was no method to this search nor was there any limit as to how much he might be willing to spend to become the one, for example, to possess a rare miniature painting, or a piece of exquisite antique jewelry being touted by the vendor as once having belonged to the czarina immediately before the Russian Revolution. I doubt if he believed for a minute such often spurious sales pitches or if he would have been impressed if the unfortunate Empress' initials had indeed been etched on the back of the piece. If he liked it, and if he thought his wife or perhaps his beloved mother might like it, he would eventually buy it, but only after some gentlemanly but ruthless haggling.

Perhaps the expression haggling is too loose a term when describing Stanley's shopping techniques. It was more like the pool game technique previously mentioned. The vendor's asking price was instantly halved by his prospective Texas client. If the vendor failed to agree to this slashed price at once, or if he dared counter at only a quarter reduction, Stanley would abruptly turn on his heel without another word and leisurely stroll away, clearly bound for a competing stall across the damp cobblestones. Nine times out of ten, the crestfallen operator of the just visited stall would hurry from behind his counter to announce that the offer made by M'sieur Marcus was more than fair and the jewelry, or rare book, or cloisonné box were his at a vastly reduced price. I suspect that even in accepting the offer of fifty percent off the original, the sly flea marketers were delighted to do business with Stanley and likely made a fair profit despite the outcome of the game of negotiated pricing which both seller and potential customer so dearly loved to play.

During the course of this first trip to France with Stanley, plans were made to announce the next Neiman Marcus French Fortnight in grand style. In conjunction with our Paris office, I took it upon myself to find a famous French celebrity who might participate in making the announcement while we were still in the city.

As good fortune would have it, a young lady in our office was a friend of someone who knew, of all people, Brigitte Bardot, then at the top of her alluring game. Mlle. Bardot, I reasoned, would give the photographers a most attractive subject to focus upon as she and Stanley Marcus smilingly announced the great international event to be staged in Dallas in the coming fall. As was not always the case, as we will see later in this book, this particular plan worked out far better than could have been imagined, at least at its outset. Miss Bardot, much to my surprise, and I suspect to the even greater surprise of the girl who claimed to know her, eagerly agreed to come to a luncheon at New Jimmy's, a well-known Parisian club. Her only conditions for this appearance were that there would be a battery of photographers there to record her dazzling entrance and that she would get a free lunch for her effort.

This seemed too good to be true and, as always, indeed it was. It later developed that Mlle. Bardot and Mlle. Regine, the proprietor of New Jimmy's, were great friends and the two had conspired to use the photo-opportunity luncheon to publicize the projected opening of yet another New Jimmy's in Los Angeles. The international prestige of the name Neiman Marcus, the two Parisian ladies had cleverly envisioned, would lend a high degree of panache and an implied endorsement of Regine's new enterprise in the United States. When I told Stanley of my publicity coup I was of course completely unaware that the two ladies were planning on using him and his store as a pawn. Never one to shy away from being in the presence of beautiful women, Stanley welcomed the news with considerable enthusiasm.

The next day, we arrived at the original New Jimmy's to find the red-headed Regine awaiting us surrounded by an army of photographers. After a suitable delay, the limousine bearing Bardot, the legendary international blond bombshell, glided to a halt at New Jimmy's entrance. As the cameramen rushed to the street, the limo door opened to reveal first one and then the other of the most photographed legs in all France. As the bulbs flashed and the shutters clicked furiously away, the rest of Brigitte Bardot quickly soon came into view.

She was stunning. Still very much the star that she had been for several years, she all but paralyzed the camera lenses with her Gallic beauty. Bardot smiled, waved, winked, and wiggled her way past the throng of onlookers that had instantly formed almost on cue in the street, and ran to the welcoming arms of her friend Regine. Still playing to the cameras with each and every one of her storied inches, she floated into the club to meet the famous American merchant prince, the one and only Stanley Marcus.

Had we left right then, I suppose, the luncheon might have been more successful, but only hindsight now makes that clear. For some unfathomable reason, the two stars of the New Jimmy's noontime meal that day took an instant dislike to one another. In fact, just as I was envisioning Stanley caught up in a welcome-to-Paris embrace with the movie star, or at least a nice-to-meet-you Parisian peck on his bewhiskered cheeks, she instead turned abruptly to one side to seek her place at the gaily decorated luncheon table. I presumed she was simply famished from a morning on the set or whatever and, to Stanley's credit, he took it all in stride and uncharacteristically rather meekly followed her to the table. Thus far, not one of the hundreds of photographic frames being snapped had managed to catch the two of them within ten feet of each other.

As Regine and I had seated them side by side at the table, it had seemed more than just probable that the much desired picture might be taken and then transmitted to Dallas for the official Fortnight announcement. With Stanley seated on her left, Mlle Bardot instantly struck up an animated conversation with the handsome and very young Frenchman to her right, in that curious Parisian patois that is only vaguely similar to the French language taught in American schools. Stanley, maybe a bit nonplussed but at least not visibly so, retaliated by giving his full attention to Regine, who was seated on his left.

There they sat, each apparently engrossed in what appeared to be the deepest conversation of their distinctly separate lives as the photographer I had retained for the occasion waited in vain for the contracted photo op to materialize. In the meantime, all of the French cameramen had accepted Regine's generous invitation to partake of the famed onion soup and steak tartare for which New Jimmy's was then justly famous. The introduction of many bottles of both excellent white and red wines did little to remind the local photographers why they had been summoned to the club in the first place. Rather than preserve for all time the glimmering image of Bardot along with her bearded American luncheon companion, they seemed more than content to just sip free wine, eat raw meat, and openly gape at the stunning movie star who appeared oblivious to it all.

My own photographer was about to join in this noontime revelry when an inspiration struck that finally got the unwilling team of Bardot and Marcus to at least look in the general direction of each other. With the invaluable assistance of Fred Izrine, our man in Paris, the chef was adequately bribed to affix spare French Bastille Day versions of Fourth of July sparklers to a small cake he happened to have on hand. Justly proud of his last minute creation, the chef carried the cake with its sputtering candles alit to the table and, thrust the confection between the two guests of honor. Somewhat startled by the flame, they simultaneously turned to look at the cake and in so doing, their eyes met for a brief, but adequate, tick of the clock. Fortunately, my photographer was in just the right location to capture the moment on film and the recorded image finally found a place in the Dallas newspapers and, as it turned out, in the *Los Angeles Times* as well.

As the little flames sputtered out, Marcus and Bardot turned back to their original conversation partners and to my knowledge, not a single word passed between them from the moment Bardot's limousine arrived at New Jimmy's until she left over an hour later. Somehow, the entire episode never came up when Stanley and I reviewed the highly successful French Fortnight many months later. This, I think, was probably a fortunate thing, particularly since Neiman Marcus got stuck with the bill for the entire luncheon and Bardot never came to Dallas.

On our last day in Paris, I was introduced to yet another Stanley Marcus trick. During dinner at his hotel, he mentioned that he had noticed that I didn't carry a briefcase to accommodate the countless sheets of notes that our visit had generated. Never fond of carrying anything even resembling an attaché case, I preferred instead to use large manila envelopes which could be filled during the trip and then stashed away in my luggage for the return flight to Dallas.

When I failed to take the bait the first time, Stanley tried again when after dinner coffee was being served. "Why not?" he asked suddenly, totally out of any context. "Why not what," I replied, genuinely at a loss. "Why don't you carry a briefcase like everybody else?" he asked again, and before I could again launch into my packable envelope explanation, he said, "Meet me in the lobby at 8:00 in the morning. I have a big surprise for you."

I stopped by the Hotel Crillion early the next morning as directed and there he sat, beaming as a trapper might as his snare snapped shut. From behind his chair, Stanley produced his old and extremely battle-worn attaché case, its handle secured by a piece of wire the hotel's always enterprising concierge had apparently found deep in the cellar of the building. "Here," he said proudly, as if he were giving me a valuable treasure from his personal trove. My feeble protests were in vain, and off I went to the Paris airport glumly carrying an empty case that deserved to be at the bottom of the Seine rather than bound for a flight across the Atlantic.

It wasn't until I met Stanley in New York City some weeks later that I noticed his lovely new Vuitton attaché case. When I complimented him on its elegant beauty, he said, "Oh, yes. I picked this up when we were just leaving Paris last week. The case I loaned you was getting old, but I'd like you to give it back to me so I can get the handle fixed. I think I like it better than this one." I had once again been duped by the master manipulator.

I never learned how to compete with him. A few months after ferrying his battered old case back to Dallas, I was called to his office. Arranged on top of the usually cluttered desk was a most amazing array of pipes. There were Dunhill's, Petersen's, calabashes, and meerschaums. Some were curved, some straight, and a few were well-used handmade Danish briars of great value. At that time, nearly all Neiman Marcus executives smoked pipes simply, I suppose, because Stanley did. From time to time, the boardroom became so smoke-filled during meetings that windows had to be opened to permit the senior vice presidents to see each other across the table.

After years of smoking, however, Stanley had suddenly decided to quit, characteristically cold turkey. Rather than throw away any of the very expensive pipes in his vast collection of nearly a hundred masterpieces, he decided to let his fellow smokers choose a couple for their own use. I was flattered to be given second choice and I selected what was known as the "President's Pipe." It had been designed by Stanley himself who had been seeking a pipe that was a bit of a hybrid having a stem that was part curved and part straight. I knew he had great pride in his design that had made the smoking cooler and the cleaning much easier. It was, I correctly reasoned, a true collector's item, never again to be smoked, but for me a lasting memento of the remarkable man who had created it.

Stanley seemed pleased that I had chosen his favorite pipe and after hearing a few words of thanks from me, the eyelids dropped and I was out the door. Two days later, I was again summoned to his office. Expecting maybe to be treated to another windfall, I hurried over to his domain. Without looking up from his standard paper shuffling routine, he let me stand in the doorway for a long minute before he spoke. "Say," he said, "let me have that pipe I loaned you, I've decided to start smoking again, and you took my favorite pipe."

To casual observers, some of Stanley's traits might appear devious or at least petty. Those who worked closely with him for long periods of time, however, viewed his tricks as just tricks. Despite the often stern visage that frequently looked more like a scowl, he possessed an almost elfin-like spirit of playfulness. He toyed with those people he liked as a cat might amuse itself with an energetic mouse.

When it came to finding a way to get his old attaché from Paris to Dallas, he could have easily had it included in the large shipments of samples and merchandise that made their way from Europe to Texas almost daily. He merely wanted to see if I would carry it for him. The select-a-pipe charade was, at least to my mind, a test of sorts designed to see which of his subordinates would take what pipe.

It is difficult to envision that a mind as brilliant as his would have had enough spare time to engage in such trivial pursuits, but to him such little feats were not trivial at all. If Stanley was fond of someone in his employ, the tests were, I think, signs of affection. Those executives whom he merely tolerated because he needed their signal contribution to the firm's profit did not share in those affectionate displays. To their bewilderment, and, I suppose, disappointment, they were excluded from his inner circle even though they were paid well and treated with courtesy.

There can be no question that since he was a demanding boss and being both a perfectionist and an erratic genius, his demands were frequently unattainable as well as inconsistent. It was this provocative scenario, played out hourly that made going to work for him each day of the week both challenging and rewarding. One never knew which of his endless dreams and concepts would have top priority on Monday morning only to be replaced by another hot idea by the time Friday afternoon came around.

Demanding though he was, however, his managerial style was softspoken and completely devoid of the ranting too often displayed by high-level business tycoons. He once told a friend that he never lost his temper in public, and to my knowledge that statement was at least 99 percent accurate.

At least he never publicly raised his voice in anger and, in fact, if speaking while upset about something, his voice became softer as his distress mounted. During a rare Executive Committee confrontation with one of his brothers, the rest of us remained mute as the two siblings voiced their totally opposite opinion on a certain issue. As the battling brother raised his tone to a level just shy of a shout in making his case, Stanley's comments soon grew soft enough to be all but inaudible. Obviously, the brother had witnessed this phenomenon before and fully understood that what could be only faintly heard clearly took total precedence over his own clamorous invective. In mid-shout, the argument came to an abrupt halt and the issue was suddenly resolved in favor of the quieter man.

If Stanley did not like something or even somebody, he did not hesitate for a second to let his sentiments be known. Criticisms were taken almost as a benediction, offered as they were by a man with impeccable credentials. The only phrase that could cut to the quick was the very rarely uttered "I am disappointed in you." Even the sting of this comment, however, was washed away with a gem of praise which, though also rare, was without question heartfelt.

Weekends were by no means considered sacrosanct to Stanley Marcus. It was a blessing to all of us who worked for him in those years that cell phones and e-mail had yet to be invented. Land lines and telegrams and even messages hand delivered to one's front door served well enough to interrupt Saturday evening dinner parties in Dallas or even a night of pub crawling in London. His communication reach was without limits and his timing of phone calls to anywhere in the world was almost always highly inconvenient. This bothered him not at all. When Stanley wanted something done, or had an idea to share, neither oceans nor time zones could stand in his way.

Creating a Christmas Tradition

alled by some of the millions of customers who receive it the Christmas Book, and by many others the Christmas Catalog, the famous annual Neiman Marcus mail order publication has become a media tradition. Although Stanley Marcus is widely held to have been the originator of this marketing masterpiece, its actual beginning can be traced to 1909, the second full year the store was in operation.

The colorful and typically hyperbolic copy was written by Herbert Marcus the company's longtime president and for many years its sole copywriter. Much of the content of that first small booklet was far more apparel related than its successors were. Ladies shoes took up over half of the space with high waisted bouffant dresses being depicted on the other pages.

If the initial Christmas mailing effort of 1909 was continued the next year is not clear, but seven years later, another yuletide-themed booklet was mailed to store customers. Again, the content was mainly apparel and while the recipients could order the shoes and garments through the mail, the thrust of the copy made it clear that customers were encouraged to come to the store to do their Christmas shopping, or at least to buy their holiday party apparel in person. Once in the store, one of the well-trained sales associates would thus have a bird in hand, ready to be smoothly persuaded to buy more than just the dress as shown in the booklet.

The Neiman Marcus Archive Collection at the main Dallas Public Library contains a few other early day seasonal mailing pieces but there is nothing about them that would even begin to hint of the future acclaim that the Neiman Marcus Christmas Books were destined to eventually achieve. It was not until 1959 that the fertile minds of Stanley Marcus and his brother, Edward, conceived the idea of adding a touch of the outrageous to what had traditionally been a rather bland combination of over-stated copy and vague sketches that afforded little in the way of specific information about an item that might be purchased, sight unseen, by an optimistic but willing customer.

The first so-called "big idea" gift was actually something of a symbol of nepotism. Edward, Stanley's fun-loving and fast-trotting brother, owned a cattle ranch to which he devoted much of his time when he was not supervising the store's merchandise divisions. His breed of choice was the popular Aberdeen Black Angus, a sturdy and reliable animal which flourished on Mr. Edward's appropriately named Black Mark Ranch located near today's Flower Mound, Texas, a relatively short distance from the northernmost edge of Dallas.

The two brothers conspired to promote Eddie's bovines in a Christmastime publication by photographing a particularly bulky looking steer and offering him for sale as "Steak on the Hoof." Alongside the unsuspecting beast was featured an elaborate silver roast beef serving cart on wheels. The complete package of living steer, serving cart and all appropriate cooking utensils were available anywhere in the civilized world via air express or, in those days, perhaps steamship non-express. For those not caring to give or receive this live animal,

Neiman Marcus, in a rather heartless and cavalier way, offered to have the animal slaughtered and then have it processed into steaks and roasts before shipping it to the lucky buyer or recipient along with the serving cart and all the accoutrements.

According to Stanley, the co-conspirator in this Wild West scheme, two orders were received for the depicted steer, but since Eddie had several hundred more head of almost identical animals roaming on his range, both orders were filled with but one hitch. An order received from South Africa had to be deferred for a full year because of the existing quarantine regulations that were vigorously enforced by the South African government.

It is only fair to note here that in addition to a keen intellect and a master showman's flair, Stanley Marcus also had an impish tendency to exaggerate from time to time. In relating the story over the years about selling two living steaks on the hoof, some of the details suspiciously changed from telling to telling. Sometimes, the quarantine rules might have held up a purchased steer on his way to Great Britain while the next time around, the Angus had to be kept in a pen for a year in a customs lot in the Philippines. Such exaggerations are forgivable, one must suppose, as each telling only enhances the salient point that Neiman Marcus with its world class storyteller at the helm could very likely sell anything to anybody anywhere on the planet.

With such tales circulating, be they slightly embroidered or not, Stanley's friends in the media came to realize that this store way out in Dallas was a great source of fodder for the public's voracious appetite for news, particularly if that news was out of the ordinary and sometimes even bordering on the outrageous. Encouraged by annual Christmas season calls from the likes of Edward R. Murrow and Walter Cronkite, Stanley eagerly accommodated their requests for interesting tidbits at a time when, at least then, fast breaking news items seemed to have been on holiday leave.

One can almost imagine the cartoon-type light bulb becoming illuminated over Stanley's head as a direct result of the phone calls. If these famous opinion makers and trendsetters wanted something to talk about, it would be theirs for the asking each year, he reasoned, particularly if the nation's media spotlight might be made to shine even more brightly on Neiman Marcus located in the middle of nowhere.

The master showman was soon hard at work on his latest brainstorm. As he notes in his autobiography, he established as his main news making guideline that the item have a degree of credibility ("however faint"). The parenthetic is his direct quote and it sums up in a mere two words the key to the early success of what came to be called "The Neiman-Marcus His and Her Gift of the Year."

By offering whatever it was in the form of a gift for the "Him" and a matching gift for "Her," Stanley improved upon the time-honored desire to kill two birds with one stone as far as the media was concerned. What loving husband could possibly deny the impulse to buy a specially designed feminine-themed Ford Thunderbird for the little woman, Ed Murrow might have cynically inquired with his trademark eyebrow arched high. Walter Cronkite, it is likely, might have countered by suggesting that her vehicle would be made even more attractive were it parked next to his manly version of the same car.

People looked, read, and listened to what those impish, if high-priced, rascals down in Texas had thought up to brighten any given year's Christmas. While most had no intention whatever of buying an expensive set of gender-inspired automobiles for $25,000, they very well might share in the fun and prestige of it all, and select a little something special from Neiman Marcus to ensure a memorable Christmas for family and friends. Few, if any, matching Thunderbirds were delivered, but hundreds of thousands of elaborately gift wrapped less ostentatious other things did find their way under Christmas trees around the world. Each package, large or small, with or without wheels, bore the distinctive Neiman Marcus logotype to clearly establish that whatever was inside the expensive outer wrap came from a very special place.

As interest in the His and Her concept gained momentum, the imagination of its creator knew no bounds, and his relationship with the media became a quid pro quo arrangement. Over time, the more outlandish each year's offering was, the more exposure it received from worldwide media. As might be expected, the media coverage tended to create a feeding frenzy as newspaper and television reporters strived to outdo one another in making cute if often condescending remarks.

The 1962 Chinese Junk for either a Him or a Her offers a good case in point. In the first place, it was difficult to accept that a high fashion specialty store located in the landlocked center of Texas would have any Chinese junks to sell at all. Under the eye catching headline "Junk for Sale," the impressive catalogue photograph of an authentic Chinese Junk depicted a truly remarkable vessel. It was made largely of teak and mahogany and boasted bright brass fittings to hold fast its colorful sails on windy days on the high seas. The craft came fully equipped with feminine or masculine luggage, appropriate cruising apparel for both captain and mate, and so forth. What seems amazing, even four and a half decades later, is that the actual price of a very real junk at the time was only $11,500 with all the other items included. The media fell on the Texas junk idea like turkey buzzards on roadkill and played the story for all of its almost lunatic worth.

As always, once the novelty of the incongruous gift idea had run its course with the media, the big question was always, "How many did you sell?" Without fail, Stanley had a very generous quantity to report. Legend has it that eight of the exquisite Chinese vessels were sold to mariners who set sail from ports on Lake Michigan, both the Pacific and the Atlantic coasts, and even onto the far off Mediterranean Sea. There was even at one time a tall tale of one of the junks running aground on a reef somewhere in the South Pacific, but that story had a bit too much of Robert Louis Stevenson in it to stay afloat for long.

Transportation themed His and Her gifts seem to dominate the retrospective gift list. From airplanes in 1960, to the junks, and on to an elaborate recreational vehicle much later, the big idea items have also included submarines, balloons, parasail-boats, hovercraft, motorcycles, the Thunderbirds, and several other automobiles. Of particular vehicular interest, from the "just look how prices have increased" aspect, are the His and Her Jaguar gifts in 1968. His was a sleek Jaguar automobile offered at $5,559 while Her Jaguar was not a car at all, but rather an equally sleek, if endangered, Jaguar fur coat available for a mere $416 more than the sticker price of His shiny vehicle.

Junks and jaguars aside, one of the most popular of the big idea gifts was the pair of camels offered in the 1967 catalog. To many, the camel, be it dromedary or Bactrian, is a very funny looking beast with its haughty demeanor, sad but all-knowing eyes, and its huge clomping feet. The camel, at least when only semi-domesticated, can also be a vile-tempered animal with an alarming tendency to spit its partially digested cud in the general direction of anyone or anything that disturbs its frequent naps. The camel-keeper who satisfied Stanley's whim to feature the beasts in his Christmas Book often vented his annoyance at being the target of the Christmas camel's ire with its attendant mass of cud.

Stanley claimed later that everyone at the store and even his wife at home denounced his wild idea of offering a camel as a Christmas gift. One fearless and eventually former employee, upon learning of the camel idea, was overheard to say, "Gee, with another camel and three wise men, we could have a manger scene." Undaunted by such jibes, Stanley set about to find his camels and he soon did at a wild animal refuge in Alabama. No one, including the Phineas T. Barnum of retailing, thought for a moment that anybody would actually be foolish enough to pay $4,125 for a pair of the beasts or even $2,062 for a solitary dromedary, but there truly is, as a wise man once said, a customer out there for everything.

Seeing the animal's photograph in the catalog, the daughter of a very prominent Texas lady and an outstanding loyal customer decided that a female camel was just what her mother needed to enliven the otherwise sedate grounds of her Fort Worth mansion. Delighted that his assessment of the existing market for camels had been affirmed, Stanley had the foul tempered beast shipped by air to Dallas, a trip that according to all involved was far more unpleasant for the flight crew than it was to the haughty camel who gave the impression that she had spent more time in the air than on the desert.

If Stanley was a bit out of sorts because the camel was on camera more than he was when the animal stumbled out of the airplane at Dallas Love Field can only be assumed but, as he rightly predicted, television and newspaper reporters had a field day with the eventful arrival of this most curious of Christmas gifts. Among those watching the television coverage of the camel's arrival were the unsuspecting soon-to-be owner of the beast and her daughter who unbeknownst to Mom had succumbed to the lure of the Christmas Book to buy her the camel. As the older lady watched the debut of the camel at the airport and listened to Stanley hint, on camera at last, that some lucky person in the Dallas-Fort Worth area was going to be surprised on Christmas morning to find this wonderful animal under her holiday tree, at least figuratively speaking.

She, who was in fact that lucky person, was bemused. "What darn fool," she reportedly asked her daughter, "would buy anyone a camel as a Christmas gift?" The next morning, the daughter threw open the front door of her mother's mansion to reveal the much traveled beast calmly grazing on the capacious front lawn. Although initially taken aback, the recipient quickly grasped the conversational potential that accompanied being the owner of the only camel in the elite western suburbs of Fort Worth. As a result, the camel was named "Lucy" for no particular reason and allowed to remain at the big house for the rest of her years.

This happy turn of events gave Stanley something else to say to reporters at the beginning of countless retail Christmas seasons thereafter. Media representatives remained curious about the camel and its well-being and the annual ritual of interviewing Stanley about Christmas often began by inquiring about what a number of reporters liked to call "The camel that came C.O.D." even though it had, in fact, come air express.

The tale of the camel proved that it was the imagination and sheer whimsical nonsense of the more newsworthy His and Her gifts that generated the interest amongst the media. Some reporters tended to identify the most expensive item in the Christmas Book as their big news feature and build their story around the trite theme that for "only" a million dollars, one could pick up a really nice gift for that special someone on their shopping list. This cynical patter seemed to imply that only at Neiman Marcus would the shopper find such exorbitant gift items, thus inaccurately suggesting that it was the outrageous price tag on an item that made it worthy of prime time news coverage.

A once highly successful store in another large Texas city decided in the late 1970s that they would steal the media spotlight away from Dallas by "out Neiman-ing Neimans." The rival store's executives believed that by simply producing their version of a Christmas book laden with only the most expensive items to be found in the marketplaces of the world, they could "out Neiman" their rival. No colorful junks or laughable camels were to be offered, but instead, opulent jewels, breathtaking maharaja palaces, full size Boeing jet aircraft, and centuries-old bottles of wine just discovered in a remote French chateau, which could also be purchased.

The prices on these rare items ranged in the modestly low to the absurdly high million dollar range, but the ploy was so blatantly obvious that the media did not bother to waste much air or ink on what was clearly a very expensive publicity stunt. Even as this losing strategy was winding down, the store announced plans to present an international extravaganza obviously patterned after the Neiman Marcus Fortnights. In just a few years, both the expensive but fatally faux Christmas Book and the copycat Fortnight schemes were abandoned. Soon thereafter, for any number of reasons, the once respected store operation was forced to shutter its doors forever. The lesson, learned too late, was that Neiman Marcus was more to be admired than copied. The success of the Dallas store, and eventually all of the new units, was built upon far more than just selling expensive merchandise to wealthy customers.

Many of the items in the Neiman Marcus Christmas catalogs were found newsworthy because of the wit and imagination that had obviously made them possible. One catalog featured a thin metal rod that telescoped outward to eleven feet, obviously to be used for touching anything not to be touched with a ten foot pole.

Another book offered a silver-plated HO gauge model railroad billed as the Gravy Train. The tiny engine pulled gondolas and flatcars around an oval track carrying salt and pepper shakers, sugar, olives, and other such dining refinements. Guests seated around the dinner table had only to activate their plate-side controls to bring the train to their place at the table. An optional offering provided a refrigerated car that held a small quantity of extra ice cubes.

For those few who did not have a real one of their own to disclaim, one catalog offered a skeleton in the closet. This articulated fabric form bore the imprint of a full size human skeleton while providing a unique hanger upon which to drape suits or floor length coats. This item proved popular enough to deserve repeat appearances in several subsequent catalogs.

One of Stanley's all time favorites was a variation on the His and Her theme that featured a gift for the optimist and a gift for the pessimist, regardless of gender. For the pessimist, the catalog offered a replica of Noah's Ark, right down to its very last cubit. On board the large craft were to be pairs of every major biological species then in residence in Texas. To the mind of any dyed-in-the-wool Texan, of course, there would be little if any value in perpetuating any creature not living in the Lone Star State after the flood had abated. To accompany this fanciful floating zoo, which carried a price tag of nearly $600,000, was a Texas A&M University trained male veterinarian accompanied, we can assume, by his wife to ensure that *all* species would be around forever.

To reward those possessed of a more positive nature, the book suggested an oak seedling in the hope that the flood would never come and that the tiny little tree would find enough nourishment to survive while avoiding oak wilt. Stanley was always delighted to tell skeptical reporters that the store would have indeed built and stocked the ark on special order had any sorry pessimistic soul given us the money for it, but while such was happily not necessary, the store did sell out of the little trees and had to order a new forest's worth to satisfy the great demand.

As orders for the seedlings arrived, including one large order from Spain, one letter did arrive containing a check for the full price of the ark. Because the check had clearly been drawn by hand and bore the name of a New York City bank that research proved to be non-existent, it didn't require much thought to conclude that the offer was a sham. Just to be certain, however, the sender soon received a letter from the store expressing thanks for the check and inquiring what type of wood paneling would be preferred in the captain's cabin. No reply was forthcoming.

Not all of the big idea, or so-called fantasy gifts, have been fantastical at all. A surprising number of them over the years were on the cutting edge of what was eventually to become the craze for "living green." Such environmentally sound gift suggestions as urban windmills, fuel efficient hovercrafts, and a meditation serenity bubble have been offered.

Not all ideas were applauded. The copy suggestion that Chinese Shar-Pei puppies would make excellent gifts was roundly attacked by that breed's association, berating us for offering for sale such priceless if quaintly wrinkled little dogs to just anybody with two thousand dollars to spend. It later developed that our source for the then rare pups was a breeder who had somehow run afoul of the official breeders group and we had managed to get caught in a crossfire not of our own making.

While the offer to sell the first ever certified pure American Bison did not cause any ruffled fur, the photographing of the herd on a Colorado ranch provided colorful fodder for the media. According to the breeder, his herd was, after decades of carefully monitored breeding, completely free from any genetic taints once rampant throughout this country's buffalo herd and brought about by centuries of the unplanned cross breeding with amorous Longhorns, or shorthorns, or whatever breed bull might have happened upon a romantically inclined bison cow in the wilds.

When his claim proved to be valid, our photo crew made a springtime journey to a beautiful green meadow high in the Rocky Mountains. The large bison herd certainly appeared to be the real thing as it moved majestically about its lofty domain beneath still snow covered peaks. The calves we planned to offer at nearly twelve thousand dollars the pair could be seen at the sides of their picturesque mothers. As the Land Rover carrying the photographers moved stealthily closer to the yearlings to take their picture for the book, the motor of the vehicle simply stopped running and the car came to a sudden halt some fifty yards from the target calves and their huge parents.

As the city dwelling cameraman and his assistant climbed out to assist the frazzled driver in his motor repair assessment, a typical late afternoon mountain thunderstorm appeared from out of nowhere and began pelting the herd, the city slickers, and the now dormant Land Rover with equal intensity. Only the bison were capable of escaping the fury of this intense but short lived hail storm and they demonstrated that unique capability by wheeling about almost as one giant wooly and be-horned beast. Turning collective tail to the thrust of the storm, they stampeded directly toward the immobile and suddenly terrified trio of humans who had come to immortalize the animals in an internationally famous Christmas catalog.

Caring far more for relief from the hailstones that were stinging their thick hide than worldwide publicity, all hundred of the animals rushed toward the car which had just become something of a mobile bomb shelter, hopefully bison proof, in advance of the thundering herd. Stretched out side by side in the mud beneath the Land Rover, the three men covered their faces as four hundred hooves churned the very grass just inches away. Fortunately for both man and beast, the vehicle was not touched by the madly passing parade, but the fury of the stampede shook the car from side to side as the bison plunged past it at only an arm's length away. In mere minutes, the fury was spent and the herd, traveling at what the rancher estimated to have been in excess of forty miles per hour, had disappeared into a silvery curtain of the hail. As it developed, the herd had in fact disappeared altogether, taking no notice of a barbed wire fence that surrounded their peaceful pasture which now stood empty except for three very wet and muddy two-legged creatures that had warily pushed their way out from under a broken but thankfully lifesaving vehicle.

The crew left that very evening for Dallas, Texas, while the buffalo no longer roamed and had wandered back to their Colorado pasture. For the first time in its history, the Christmas Book that year featured a dark and obviously amateurish photograph. It was taken three days after the store's professionals had left the pasture in haste and empty handed. Eventually the rancher collected his wayward herd and used his inexpensive little camera to capture for all the world to see examples of his purebred, if rambling, American bison. The whole adventure story eventually made it into the *Denver Post*, whose editor found obvious delight in painting a tongue-in cheek word picture of brave Texans cowering in the mud before the onrushing phalanx of Colorado buffaloes.

Other animals have also created a stir through their exposure in the catalog, although one of them had been dead for over a century and a half before it stirred a sea of controversy. In 1974, the depiction of a beautiful antique ivory tusk of a long-deceased narwhal set off an unexpected barrage of letters all suspiciously carrying an identical postmark. The typewritten and unsigned letters attacked Neiman Marcus for profiting from the death of an endangered specie, namely this single-tusked narwhal which appears to the unscientific eye to be an unlikely cross between a medium-sized whale and an enormous ocean going unicorn.

Hoping to calm the unfounded fears of the unknown writer, and to generate some publicity, of course, the store ran a single column ad in the newspaper of the large city close to the postmarked source of the fifteen or so letters. In the ad, the facts were made known that the trophy was indeed an antique that carried credentials confirming its age, the name of the firm that had created the trophy in the early 1820s, and disclaiming any intent to rid the world of any other narwhals that might have still then been extant. Two weeks later, much to the delight of those responsible for the disclaiming little ad, a single envelope arrived bearing the same postmark and addressed to Mr. Neiman Marcus. Inside, was an anonymously typewritten letter comprised of one magnificently succinct line. It read, "I don't believe you." No further communication on the matter was ever exchanged.

Another credibility issue arose a few years later when the store offered an attractive chrome plated ice bucket in the catalog. The bucket appeared to be a nearly foot high statue of a penguin rather than an ice container, but its snugly fitting top was easily removed to reveal the insulated interior with a capacity to hold over three pounds of cubes. The item was shown as being available for a mere $450 unless the purchaser decided to add an optional feature to the ice bucket, namely ice. In a rush of news-making genius, the writer of the copy decided that such an attractive Antarctic-themed item should come with genuine Antarctic-produced ice. A few well-placed phone calls yielded the fact that ice from the South Polar Cap was indeed available via the mail plane that flew north, the only direction it could fly, of course, on a regular schedule.

The estimated final cost for a small three pound supply of real penguin-variety ice was placed at $2,950 FOB Panama City with another fifty dollars or so added on to the bill to get the ice on its way to almost any city in the United States. After a test run confirmed the validity of the cost estimate, it was determined that the $450 little ice bucket filled with certifiably authentic ice from the homeland of the penguin should appear in the Christmas Book for $3,450. Sometimes such ideas truly took on a life all their own.

This took place before any public concerns about global warming had been widely voiced and if fears existed about the shrinking South Polar ice cap, no one in the Mail Order Division at Neiman Marcus had been so informed. Within a week after the Book had been mailed, the store received first an angry phone call demanding that the item be pulled immediately from inventory. This was followed by an even angrier letter that pointed out, none too convincingly, that removing even tiny buckets worth of ice from the gigantic shelf would add incalculable momentum to what the writer, well ahead of his or her time, viewed as the beginning of the end of the world due to the disappearance of polar ice.

Curiously, this letter, as was the one regarding the narwhal tusk, had been mailed from Boston but in this case we did not invest in a newspaper column to defend our stance. As things developed, the store sold eighty-seven penguin buckets, but not a single crystal of Antarctic ice was ever ordered.

As Stanley devoted much of his later years at the store dealing with the myriad of problems stemming from merger issues and the challenges of rapid expansion, he for the most part delegated the creating of the big idea items to a few handpicked associates. He usually accepted our ideas without comment, but on a few occasions, he could not resist slipping back into his old micromanaging ways.

Among the more memorable of these rare instances was the infamous NM Mouse Ranch that appeared in the catalog in 1975. This highly unique idea was based on a terrarium theme and featured a very large Lucite container filled with genuine Texas soil. Placed here and there on the surface of the impacted dirt were tiny windmills, a small mouse-sized ranch house, corrals, barns, and, of course, a traditional Texas-style ranch gate that could be personalized with any name or brand.

The basic ranch idea held at least some potential for amusement, it was assumed, but it was the long-tailed livestock that offended not only Stanley but apparently hundreds of good customers all across America. As the headline on the catalog page stated, this was a ranch for raising mice and therefore we had to establish our herd with good breeding stock. Based on the suggestion of a local biology teacher, we chose white laboratory mice to populate our ranch. The operable word in that misguided ambition was "populate" as we very rapidly discovered that mice are exceptionally good at increasing the population of their species at an astounding clip. Well-fed and watered in their secure environment, the mouse herd quickly doubled and then redoubled almost to infinity. As a result, the herd capacity of the little mouse ranch quickly proved to be grossly inadequate. Culling the herd proved to be a stressful chore for the faint-hearted copywriter turned wrangler who was assigned the responsibility of controlling the head count.

When Stanley appeared with Johnny Carson on the *Tonight Show* to talk about the Christmas Book that year, it was quite obvious that the concept of the mouse ranch was not high on his list of really great ideas. To his amazement and to our immense relief, Mr. Carson's dead-pan analysis and description of the ranch, its tiny buildings and authentic if miniature watering troughs produced gales of laughter from his audience. Despite his original and rather heated negative observations, the master showman from Dallas quickly recognized that the audience was in his hands. Apparently suffering a momentary lapse of memory, Stanley took full credit for the mouse ranch idea and all but matched Johnny Carson in poking good natured fun at the smallest ranch in all of Texas. The final result of the whole escapade yielded zero ranches sold, but untold amounts of free and, curiously, favorable publicity. Not one letter of complaint was received from Boston.

Sometimes, the publicity value was less fortunate. In 1980, the catalog featured His and Her ostriches as the big news making items of the Christmas season. The price tag, at fifteen hundred dollars each, seemed reasonable enough at the time and the team choosing items for the catalogue assumed that ostriches were every bit as funny to look at as camels were. Since the long ago camel caper had been a great publicity engine, it was reasoned then the bizarre looking giant bird, offered at such a relatively low price, was sure to appeal to the masses and the media that kept them informed if not inspired.

The big birds were photographed on location in Oklahoma at a session marked by ostrich attacks upon the very same cameraman who had survived the buffalo stampede in Colorado some four years earlier. After suffering several severe pecking thumps to his bald head, the photographer finally located a construction helmet which he wore for the duration of the shoot. The photographs were excellent despite the painful encounters involved in taking them. When the catalogs went into the mail, our publicity people sat eagerly by their phones, awaiting an opportunity to extract all possible benefit from our clever choice of the weird bird as the store's leading Christmas item.

If we were seeking headlines, we certainly were not disappointed. Within days, such pointed banners as "Neiman Lays an Egg" and "NM Gives Us the Bird" appeared across the land. Inadvertently and inadvisably, the store, it later developed, had stumbled into a raging national controversy surrounding ostriches. The bird was just then being touted by its breeding association as being the utility animal of the century. From its supposedly tasty meat to its undeniably boot quality hide, the ostrich properly raised and hatched from hand inspected eggs, were all but priceless, or so said the professional breeders association. A good blue ribbon quality ostrich chick was worth, some advocates said, at least five thousand dollars, but only if it received the proper care in the right environment. "Neiman Marcus," ran an article in one newspaper, "was trying to undercut the market" as well as encouraging the unqualified raising of the breed by just anyone anywhere with fifteen hundred extra dollars to spend capriciously.

For the first time ever, Neiman Marcus was being publicly accused of selling something at too low a price! Our publicity people were dumbfounded at this totally unexpected reaction, and since our corporate playbook did not include any directions about how to deal with customer claims of being undercharged, we adopted a low profile approach and tried with only limited success to divert the public spotlight to other more typically priced items in the Neiman Marcus tradition.

The flurry of negative, if organized, public outcry quickly faded. As it was, only two ostrich chicks were sold to a lady in Omaha who, after naming them for her two children, donated them to a zoo in Iowa. Much more favorable publicity attended that generous but previously unplanned newsworthy event.

Of all the memorable unplanned Christmas Book happenings, however, Stanley favored the tale of the mysterious mummy. It began in the late 1960s when an antique dealer living in London approached him about buying an Egyptian female mummy case. At the time,

Stanley was vigorously upholding the strict His and Her concept for the big idea gifts, and as the dealer did not have a case constructed for a long-deceased Egyptian man to match the obviously female case he was offering, the deal fell through. Disappointed, the Londoner vowed to keep looking in order to find a proper "His" case to complement the "Hers" that he promised to keep in storage to someday accommodate the whim of the famous Stanley Marcus.

Several years passed before the man called again to joyfully announce that his long search had borne fruit and a case clearly made to contain the mummified body of an Egyptian male had been located and acquired. As promised, he had kept the female variety safe in his vaults and he was now prepared to offer the complete "His and Hers" mummy case set to Neiman Marcus.

Just how he found the larger second case that was decorated almost exactly as was the first smaller case was a question which Stanley did not wish to pursue. The fact that the dealer lived directly across the street from the British Museum might suggest an answer to those with a suspicious or inquiring mind. By viewing the two beautifully ornate cases standing side by side, it was easy to recognize that they were closely related. The painted expressions bore the same quizzical look, the gilt edged necklaces imprinted on both cases had the identical pattern and even the twenty etched fingernails were the same although distinctly different than those found on any other cases to be seen at the British Museum or elsewhere. The modern day Egyptian government has long and steadfastly forbidden any such treasured antiquities from being exported. With an estimated age of well over four thousand years, both cases were clearly antiquities that would have been denied any legal exodus from the land of the Pharaohs. Their source remained forever a mystery.

With all that noted and likely pondered by Stanley, the deal was closed over international telephone lines but only after color photographs of the two exquisitely designed items had been received and studied in Dallas. Although the purchase price, at wholesale so to speak, was never disclosed by the purchaser, it is easy to estimate the amount based on Stanley's propensity to throw caution to the wind when dealing with a one-of-a-kind, or in this instance, two-of-a-kind items. As the retail price in the 1971 catalog was six thousand dollars for the pair, it is likely that the London dealer sold them for around twenty-five hundred to three thousand dollars for the set. Knowing something of Stanley's legendary ability to make a good deal even better, the seller most likely was quietly browbeaten into paying all shipping costs.

At any rate, after two weeks at sea on board a slow moving English freighter, the two cases, one nearly six feet in height and the other about eight inches shorter, arrived at Port Everglades near Miami, Florida. The company had but recently opened its first store ever outside the borders of Texas in Miami and it was hoped that through displaying the two cases in the store, the initially somewhat disappointing traffic and sales levels there might be substantially increased.

Once carefully lifted from their protective shipping crates, the cases then came under the scrutiny of United States Custom Service agents. According to records, these were the first two such antiquities to enter Florida by sea for over fifty years, and as such an unusually large platoon of agents gathered around to study the strange markings and fascinating hieroglyphics that adorned each of them.

Mummy cases are, after all, ancient coffins and despite their age and many mysterious journeys taken long before modern times, these two were still faintly redolent of an odor that vaguely hinted at their original usage. Perhaps this explains why no one ventured to open either case to peer inside before all the shipping manifests had been duly signed and vigorously and repeatedly stamped with official federal symbols of approval.

A store truck had been sent to the Customs building at the port, and after a three hour wait, the driver had helped load his ancient cargo and promptly delivered it to the freight dock of the new store located just north of Miami proper. Obviously more curious than the jaded customs men, the store manager could not resist looking inside the old mummy case. One can only imagine his shock and disbelieving horror when he found inside the two thousand year old mummy case a two thousand year old mummy.

Once the dim lights of the store's dock had been turned up to confirm the gruesome discovery and to calm the understandably agitated discoverer of the ancient corpse, it was soon determined that this was, or rather once had been, a man. For all of his twenty centuries of wear and tear, he was in good condition, a fact that did little to calm the nerves of the store manager who still found it difficult to accept that he was indeed peering at a dead human body. The nose was still prominent, the ears only slightly eroded by soundless time, the eye sockets frighteningly discernable but blessedly empty, and a surprisingly full head of hair still clung to the ancient skull. Teeth could be seen behind the slightly parted lips. The absence of most of the wrappings generally associated with ancient mummies only enhanced the awful truth that an unidentified corpse laid amid the packing straw in a Neiman Marcus store.

What to do? Reacting in an almost Pavlovian manner, the unstrung manager rushed to the nearest phone to call the man in Dallas who had at least indirectly caused him all of this day's shock and woe. In writing of that phone call, Stanley casts himself being, as usual, the cool captain in charge of every situation. In his version, he commanded the hapless Floridian to call a doctor, call the police, but by all means not to call the newspaper. In truth, Stanley himself called a friend who was then the editor of Miami's leading newspaper and, with the shining eyes of a Phineas T. Barnum who had just discovered Colonel Tom Thumb, told him the entire story to ensure front page coverage.

The manager did call the store's appointed physician who arrived at about the same time as the officers of the local constabulary who found the whole matter beyond their limited comprehension. The forms they were required to complete contained no provision for identifying the remains as having been obviously dead much too long to suggest any recent foul play. As they puzzled over how to fulfill their responsibilities, the bemused doctor went about his duties in an effort to prove beyond the shadow of a doubt that the poor shrunken figure in the case before him was truly dead.

When no fog of condensed breath appeared on the mirror held in front of the mummy's darkened lips, and only after no reassuring heartbeat was detected nor pulse felt through the parchment like skin, the nameless ancient wanderer was pronounced to be legally dead by unknown causes. Convinced that opening an investigation into the death of this illegal alien would lead nowhere, a policeman suggested that the relic be wrapped in a sheet, secured back into his centuries-old traveling case, and sent to the nearest mortuary just as soon as possible.

In the meantime, the newspaper reporters had arrived to write the story of the long-dead Egyptian who had come to Florida for Christmas. Upon the visitor's arrival at the mortuary, he was placed in a cold storage unit as a matter of routine procedure although to many it seemed unlikely that refrigeration was going to be of much value to his desiccated mortal coil.

The case, empty one supposes for the first time in thousands of years, remained in the Florida store where, on display alongside its fortunately empty companion case, it did in fact prove to be a potent stimulator of crowds of curious onlookers. The story was carried around the world, just as Stanley had hoped. Rumors of an investigation into the ethical deportment of the London antique dealer drifted past from time to time, and the efforts of well-intentioned researchers to seek and perhaps find the identity of the really old Egyptian eventually went for naught.

The mummy itself stayed in the Miami area mortuary for nearly a year while its case and its companion piece came to Texas to be displayed before being photographed, at long last, for an appearance as the "His and Hers" gifts in the Christmas catalog. At a mere six thousand dollars for the pair, which Stanley refused to separate, interest ran high. Ultimately, an obscure California-based religious order sent its representative to Texas to view the cases. Claiming some mystic relationship to ancient Egypt in their frequent magazine ads at the time, the brothers of the order finally came forth with the adequate cash to buy the "His," and in time, with the stipulation that its original occupant be returned to it. The "Her" case was also soon paid for entirely and shipped to the order's West Coast headquarters. Although federal law made it illegal to transport a dead body across state lines without a certificate that clearly states the cause and time of death, the posthumously wandering Egyptian was allowed to be air shipped to California where his case awaited him. In keeping with his well polished instincts Stanley made sure that all expenses involved in the shipping of one mummy and the two cases were fully absorbed by their new owners in sunny California.

Each year, the Christmas Books gained an increasing amount of publicity across the nation and around the world. Unforeseen happenstances such as the mummy issue and the ostrich flap seemed to inspire the media to devote more interest and time to such unplanned events than it might to an obviously contrived stunt. Newspaper readers and television viewers alike appeared to find a good deal of humor of things gone awry at the high and mighty Neiman Marcus. One might easily compare such a reaction to that of an audience at an old time silent movie laughing wildly at the sight of a haughty society matron catching a deftly tossed custard cream pie in the face. Things seldom went even slightly wrong, but when they did, the media lapped it up. The irony of it all was that the media was almost always tipped off about the story by the society matron who had been smacked with the pie, in the form of the Neiman Marcus publicity office.

One of the time-honored ways to ensure the popularity of any publication is the inclusion of lovely ladies within its covers. The Neiman Marcus Christmas Book is no exception to this practice and such famous models as Cindy Crawford, Andie MacDowell, and Heidi Klum have been seen over the years. Audrey Hepburn, another famed beauty, once appeared in the catalogue but on behalf of her pet charity rather than as a fashion model.

As the book took on an international persona, it became necessary to improve its front cover. In the highly competitive mail order business, every book is in fact judged by its cover and it had become obvious that the artwork created by the store's advertising staff was not quite up to demanding international standards.

Out of this realization was born the high quality magazine cover art for which the Christmas Book became widely famed. Over the years, such noted artists as Robert Indiana, Victor Vasarely, and Bjorn Wiinblad have seen their cover designs accepted and then reproduced literally more than a million times over. At least until the mid-1980s, each of these and other famous designers agreed to accept the contract for the Christmas cover for a fee far less than that which their work would normally command. In order that their work could appear on such a widely distributed and well publicized publication, each artist agreed to accept a flat fee of twenty-five hundred dollars for the design. Sometimes, rather spirited discussions about this relatively modest fee took place, particularly with those artists who had not yet reached the generous compensation levels of a Vasarely or a Ben Shahn, but upon hearing that the proffered fee was not negotiable, the artist usually agreed to proceed with his design.

One cover artist became so enamored of the project that he offered to work for no fee at all. His generosity was rebuffed, and with the nominal fee in the bank, the Oscar-winning artist gave the catalog cover a unique look it had not previously shown. That famous designer was Chuck Jones, the creator of such cartoon characters as Bugs Bunny, the Roadrunner and, of course, the ever popular Wile E. Coyote. The Christmas Book had never been graced by a cartoon figure before, and while Stanley Marcus did not initially enthusiastically embrace the idea of a coyote and a bird on the cover, the store's clientele found it to be totally unexpected and refreshing.

Working with Chuck Jones on the project was every bit as entertaining as watching his lively creations play across a movie screen. His personal sense of humor was even more cynical and capricious as those of his universally admired animated characters. Pixie-like in appearance, he seemed out of place in the Fort Worth steakhouse where we lunched during his visit to North Texas. The place was full of cowboys, both real and imagined, and Jones in his California sportswear gave irrefutable evidence that he was neither a horseman nor a caretaker of cows. It was not until he autographed the back of the luncheon check with a likeness of his Yosemite Sam character that our waitress realized who he was. In the manner of many waitresses, she made certain that word of his presence spread through the crowded Cattleman's Steakhouse. Instantly, other diners came our way, holding napkins and note cards for him to autograph. He joyfully obliged and even drew for one youngster a full face portrait of Bugs Bunny that would be worth a hefty sum today.

As popular as the Chuck Jones cover proved to be, it was the work of artist Paul Davis that spawned a new gift campaign within Neiman Marcus stores. Contracted to submit a cover design, Davis complied by sending a color portrait of an expressionless but irresistible cat. The only hint that the animal had the slightest relationship with the holiday season was a touch of mistletoe and a tiny sleigh bell at his throat. At first, the staff's reaction to the drawing was mixed, but upon further study it became apparent that there was an hypnotic but typical "I am a cat and you are not" quality in the animal's blank expression. The effect was so unusual that it seemed worth the risk to pay Mr. Davis his $2,500 and make the Christmas cat the star of the annual book.

Our confidence in the appealing feline was such that we took him, or actually a living cat that was a dead ringer for the one Davis had drawn, to every Neiman Marcus city to launch the catalog. In a chartered jet, with the Neiman Marcus logo emblazoned on the fuselage, we transported the fortunately good natured animal to such cities as Miami, Atlanta, St. Louis, Chicago, Los Angeles, Washington, D. C., and even to New York City to meet the likes of Dan Rather and Barbara Walters. At National Airport in Washington, D.C., the cover cat had the unexpected opportunity of meeting Senator Barry Goldwater who proved to be totally unimpressed with the whole scene, which was unplanned anyway.

In Los Angeles, our star met the charming Dinah Shore backstage at her television show. Unlike certain late senators from Arizona, she fell in love with the cat and insisted on holding him on her lap during the taping of our segment of the show. He seemed to enjoy the experience immensely.

The media of each stop covered the landing of the Neiman Marcus plane, the interviews on the airport ramps, and followed up with their cameras as our limousine hurried us to press conferences in the various downtowns. It is fairly safe to assume that the Christmas cat was the first such animal to be warmly received in the editorial offices of the *Atlanta Constitution*, the *Chicago Tribune*, and the *Los Angeles Times*, to say nothing of the CBS Studios in both Los Angeles and New York.

The wave of public acclaim for both the painted cat on the cover of the book and his real life stand-in was without parallel. The store received countless fan letters addressed to MR. NM CAT or Miss Neiman Cat, etc., proving that while it is sometimes difficult to determine the gender of any feline at first glance, the appeal of most felines is universal.

Because of the popularity of the cat cover, it was decided to capitalize on the design by offering reproductions of it on Christmas tree ornaments, holiday candles and so forth in the subsequent catalogs. The success of that idea generated the continuing tradition of offering versions of the Christmas cover design on all manner of holiday merchandise.

Though widely imitated but never emulated, the Neiman Marcus Christmas Book/Catalog, has become over the years, the media's universal focal point by which to launch the most important retail shopping season of the entire year. Although a handful of commentators may complain about what they view as the premature timing of the book, or make a snide remark or two about any price tag they might deem to be excessive, the fact remains that members of the media cult seem virtually compelled to say something about the Book even if it is not always kindly said or well-intentioned. To any publicist who knows his business, that mention, good or bad, is all that really matters. As long as the "E" in Neiman came before the "I," we were delighted with the coverage.

Courting Celebrity

As the reputation of Neiman Marcus grew over the decades, its brilliant glow attracted celebrities from far and wide. At the center of the retailing universe he had created was Stanley Marcus and into his web, movie stars, foreign dignitaries, and the leading lights of international society gravitated in endless numbers.

They came asking for his endorsements, his money, his advice, and most often, his patronage for their favorite cause, be it their own career or a charitable project that might benefit from his recognition and support. Giving away great sums of money to unfamiliar entities was not one of his more obvious traits, and unlike some other American retail operations at the time, Neiman Marcus was not publicly known for its overtly generous philanthropy. Charitable functions in Dallas were very often sponsored by the store but its principal contribution was the considerable time and matchless expertise of Stanley's staff rather than any large scale monetary gift. As the company expanded across the United States, from Honolulu to Miami and from San Diego to upstate New York, the same pattern of in-kind charitable and civic contribution was maintained. In later years, however, the company became more generous in its support of worthy causes.

Because of Stanley's acquaintance with famous celebrities in all parts of the world, the store was often instrumental in bringing to Dallas a great many headline-makers who could transform a charity ball into an international event just by making an appearance, aided immeasurably by the well-oiled publicity process of Neiman Marcus. Some of those appearances are still the stuff of legend, as follows:

✍ John Wayne ✍

The Duke hit Dallas, Texas, with all the force of the University of Southern California football star he had once been many years earlier. Although he had often been in Texas to make motion pictures, his first official visit to Neiman Marcus was in October of 1970.

John Wayne and Stanley Marcus probably did not share a single political or philosophical tenet. While Stanley might have rated Karl Marx as being an arch conservative, Wayne would have considered Attila the Hun to be a liberal poster boy. When the two met for the first time during that visit, they approached each other with a wariness that was sheathed in a cool courtesy. The reputation of each legend had preceded him and when the initial conversational ploys confirmed the left and right polarity of the two, they politely avoided each other for the rest of the evening. When Wayne came to visit the store as the star attraction of a fundraising event, Stanley greeted him with a formal courtesy that was devoid of any sign of his usual warm cordiality. Mr. Wayne, it appeared, could not have cared in the least if in fact he noticed his rather cool reception. As the party raged on until well past the early morning hours and the specially ordered Commemorativo Tequila flowed without restraint, the looming movie giant clearly enjoyed himself immensely even though he was celebrating in the palace of the city's most liberal philosopher. As long as that philosopher was providing the tequila, Hollywood's most visible conservative symbol was bound to have an uproariously good time.

The Wayne visit to Dallas and Neiman Marcus had begun with as much tequila as a lubricant as the big party that ended it. He was on location in Durango, Mexico, shooting a picture titled "Big Jake." Persuaded to come to Texas and Neiman Marcus by his wife Pilar whose favorite cause was to benefit from the store event, Wayne suspended the filming to make the weekend trip to Dallas. A private jet was found to ensure the star would be away from the location for just a few days and, being nominally in charge of the overall care and feeding, and watering, of such celebrities in general, I appointed myself to fly down to Mexico to accompany Wayne on his flight.

Hoping to earn his approval, I arranged to have two bottles of his favorite tequila on board along with a case or two of beer and, for some curious reason that now escapes me, a six-foot-long-hero submarine sandwich that I was presumably sure would delight the six-foot-four-inch tall superhero himself. As best I can recall, the sandwich remained untouched by the movie star, his ten-year old son, and the official if self-appointed Neiman Marcus escort. All of the tequila and eventually most of the beer, however, seemed to evaporate as the jet made its way from Durango to Dallas.

International flight regulations at the time for some reason made it mandatory that all flights from Mexico to Texas stop first in Monterrey and then in Brownsville, on the American side of the Rio Grande. As our jet pulled up to the terminal in Monterrey, swarms of John Wayne's Mexican fans stood waiting. At the sight of the fedora-wearing star, the crowd whistled, cheered, and clapped while following him to the door of the caballero's rest room. A uniformed airport security man thoughtfully restrained the army of fans until the Duke emerged and made his way, with some difficulty, through the crowd and back to the aircraft. Along the way, he tossed small pre-signed "Duke

Wayne" cards to his admirers who showed admirable athletic ability in snatching the cards out of the air.

How the fans knew that John Wayne was to land at the Monterrey airport has always puzzled me. Maybe such a sizeable number of his admirers gathered there every Saturday in the unlikely chance that he just might pass through or maybe Wayne's publicity folks had sent the word on ahead. At any rate, it was apparent that the star was immensely popular in at least that part of Mexico even though his "Alamo" film had been initially banned by the Mexican government.

The short flight to Brownsville afforded us an excellent opportunity to tap into yet another bottle of tequila, with a side order of sangrita, the spicy tomato juice often consumed with the fiery Mexican liquor. At the Brownsville airport, the Monterrey scene was repeated although by this time Mr. Wayne and I were about to reach a point of not really caring all that much about our reception or, in fact, much of anything. Once again, the movie legend expressed a desire to quickly find the men's room. As we made our by now somewhat weaving way toward the customs facility and, hopefully, a restroom, throngs of young fans, both Americans and Mexicans, ran onto the airfield to greet the famous visitor.

In his haste to leave the plane, Señor Wayne had left his snap brim hat behind but fortunately the hairpiece he hated to wear was in place, albeit slightly askew. This toupee, I like to think, is the same one he wore when he famously, or infamously, visited the unfriendly environment of Harvard University some time later. When asked if that which covered his head was real hair, he replied in his best John Wayne voice, "It sure is real hair, but it's not mine."

Once again, he threw handful after handful of the little autographed cards into the air to the delight of his fans. Back on the plane, we set about reducing the beer inventory seeing as how all of the tequila had disappeared. Throughout the entire flight with its somewhat epic consumption of alcohol at high altitude, John Wayne never ceased to be John Wayne. The persona he displayed in real life was identical to the roles he played out on film. If there was an original person inside him somewhere, a Marion Michael Morrison from Winterset, Iowa, it never emerged during that long flight. By the time our jet touched down at Dallas Love Field, "The Ringo Kid," "Sergeant John Stryker," and "Rooster Cogburn" and I were ready to deplane to prepare for that night's private party.

Pilar Wayne was there to greet her husband and her son, who had slept almost all the way. Somehow, the effects of the long and well-lubricated voyage from Mexico had all but dissipated, but Pilar seemed to suspect that we might have enjoyed our trip a bit more than was necessary. That evening, apparently none the worse for his long and liquid flight, the big man kept partying until the sun rose over the Dallas skyline.

✍ Lord Mountbatten ✍

If John Wayne was the salt of the earth, then Admiral of the Fleet, Earl Mountbatten of Burma, KG, PC, GCB, OM, GCSI, GCIE, GCVO, DSO, and FRS must be considered the cream of the crop. The great grandson of Queen Victoria, Lord Louie as he was more familiarly known, was born in 1900 and given the unwieldy name of Albert Victor Nicholas Francis of Battenberg but called Dickie by the family.

When Stanley and I were invited to his home in the south of England in 1973, Mountbatten was the sole survivor among the very highest level of Allied commanders of World War II. The reason for our visit was to persuade him to come to Dallas as the guest of honor for the British Fortnight scheduled for later in the year.

The magnificent home is known as "Broadlands." Once the private home of Lord Palmerston, longtime prime minister of the Empire, the house and grounds had been acquired by Mountbatten's wealthy father-in-law, Sir Ernest Cassel. As our limousine pulled to a stop, the tall still strikingly handsome seventy-four year old Admiral of the Fleet, literally bounded down the front steps to greet us. While cordial, he was still very much a "Royal" and even more so, still the highest ranking officer of the British Royal Navy, even in retirement.

Before luncheon, he conducted us on a tour of his historic home, filled with hundreds of photographs of the royal families of nearly every country in Europe most of whom were his close relatives. Full length portraits of Queen Victoria and her consort, Prince Albert, hung in the library, while other oil paintings featured the Admiral's cousin Nicholas II of Russia and his uncle Edward VI. A beautiful portrait of his wife, the late Edwina Mountbatten, greeted visitors in the great hall.

The luncheon was one of those famous but often difficult English so-called informal events in which a corps of servants stands by impatiently as the diners help themselves to the contents of the countless dishes and platters being held for their convenience. The fare was typical, I can only assume, as dining in English estate manor homes is not a frequent pastime. There were little game birds and cuts from the loins of deer, all "taken," as His Lordship put it, on the estate itself. We used the most elegant of silver utensils to take for ourselves roast potatoes, tiny green peas, and eventually, clusters of delicious grapes, also presumably "taken" from the estate, which we transferred to our plates only with great difficulty by using tiny silver scissors to awkwardly snip each grape from the cluster held by a disdainful servant.

Stanley and the Admiral bantered to and fro about art, a subject dear to the heart of both. During a lull in the conversation, I snuck in a query about our host's opinion of Winston Churchill. The Admiral was not at all generous in his heated response. A question about who in Mountbatten's view was the best of all Allied commanders in World War II yielded the name Field Marshal William Sim. His views on Field Marshal Montgomery were not favorable, while Dwight Eisenhower got off fairly lightly, probably because of the nationality of his luncheon guests.

At some point between the turtle soup and the small green salad, there was a perceptible chill introduced in the atmosphere of the dining hall. Either Mountbatten or Marcus had said something that temporarily distanced one from the other. Stanley, usually a brilliant conversationalist if so motivated, fell strangely silent. When asked about Dallas, Texas, a subject totally alien to the Admiral who was seeking information, Stanley offered only the briefest of descriptions. Mountbatten, obviously baffled by this sudden turn of events, looked at me as if I held the reason as to what was not being said. Quickly sensing that I was as clueless as he, the Admiral in the best tradition of the Royal Navy took the offensive to steam full speed ahead. Grasping a pair of the awkward little grape scissors, he deftly snipped a tiny red tomato from the cluster that he had placed on a side dish. "I say, Alexander," he bellowed in his best royal anchors aweigh voice, "do you know what these are?" Before I could answer, he flung the little tomato at me the length of the dining table. Had the distance of his throw been shorter, I would have likely failed to catch the small red missile, but as it was at least twenty feet from his place to mine, I caught it without difficulty. "That, sir," he roared with delight, "is a tree tomato (pronounced 'tomahto' of course), I brought the plants with me from India after I was Viceroy." Although the servants seemed mildly stunned at this highly unusual display of noontime athleticism, the Admiral was apparently very amused at his stunt while I was overjoyed that the flying tomato had been prevented from splattering what appeared to be an original Hogarth painting that adorned the wall just behind my chair.

This strange interlude also served to break the frigid mood that had briefly descended over the table. Stanley had watched the launch of the tomato and the successful termination of its flight in my outstretched hand. Whatever had caused him to abruptly halt his participation in the lunchtime conversation seemingly dissolved as quickly as it had arisen.

Over the years, I noticed this unusual quirk in his behavior on several occasions. I can only assume, in distant retrospection, that he was uneasy when being upstaged. Without doubt, the Admiral of the Fleet was a powerfully charismatic figure. Historians of the war in which he distinguished himself as well as of his service in India as the last Viceroy, while not always agreeing about his abilities, are unanimous in their evaluation of the sheer magnetism of the man. Perhaps, even briefly displaced as the center of his immediate universe, Stanley unconsciously withdrew into a rarely occupied shell. The retreat, if that is indeed what it was, did not last for long and his interest in the luncheon's discourse returned almost as rapidly as the tree tomato made its flight over the long linen covered table.

By the time Admiral Mountbatten arrived in Dallas for the opening of the Fortnight, the two men had become good friends through their exchange of correspondence. Those letters had persuaded Mountbatten to bring his dress uniform with him to wear to what was up until then the only white tie event the store had ever staged.

At the age of seventy-four, the Admiral was naturally not quite as erect in stature as he had been as the Supreme Commander of Allied Forces in the Far East during World War II. When he was in "full fig," as he called it, the Admiral in formal uniform seemed to instantly regain every inch of his earlier height. Aglitter in gold braid, stripes from cuff to elbow, and no less than eleven full rows of ribbons and medals, Mountbatten's uniform made him appear to be at least twelve feet tall.

The event of which he was guest of honor was held, appropriately enough, in the Imperial Ballroom of Dallas' Fairmont Hotel. It was agreed that the five hundred guests at the banquet be seated before the Admiral, in his "full fig," would make his grand entrance. As a beaming Stanley Marcus, himself a fine figure in white tie and adorned with his own splendid array of decorations, looked on from the head table, a spotlight suddenly played on the very tall closed but majestic doors to the ballroom. As the orchestra launched into a rendition of "Hail

Britannia" worthy of the Black Watch Band, the doors swung slowly open to reveal this last towering senior commander of what many call the last good war. On his arm was the diminutive Minnie Marcus, widow of the store's founder and mother of the man who could bring about such a wondrous event in the once remote State of Texas.

The audience rose as one without prompting, and with every medal and each stitch of gold glittering in the sweeping arcs of light from a battery of spotlights, the Admiral and his lady-for-the-ball made their way majestically toward the head table where Stanley stood, leading the cheers and applause beneath a massive Union Jack of the British Empire that stretched from ceiling to floor.

It was by all accounts a grand night, at least by the standards of the mid-1970s. Times were different, Dallas was less sophisticated, entertainment was less dramatic, memories of that pivotal war were still relatively fresh and, in short, people expected less and were over-joyed when they received more. Such a spectacle as that memorable procession by the wartime hero and the matron of legend would likely not impress the more worldly society of today, but as the Admiral him-self wrote so long ago in a letter of thanks, "What a night it was!"

✒ Sophia Loren ✐

Experience teaches that motion picture stars come in all shapes and sizes and with personas that ebb and flow in relation to the occasion or the size of the crowd. Sophia Loren was, in my view, the consum-mate screen star, both when it came to shape and her warm personal charm that she radiated regardless of circumstances. Stanley Marcus, the ultimate connoisseur of all things beautiful, once proclaimed Sophia to be one of only two things he had encountered in his life that exceeded his expectations. The other superlative was his visit to the ultra-elite Bohemian Grove in San Francisco.

Sophia arrived in Dallas as the guest of honor of the Italian

Fortnight of 1975 accompanied by her husband, Carlo Ponti. She deplaned at the airport to find Stanley, her longtime admirer, awaiting her. It was a rare event when the boss himself took the time to go to the airport to meet a guest of the store. Such routine duties were usually assigned to functionaries such as me, but the arrival of such a luminous star as Sophia Loren clearly demanded the personal attention of the man who had somehow persuaded her to come to Dallas.

Sophia in the 1970s was one of those unique individuals whose charm seemed to burst outward from her very soul. She was gracious, funny, and, in a way, something of a naïve schoolgirl despite the often torrid earthiness she usually exuded on the screen. Unlike many celebrities of the time who avoided large gatherings of media representatives in favor of more intimate and more easily controlled one-on-one interviews, she asked for and received a full-blown old-fashioned press conference the day after her arrival in the city.

A large ballroom of the Fairmont Hotel was provided so that television and newspaper reporters could have an opportunity to ask the then forty-one year old superstar any questions they wished to hurl in her direction. Nothing was to be off limits or off the record the overflow crowd of news hawks had been assured, and as soon as Miss Loren arrived, they could fire away.

She kept them waiting just long enough to ensure that all of their attention would be focused directly on her and when she smilingly entered the room only five minutes behind schedule, all eyes and all cameras were indeed focused on the Neapolitan beauty.

The media of any city are a tough bunch. In Dallas, that was particularly true in the 1970s. It had learned to be tough when a president was shot dead at their city's gate. As the world turned its back on Dallas on those dark days in late 1963, the media had risen up in a rare display of unity to defend its town, all the while questioning and probing to determine how this dreadful act could have occurred in Dallas, Texas.

Most of the Dallas press corps, then, had experienced much, but few if any had ever seen anything quite like Sophia Loren. Reporters had come from all across Texas and from out of the state primarily just to see her, never for a minute fully expecting her to be able to string enough English words together to utter a cogent sentence. To the collective dismay of the assembled mass of instantly captivated former tough guys, she began to systematically make a conquest of each and everyone in the room.

Sophia regaled them with stock stories of how she broke into the movie business, shared her views about her many co-stars, expressed her opinion about Dallas, and in so doing, left the usually sharp-tongued media without breath enough to ask many questions. When she laughed her contagious earthy laugh, the reporters laughed with her. When she grew serious in talking about how her Oscar-winning performance in *Two Women* had changed her outlook on life, the media folk leaned forward to catch every single nuance behind each word. For over two hours, Sophia held this traditionally rowdy and cynical band of professional sensation-seekers spellbound. There were a few innocuous questions about her children and what her next film was going to be and such, but for the most part, the hours were filled by her solo performance.

As the morning drew to its close, she asked if anyone had anything else to ask. From the back of the room came a request that could barely be heard. "Might I come closer?" a shaky tenor voice asked, and when encouraged to do so, the questioner moved through the crowd toward the graciously smiling star. Hotel and store security personnel relaxed as a tiny fully frocked Catholic priest made his way down the narrow aisle.

When he came to within steps of the star who towered over him by at least a foot, he broke the hush of silence that had fallen over the crowd. A priest at a Dallas press conference? Impossible! Yet, it was possible after all. "I am Father Dominic," he said in a wee little voice that must have caused concern on Sundays for those members of his flock whose hearing had diminished. "I have come here from Corpus Christi," he went on, "In fact, I have walked a great deal of the way just to thank you for coming to Texas, and I do thank you." With that simple statement, he turned and left the room presumably to begin his return journey to Corpus Christi, many miles to the south. The little holy man was obviously her true fan.

Stanley, who had smilingly watched the media become essentially mesmerized by Sophia, took his eyes off her beaming face to shoot a look in my direction, asking without words if the hiking priest was in fact some homeless chap I had hired to bring a resounding climax to the media event. As I had never before seen the little man, my innocence must have shown forth, and Stanley then moved to stand next to his guest who had completely won over one of the roughest media gangs in the country.

Later the same day, a limousine carrying Miss Loren arrived at the entrance to Neiman Marcus. As I waited for the vehicle to come to a full stop, I looked up at the towering bank building that stood across the street from the store. As far as I could see, every office window was occupied by at least one long-distance viewer eager to catch a glimpse of Sophia as she entered the store. Ever the star, she somehow sensed the presence of this tower of glass filled with fans, and turning her face in their collective direction, she blew them all a kiss, straight from the heart of Naples.

After a whirlwind tour of the store which was festooned in all its Italian Fortnight finery, Miss Loren was driven back to her hotel accompanied by a Dallas police office named, appropriately enough, Lieutenant Hawke. Officer Hawke had come to my office a week before Miss Loren's visit and asked if I would make a formal request to his superior that he be assigned as Sophia's official personal security agent during her stay. I did so and the request was granted after Lieutenant Hawke assured us all that his eyes would not lose sight of Sophia Loren as long as she was in Dallas.

He was true to his word. The next morning, rumors began circulating that the star, apparently grown weary of the well-intentioned but often stuffy conditions she had experienced since her arrival, had gone out on the town. Her director, Zev Braun, had accompanied her to who knew where, as had other members of her entourage all under the watchful eyes of Lieutenant Hawke.

While no details ever surfaced of the Loren night out, Neiman Marcus had a friend for life in the police lieutenant. If a problem ever arose due to a misunderstanding between the Dallas Police Department and the store in the future, a quick call to Lieutenant Hawke would bring a swift and always favorable resolution to the problem. On one memorable occasion, the store staged a late night social event in a building on a remote corner of Dallas Love Field Airport. The road to the scene of the party was long, dark, and usually deserted. Advance word of the gathering somehow reached the police traffic division where it was correctly assumed that many of the departing celebrants might attempt to outrun the many beverages they had consumed by rushing down the lonely road at speeds well over the forty mile per hour posted limit.

As the party began to dissolve in the early hours of a Sunday morning, a bevy of police cars lurked in the darkness, their interiors illuminated only by the digital read-outs on their radar devices. Their wait was not in vain and in a matter of minutes, nearly thirty vehicles, more than usually traveled the roadway in a week, had been flagged down by the crafty traffic patrolmen whose trap had successfully been sprung. Although it was nearly 3:00 A.M. when Hawke's home phone rang, he responded with more than the promised alacrity. Literally within minutes, all the speeding tickets were cancelled, and the drivers set free to wend their merry way homeward. The police cars left the area to seek less protected prey. Sophia Loren, by this time safely at home in Italy, had no idea how much influence she still had back in Dallas.

❧ The Spurious Prince ❧

Sometimes, the magnetic force that was Neiman Marcus attracted people that probably should have stayed away. One such character was Prince Tachibana of Tokyo, Japan.

The decision to stage a Japanese Fortnight had been fraught with emotional arguments on both sides of the issue. Stanley, always keenly in tune with sensitivities of his clientele, worried that veterans of the war in the Pacific might resent such a promotion that would advocate and endorse the culture and products of their one-time enemy. Others reasoned that enough years had passed to at least add some soothing balm to the scars of war. In the end, those who saw the bright and positive side of the matter prevailed and their assessment proved to be correct. It was, in fact, one of the most successful of all thirty of the Fortnight events.

Getting the event approved for funding by Japanese governmental agencies was not easy. The agencies in question were rigidly structured from the bottom up and to gain official endorsement from the top level in Tokyo, it was required to start at the bottom tier which was the regional trade office located in Houston.

It fell to my office to make the necessary exploratory trip to Houston to determine if Japan indeed wanted to entertain thoughts of sponsoring a Neiman Marcus Fortnight even though we had convinced ourselves, and our leader, that such an event was now appropriate. When I arrived at the trade office, I was not aware that at some time in the distant past, possibly just following World War II, Stanley or perhaps one of his brothers, had made a disparaging remark about Japanese merchandise or maybe even about Japan in general in public. I was also unaware that most representatives of the Japanese government at the time had extraordinarily long memories.

This was soon made clear to me when I entered the office to be introduced to the regional director. He bowed, I bowed, we shook hands,

we sat down, and he began to hiss. It was not a subtle sort of reptil-
ian hiss, but a full-blown exhalation that one might expect to en-
counter at an old-time one reel movie when the top-hatted villain lays
the distressed damsel on the railroad tracks.

The manager's assistant was in the office, and the two of us sat in
silence as the man in charge continued to hiss away without making
eye contact with me. For awhile, I thought the poor fellow had sprung
a leak of some sort, but after nearly three minutes of this curious east-
meets-west tableau, the sibilant sounds began to lose their force, much
as a teakettle does when the heat is turned off.

His own heat apparently much lessened, the manager permitted
himself to smile somewhat wanly in my direction and from then on our
business was conducted in a more normal manner, devoid of any further whistling sound effects. The gentleman was, in fact, very interested in our proposal and promised to send it on to higher headquarters with his enthusiastic endorsement.

Our interview over, he stood, I stood, we shook hands, he bowed,
I bowed, and I walked to the door. Outside, I asked his bright young
aide de camp about the significance of the hissing bit. "Mr. Ito is very
emotional for Japanese," the Harvard educated young man told me
"and his country having been insulted by your company long ago, he
was still too angry to speak of it for awhile." In the many dealings I
later had with Japanese over the years, only one other person found it
necessary to blow off steam before speaking, so I presume it is not a
common social characteristic in that country.

After a few more successful fully verbal meetings with Japanese officials in this country, it was clear that the event would be endorsed
and funded by the government as well as by many private corpora-
tions. Upon hearing the news, Stanley made arrangements to fly to
Tokyo, the capital city of one of the few countries he had yet to visit.
The plan was that he would go on ahead and then I would join him
there in a few weeks time. With memories of his performance in

Australia a few years earlier, I sensed that I would be well served to catch the soonest Japan Airlines flight out of San Francisco, lest I again become like the shovel brigade following a parade of cavalry horses.

Arriving in Tokyo only a few days following his arrival, I called Stanley's room at the Imperial Hotel. He asked that I come see him so that we could plan our schedule for the next week. Upon entering his suite I found it difficult to see either him or any furniture as the entire space was filled with stacks and piles of merchandise samples that Japanese vendors had brought to his hotel for his expert consideration. It was clear that the government's trade organization had circulated the news about the Fortnight and about the Tokyo visit of America's merchant prince.

The suite was even more cluttered than his desk back in Dallas. He was all but knee deep in excelsior and wrapping paper, with brightly colored silks spilling off the leather chairs to cascade down to the sea of cardboard boxes that engulfed the floor. If there was any order to it all, it escaped the eye of the casual observer, but it was very clear that he was in his heavenly element. Here was the merchant personified, up to his knees in silk and his eyes aglitter at the sheer splendor of the many treasures of the East. It was much the same as watching a Van Gogh cast his eyes across a sea of yellow flowers. Arrayed helter-skelter within his expert reach, were the colors, the fabrics, and the talented craftsmanship from which he, the master, could create a tapestry of mercantile success.

As we talked and planned, he continued to prowl the suite, stopping to exclaim over a deftly carved Noh mask or an ornately wrought miniature Samurai sword. As twilight does not linger for long amid downtown Tokyo's brilliant neon glare, it became dark quickly and time to substitute the joy of merchandise for a good supper hopefully of equal pleasure.

Stanley did love to eat, perhaps almost as much as he liked wading about in beautiful merchandise, so we hastened to the lower levels of the fabled Frank Lloyd Wright-designed Imperial Hotel. Of the various dining venues offered within the building, Stanley chose the one featuring authentic Chinese food. Although some of our fare was too far removed from the American style chop suey that my simple tastes preferred, Stanley fell upon each of the many courses with his customary gastronomic gusto. The more exotic it appeared to be, the more he seemed to relish it. Each course was accompanied by a different brand of the fine beers of Japan. Asahi, Kirin, and other notably labeled bottles were brought to us by the giggling waitresses who seemed amused as well as aghast at the volume of food being consumed by these two American gluttons.

For a man who really never drank much in the way of alcoholic beverages, Stanley did love to drink beer. Aside from wine, I saw him only on occasion take a glass of Cointreau or such, but nothing stronger. In France, Germany, England, and certainly in Japan, the local beer was his beverage of choice.

All good things must come to an end, and sure enough, the headwaiter soon materialized with the dinner bill in hand. In those days, some thirty years ago, prices in Tokyo had not climbed to their later astronomical levels and even though many empty plates and drained bottles had been carted off by our bevy of gigglers, the amount due was surprisingly low, probably less than thirty dollars in American equivalents.

I made a gesture at reaching for the check as the headwaiter placed it upon the table, but as it was truly closer to Stanley and, I maybe subconsciously reasoned, he was after all Stanley Marcus, the famous and wealthy legend of high-end retailing. Consequently, I did not try too hard to reach the check first and, besides, he beat me to it. Thanking him for his generosity in providing me with my first meal in Japan, we parted ways after planning to meet early the next morning to start making our rounds of calls on governmental and private offices.

The next day was very productive and on the drive back to the hotel, Stanley said, "That was good fun last night. What do you say to eating together again tonight?" I was pleased to accept this suggestion, of course, and within the hour we were on our way out on the big glittering city once again.

Stanley announced that this night's destination was to be one of Tokyo's most famous Kobe beef steak houses. Kobe beef is said to be among the finest in the world. The animal from which the steaks would eventually be taken was fed the fermented hops residue left over from the beer brewing process or some other similar highly enriched grain. Each day, the living steer was hand massaged to stimulate the layers of inner tissue fat that might give American nutritionists nightmares but most certainly gave each cut of Kobe beef a flavor unmatched by any Western steak.

The only drawback to the enjoyment of this absolutely wonderful taste delight was that someone had to pay for all that rich cattle feed and the tedious labor involved in massaging a cow for hours on end. As was only right, the one who was given the privilege and the responsibility to cover all of the expense involved in the entire Kobe process was the end user of the product, the diner in a Tokyo restaurant.

Even by the moderate standards of the mid-1970s, the price of a small slab of the massaged meat often ran as much as one hundred American dollars. When combined with a tsunami of Japanese beer and a touch or two of sake, the tab for a dinner was just short of astronomical.

Stanley and I, oblivious to the cost involved, ate our Kobe and downed our Kirin with a gusto accompanied by good conversation and laughter. As the last morsel of beef disappeared and the beer glasses contained only a trace of foam, Stanley said, "You know, that was really good. Do you want another steak?" Well, why not! Each steak was probably less than four ounces in weight, and liter bottles of beer presented little challenge, so we gleefully ordered another round of the whole thing, blissfully unaware of the cost involved. Steak and beer and good company! What more could anybody want?

The moment of truth came after several hours in the steakhouse. The bill arrived on a silver tray borne by a far more impressive gent than the one we had encountered the previous evening. He placed his little tray directly in front of Stanley, apparently presuming that he appeared to be the more likely of the two of us able to pay. Remembering my fellow diner's generosity in picking up the tab the night before, I gallantly asked if it was permissible to treat the boss to dinner. "It certainly is," laughed the boss almost to himself, deftly pushing the tray to within my easy reach.

As opposed to the Chinese feast at the Imperial, this Kobe banquet had worked itself into a stunning level of expense. It was, as I hazily recollect, in the neighborhood of $450, or about fifteen times greater than the previous meal. I never knew if it was the expression of shock that must have flashed across my face when I saw the total amount due, or if it was because he had outfoxed me yet again that prompted him to smile broadly and contentedly. It was all in fun, of course, as we were dining on Neiman Marcus expense account dollars, but to him, regardless of whose dollars were involved, it was another victory in our undeclared game of chicken and fox. It was a game I was never to win.

After a few more days in Tokyo, but with no more expensive dinners, we went our separate ways. Word of the Texas event was still spreading throughout the capital and beyond into the hinterland causing all manner of interested folk to show up at the Imperial to discuss how they might become involved.

Among these was a tiny Oriental lady in western dress who presented me with a card identifying herself as "The Princess of Korea." She was not interested, she said, in talking with me in her role as a Princess, however, but rather as the good friend and "constant affectionate companion" of His Royal Highness, Prince Tachibana of the

Imperial household. Honored to have an opportunity to visit with such a noble dignitary, I agreed to meet him the next day in the lobby of the hotel.

The princess, wearing a "Beverly Hillbillies" style hat with a large artificial daisy sprouting from it, arrived at the appointed hour to say HRH could not possibly appear in so public a place as a hotel lobby full of tourists. Instead, we were to meet him in a nearby park. Although the logic of this curious protocol escaped me, I agreed and we set off on foot to meet the prince.

Tachibana was waiting. He stood about five feet four inches in height. Small though he was, the man appeared to be a somewhat shrunken version of Clark Gable. His eyes were just barely similar to those of most Japanese and his skin very light. He even had a thin Gable-like moustache and his hair was worn very much in the style of Gable in his role as Rhett Butler.

The prince wore a plain black kimono that bore over his heart the distinctive golden chrysanthemum design of the Japanese Imperial Dynasty. He spoke no English, but his "constant affectionate companion" told me that Tachibana was in fact the illegitimate son of the late Emperor Meiji. Since Meiji apparently had countless illegitimate children lurking about in Japan, his spokeslady said that although he held no official position in the current royal household he was permitted to wear the chrysanthemum design to indicate that at least half of his blood was imperially divine.

It soon developed that his willingness to meet me had something to do with money. This was not at all surprising, but it soon developed that the prince was an artist, with his specialty being the creation of massive silken screens of traditional design. Six of his screens were then and still are, located at the Panhandle Plains Museum in Canyon, Texas, of all places. If Neiman Marcus would transfer his screens to the Dallas store and offer them for sale, it was suggested, Tachibana would be willing to represent the Imperial family at the Japanese Fortnight providing we would pay for the airline tickets for the royal duo, meaning that the princess of Korea would be coming along as well.

I promised the alleged prince and his princess that I would look into the matter and be in touch with her before I left Tokyo. A phone call to Dallas led to another phone call to the museum in Canyon where it was confirmed that six of the Tachibana screens had truly been acquired by the museum at the end of World War II. As Japanese motif works of art did not easily fit into the museum's traditional displays of western life and Native American culture, the large screens, absolutely beautiful though they proved to be, remained safely stored in the museum vaults.

Another phone call, this time to a local Tokyo associate, produced the knowledge that the prince was something of a charlatan and that his claim of imperial blood even acquired without the formal benefit of Shinto clergy was dubious at best and spurious at worst.

One of the store's art experts made the trip to Canyon to evaluate the screens while I was still in Tokyo. The message soon came through that the screens were in fact quite magnificent and that the museum would be overjoyed to let us borrow them for the Fortnight. If a buyer were to surface during the event, something could surely be worked out whereby everybody would be more than satisfied. "Prince" Tachibana had told me that each screen carried a price tag of $6 million. When I seemed surprised at this high evaluation, he told me in a Zen-like statement translated through his princess that they were "either worth $6 million or they were worth nothing."

Acting upon the intelligence I had received from both Canyon and Tokyo, I struck a deal with Tachibana. We would use his screens in our store during the Fortnight and make them available for purchase, but it would not be at all necessary for him to come to Dallas to open the event. Other arrangements had been made for the guest of honor requirement, I told him in all honesty, and to my delight he agreed to this plan and hurried off, arm in arm with his Korean sidekick.

The months passed quickly. The Fortnight was officially opened by the daughter of Japan's late but legitimate Prince Konoye, as arranged by the Imperial family. As she spoke to the opening morning crowd, the honorees' eyes could not have missed the six screens of Tachibana, each towering well over ten feet on raised platforms on the store's first floor. As all who had seen them had previously concurred, the screens were truly magnificent works of art, regardless of the paternity of their creator.

All went well during most of the Fortnight. At the beginning of the event's final week, however, my secretary burst into my office to exclaim with wide-eyed wonder that a Japanese prince was said to be in the store and headed toward the executive suite. I knew it could only be Tachibana and I quietly wished I had one of his screens to hide behind should he find his way to me.

Unfortunately, he did find the way. Without pausing to announce himself to my secretary, he bounded into the office and, scowling, he made his way around the desk and simply picked me up. Tachibana did not hiss to show his displeasure at not being invited to open this event which did at least feature his beloved screens. Rather, he merely picked me up as one might lift a sack of rice by its upper edges. Once I was aloft, the prince carried me effortlessly around the office for a short time before depositing me back behind the desk. With that, he bowed rigidly and turned on his heel to rejoin his princess who had wisely awaited him in an outer office. I was totally unhurt but highly surprised to say the least. The little Gable-like-man was enormously strong and, had he been really angry, could have easily thrown me through a wall before I would have had time to react.

Apparently, the spurious, if not downright bogus prince had thought I had treated him foully by not inviting him to come to Dallas even though I had told him, through his own Miss Korea, that no invitation would be extended. Perhaps something got lost in the translation from the princess to the prince. At any rate, his screens were a big attraction but when no buyer came forth to come up with the required $6 million to buy even one of them, the collection went back to the museum in Canyon and presumably they are there to this day.

✐ Jack Benny ✐

Fortunately for Japanese-American relations in general, Stanley had not been directly involved in the Prince Tachibana affair. While he had counseled against having the so-called Prince serve as the official guest of honor of the Fortnight, he had missed out on the little screen maker's impromptu visit to the store. Had Tachibana decided to storm into Stanley's office in order to show his displeasure, I suspect I would have needed to call my lieutenant friend at the Dallas police headquarters to restore order.

As it was, the Japanese Fortnight was successful, as already noted but also a memorable event. In addition to the spurious prince episode, the celebration was in one aspect a sad occasion. Hard pressed to find a notable Japanese entertainer to be the big name ticket-selling performer at the opening gala, it was finally determined to book a well known celebrity to ensure a good attendance at the charity event.

The chosen star was the famous Jack Benny, the legendary entertainer who was so obviously devoid of any relationship with Japan that his appearance during the Fortnight would in itself be humorous. When I told Jack the international significance of the black tie event at which he was to perform, he laughed and said he would have his writers work up a few jokes along the lines of having misplaced his trademark violin in the Tokyo airport, or some one-liners about Japanese food and so on. If those quips were ever written will never be known, because, the Jack Benny Show in Dallas did not happen. In the hotel elevator, somewhere between his penthouse suite and the ballroom floor, Jack Benny's career in show business came to its abrupt and tragic finale.

He had seemed in great shape as I rode in his limousine from the airport en route to the Fairmont Hotel the day before the event. As a youngster, I had been a regular listener to his Sunday night radio show and he appeared pleased that we shared memories of some of the still classic characters from that long-running show.

The next morning, he rehearsed his violin routine with the orchestra that would be backing him later that evening. Jack Benny was a funny man even away from the microphone and the camera. When word spread throughout the hotel staff that the great comedian was rehearsing in the Imperial Ballroom, a large crowd of maids, bellmen, and executives soon filled the room and between musical rehearsal segments, without benefit of any visible script, he made jokes about Texas and even about Neiman Marcus and its fabled leader, the two having known each other for a number of years.

When the time came to launch into his signature off-key violin rendition of his theme song, "Love in Bloom," Jack told the ad hoc audience of how he had perfected the routine some fifty years earlier and how, he cracked, even those who paid dearly to hear him perform still loved it. With that, he tucked his truly rare violin under his chin and began to play. To the amazement of his listeners and particularly the members of the house orchestra primed to be his musical safety net, he lured from the strings a dazzling and highly professional rendition of "The Flight of the Bumblebee." The speed and dexterity of his playing was just short of virtuosic and when he had completed the frantically paced work, even the orchestra stood to applaud and cheer the performance.

He bowed, smiling broadly, and began again, this time scratching out the studiously and deliberately misplayed version of his theme song that he had finally turned into a classic masterpiece of discord over a long half-century in show business. The rehearsal was over in about an hour and the shining violin was placed back in its case. Mr. Benny would never play it again.

I was in the hotel's ballroom around nine o'clock, some thirty minutes before Jack was scheduled to perform. He had participated in an excellent television interview earlier and it had been widely seen. A full page newspaper story about him had appeared that morning causing considerable anticipation among the hundreds of formally attired guests.

One of my associates found me with an urgent summons to come backstage to the Green Room where Mr. Benny had just arrived. I entered the room and my eyes met those of Jack Benny. It is a look I will never forget.

Coming down in the elevator, he had apparently felt a sharp pain in his right arm and by the time he had reached the backstage room, the arm hung limply at this side. When I came into the room, a doctor had already been summoned from the ballroom, but the star of that evening's show probably already knew the diagnosis he was about to hear. There would be no "Love in Bloom" tonight and no funny lines about Japan. He knew what was happening and his eyes said it all. He had suffered the first of a series of strokes that took his life just days later at his California home. Rushed to Parkland Hospital from the hotel, he soon lapsed into a coma from which he never fully awakened. A private plane took him back home to California for the last time the next morning.

I hurried to find Stanley to tell him what had just occurred and as he stepped to the microphone to tell the large crowd that Mr. Benny was indisposed and would not be appearing, I was off in search of a stand-in act to give our high-dollar audience at least some entertainment return on their evening's investment.

As great good luck would have it, Miss Pearl Bailey was starring in her own show in another entertainment venue within the hotel. A friend of mine was general manager of that room and with his assistance and co-operation, Miss Bailey quickly agreed to come do a show in tribute to Jack. Along with her husband, drummer Louie Belson, the remarkable song stylist hurried to the ballroom to present a full hour of songs that completely entranced her audience. She did an encore or two, said a few kind words about the fallen legend she had so graciously replaced and then literally ran down the long hallway to get back to her own paying audience who received her there with a standing ovation.

After going to the hospital and learning the sad truth about Jack, I drove back to the Fairmont to find Pearl making her final curtain call. I had come to tell her that even though we obviously had no contract with her, we would happily pay her whatever such a contract would have stipulated. "Are you kidding me, honey," she responded in her very best Pearly Bailey voice, "I did that show 'cause I love that man." I guess we all did, and after that unforgettable night, we all loved Pearl Bailey, too.

❧ The Queen of Thailand ❧

One of the more fascinating behind-the-scenes aspects involved in the production of the Fortnights was security. When a guest of honor was, for the first time ever, the queen of a foreign country, the planning for tight security precautions became even more fascinating than usual.

Queen Sirikit of Thailand could easily star in the leading role of a motion picture about her life. Powerful and influential in the internal affairs of her country, she is both beautiful and gracious in person. To her people, she and her husband, the King, are revered as deities but away from the throne she is more inclined to talk about her grandchildren and their antics than about the seemingly endless political strife of her part of the world.

When she agreed to come to Dallas in 1985 to be the guest of honor at the store's Orientations Fortnight, the American State Department expressed its official displeasure over the fact that Neiman Marcus had invited a nominal head of a foreign nation to come to the

United States without getting prior approval. The invitation to the queen had in fact been informal and extended to her in person by Stanley's son Richard while in Bangkok. She had accepted instantly, without asking her husband about the matter, though one suspects that even the king would not have dared to decline her enthusiastic proposal to travel to the United States.

Despite its collective hurt feelings, the State Department did fully cooperate in all aspects of the impending royal visit. Special security details came to Dallas many months in advance of the event to undertake covert intelligence investigations to determine what level of danger might threaten the royal party while it was in the city.

Thailand, then as now, was riven with all manner of political intrigue with various groups seeking to overthrow the royal family's symbolic rule and replace it with either an Islamic or Communistic form of government being fostered by different groups with varying goals and agendas.

The monarchy of Thailand seemed almost as concerned about the very real possibility that some crass Texans might inadvertently violate the strict code of decorum that surrounded the Queen/Goddess than the remote possibility of enemy action. To keep the perceived savages of Texas on the straight and narrow pathways of Royal Thai etiquette, the monarchy sent to Dallas an advance agent in the form of the High Lord Chamberlain himself, a diminutive chain-smoker named Poonperme.

Lord Poonperme, it soon developed, was far more interested in studying the crass ways of the savage Texans, indeed to participate in them, than he was to teach any lessons about the courtesies demanded by royal etiquette. As a result, his Lordship spent much of the time, day and night, lounging about the barroom of the Dallas Mansion Hotel, sipping single malt scotch and peering through his thick eyeglasses and clouds of cigarette smoke at the assortment of local ladies he had managed to attract. From time to time he would bestir himself, from the perch he was to occupy for nearly two weeks, long enough to inspect the sites the Queen was scheduled to visit in October.

To his credit, Poonperme did sponsor one session for store executives on royal etiquette during which he pointed out that the soles of one's shoes should never be visible to Her Majesty, that she was never to be touched even if she offered her hand, and so forth. For the most part, everything he advised was promptly forgotten and the Queen, once she arrived, proved to be so very American-like in her demeanor that all such ritualistic deference might likely have embarrassed her.

When the Queen's chartered Royal Thai 747 aircraft landed at the Dallas/Fort Worth Airport, it was greeted by a horde of screaming well-wishers. Although security officers were on hand in ample numbers, no terrorist groups were among the greeters. The plane was filled with media people from Thailand and the Queen's own large retinue of ladies in waiting, hairdressers, secretaries, and a small army of unusually large Thai men obviously carrying unusually large handguns under their unusually tight jackets.

As soon as Sirikit appeared from the end of the jetway, the worshipers of the Royal House prostrated themselves on the terminal floor, leaving only the Neiman Marcus welcoming party standing full upright, looking for all the world like the only stalks of corn spared by an otherwise merciless Texas windstorm. Her Majesty saved the situation by quickly motioning for her minions to stand. She then moved through the crowd of Thais smiling at each one who had come to welcome her.

For the next three days, the Queen was kept busy visiting sites in Dallas and Fort Worth. Although there were no untoward events during her travels around the Metroplex, rumors did begin to filter in that one radical group, known as "17 September," was planning to come to the area with some undisclosed evil intent. As a result, even more State Department security details converged to gather around the Queen whenever she appeared in public. No danger ever came her way.

She had expressed an interest in visiting a real Texas cattle ranch and in response, it was arranged for her, along with her retinue, to fly to the famous 6666 Ranch near Guthrie, Texas. We assembled a small fleet of sixteen aircraft to ferry the party to the sprawling ranch for a barbeque and what was billed as a hoedown.

It was at the so-called hoedown that Her Majesty was confronted by the only visible breach of royal etiquette. She had gamely endured the sight of many square feet of Texas shoe and boot soles and had her hand vigorously shaken by well-meaning good old boys from Dallas and Fort Worth, but on the outdoor dance floor at the 6666, the Queen was fair game to two-stepping cowboys.

They all wanted to dance with her. To the tune of "Cotton-eye Joe" and other rollicking favorites, the hands, well-turned out in bright white shirts, stiffly starched Wranglers and high-top boots with spurs a jingle pranced the Thai beauty across the floor. She who had waltzed with presidents and perfected the foxtrot with prime ministers seemed to relish the fast-paced rather rustic two-step born in Texas dancehalls.

Later, some of the cowboys seemed to lose sight of the fact that they were holding a certifiable goddess in their arms under that big Texas moon. Each time her partner's hand tended to slip anywhere near her beltline on her back, she would with great grace and aplomb reach around with her free hand to politely but firmly push the cowboy's ham-sized mitt back to its proper and much higher position between her royal shoulder blades.

There can be little doubt that the Queen and her ladies in waiting found much to talk about on their luxurious flight back across the Pacific. Some of those young and attractive un-royal ladies had also been in the arms of the tall Texas cowboys that same moonlit night and any straying of hands, innocent or otherwise, might not have been all that unwelcome.

෨ Princess Margaret ෧

Stanley had for many years attempted to successfully invite a major member of Britain's Royal Family to Dallas. We had nearly succeeded with Princess Margaret on an earlier occasion, but in 1984, the right regal buttons were identified and duly pushed.

Princess Margaret, the only sister of the Queen of England, had become a somewhat tragic figure. Once beautiful and the vivacious center of London society, she was more or less a royal ribbon-cutter but the most likely member of the Royal Family to show up for the dedication of power plants, new schools, and such.

However, who she was and what she had once been still lent her an aura of international recognition and celebrity that made her comings and goings front page news. Often photographed at her Caribbean retreat on the island of Mustique, Margaret appeared to be fairly content in her role as royal sister and, according to some reports, she who wore the crown listened to what her sister had to say on many matters in the court.

In person, the fifty-four year old Margaret seemed younger than her photographs might have indicated. Still a chain smoker, even though her father had died of smoking induced lung cancer, her skin did not have the telltale signs of one who purportedly incinerated over sixty cigarettes each day. She was tanned and, with one exception, in a good mood during her three day stay in Dallas.

It was at a formal dinner at the Mansion Hotel, hosted by Stanley, that her royal feathers became ruffled, albeit with excellent reason. The party had started well enough, even though Margaret was nowhere to be seen until all the guests had arrived and had been seated. She must be forgiven that, since for a time some years before, she had been but a heartbeat away from occupying the throne of Great Britain.

Just as members of the famously impatient higher reaches of Dallas society had reached their breaking point, the Princess appeared. Exquisitely dressed all in white, she suddenly materialized in the hotel courtyard and, unescorted, entered the dining area. This was exactly as she had said she wanted her entrance to be arranged and it was most effective.

Richard Marcus then rose and escorted her to her seat as the guests stood rewarding her with a warm and genuine applause. She smiled and nodded in an almost queenly manner until she was finally seated. As the other guests began to devour their salads and empty their only briefly unfilled wine glasses, the Princess felt the urge to have a cigarette. The Mansion then as now had a no-smoking policy throughout the hotel, but this had been waived for the royal guest's convenience at least within her top floor suite.

It is interesting how rapidly the offending smoke from a single cigarette can flood even a vast outdoor area in which no other cigarette is afire. An international incident seemed imminent. The undeniable fact that someone was befouling the atmosphere in a no-smoking area was offset by the equally undeniable fact that the offender was the sister of the Queen of England.

A crude solution to this dilemma was quickly attained through the direct intervention of no less than J. R. Ewing himself, that is to say the actor Larry Hagman who had portrayed Mr. Ewing in the television series entitled *Dallas*. An absolute zealot on the subject of the enforcement of no-smoking regulations, Mr. Hagman carried with him at all times a small battery operated fan with which to both disperse the smoke and send a clear message to the offender. As Mr. Hagman had been seated next to the Princess, at her specific request, the surprisingly stiff breeze put forth by the tiny fan had only a distance of a few feet to travel to blow all of the smoke directly back into her face.

It was a scene that could have played well in Mr. Hagman's long running series. There he sat, expressionless, holding his efficient little fan not a full yard away from the face of a Princess of royal blood. She, too, was without facial expression as she stared through the smoke and into the whirring blades of the fan aimed directly at the cigarette that continued to hang defiantly, without charm, from her heavy, rounded lips.

Every movement in the room seemed to freeze as this tableau ran its course. Just exactly how long that actually took is unclear, but in the end it was the Princess who blinked. Taking the half-smoked and unfiltered but no less offending object from her lips, she ground out its burning end in a saucer, there being no proper ashtrays in sight. Ever the gentleman, Mr. Hagman obligingly turned off his little fan, put it back in the jacket pocket of his tuxedo, and began to sample the slightly wilted romaine lettuce of his salad.

Without a word, the Princess followed suit. An unusually perceptive waiter deftly replaced the saucer containing the discarded cigarette with a fresh one holding a coffee cup. Mr. Hagman turned away from the Princess to launch into a humorous discourse about life on Malibu Beach while Margaret focused her startling blue eyes on the gentleman to her left who seemed fascinated by tales of the Court of St. James. She did not smoke at the table again that evening, but neither did she accept Mr. Hagman's proffered hand when she later rose to retire to her suite, presumably to chain smoke the night away.

⋙ Other Celebrities ⋘

Countless other celebrities came into the Neiman Marcus orbit over the years, frequently because Stanley would simply invite them to do so. His personal phone list contained the private numbers of presidents Eisenhower, Kennedy, Johnson, Nixon, Carter, and George H. W. Bush, but not that of Ronald Regan.

Such show business luminaries as Joan Crawford, Gloria Swanson, Bing Crosby, Edward G. Robinson, and Kirk Douglas were listed in his book as were Bob Hope, Red Skelton, Greer Garson, Irving Berlin,

Richard Rodgers, Mary Martin, and Humphrey Bogart. Politicians such as Barry Goldwater, surprisingly, and John Connally, Hubert Humphrey, Adlai Stevenson, William Fulbright, and Sam Rayburn were also on his personal list.

From time to time, he was in touch with the likes of David O. Selznick, Samuel Goldwyn, and Ed Sullivan, perhaps to discuss broader entertainment issues. J. C. Penney's private number was on the list, along with Henry Ford, Conrad Hilton, Truman Capote, and Danny Kaye.

His pursuit of famous people was relentless and, in return, they often came to him with a matching tenacity. By the time he was forty, Stanley Marcus himself had become a celebrity.

Branching Out

For many years, from 1907 until 1971, Neiman Marcus was exclusively a Texas store with an international reputation for selling nothing but the best. When the Marcus family and a closely knit group of other share holders agreed to sell the company to a California retail conglomerate, however, things began to change.

With stores located only in Dallas, Fort Worth, and Houston at the time of the merger with Broadway Hale Stores in 1969, Neiman Marcus began an expansion program that would over the next four decades increase the number of store units tenfold. In the process, what had for over sixty years been a family operated luxury fashion business was transformed into a trendsetting and largely exclusive national chain of elegant and exquisitely designed stores.

The expansion of any successful business is a risky undertaking, particularly if that business has superlative customer service as one of its fundamental tenets. Herbert Marcus did not believe that the store which carried his name was a good candidate for expansion. Despite the fact that countless invitations to bring a Neiman Marcus to other cities often came his way, he declined them all, fearing that the lack of properly supervised personnel in some far away store might dilute the high standards for customer service he so adamantly demanded.

Throughout its long history, cities all across America and in foreign lands have solicited the interest of Neiman Marcus executives in expanding to their locale. Small towns in Missouri and Arkansas competed with New York City for the next Neiman Marcus store. Even the city of Riyadh, in Saudi Arabia, once made an impassioned appeal for a store, but until a mass infusion of merger-acquired conglomerate cash changed the course of the company's policy, Neiman Marcus remained solely a Texas entity. Once the policy was changed, however, Neiman Marcus entered into the business of expansion in its own legendary style.

In keeping with its well-earned reputation for showmanship gained from its Dallas Fortnight extravaganzas, the company opened each of its new stores with flair and excitement. Such mundane and shopworn opening acts as the mere cutting of a ribbon were never considered acceptable by Stanley Marcus. Instead, the new Neiman Marcus stores that opened in Florida, Washington, D.C., and other locations did so with events that were both spectacular and, somewhat surprisingly to some, very Texan in nature.

Although it was without any doubt native Texan by birth, the company had not previously wrapped itself in the ten-gallon hat and high-heeled boot syndrome that many believe to be an integral part of the Texas legend. Customers who came to the Neiman Marcus stores located in Dallas, Houston, and Fort Worth in the pre-merger days expecting a Lone Star theme to prevail would only have been disappointed.

There were no cowboy boots to be seen, either for sale or on the feet of the store employees. The men's hat department offered nary a broad-brimmed Stetson, featuring instead stylish snap-brim fedoras and, for those gentlemen who wished something a bit more continental in style, a Homburg or perhaps even a satin top hat.

With exportation of the store beyond the Texas borders, however, that began to change. Even before the out-of-state units were actually opened, the store's senior executives came to realize that customers in the new stores yearned to see some manifestations of the Texas heritage that they anticipated. After all, by 1970 most high-end retailers were carrying many of the same lines as their competitors. Chicago had its famous Marshall Field and Company, for example, and in opening an eventual three stores in the Windy City, Neiman Marcus could offer very little merchandise not already available at such long established retailing institutions as Fields.

It soon became highly apparent that customers in Florida, Illinois, New York, Massachusetts, Georgia, and California, to name but a few of the states soon to have a Neiman Marcus, fully expected the store from Texas to bring them at least a taste of Texas. To satisfy this expectation, the company's marketing department developed a store opening feature that focused on that most obvious of all things Texan, the oil well derrick. Workers quickly fashioned a replica of a typical derrick of wood and metal. Standing just over sixteen feet in height, the structure rested on a solid platform of another five feet giving the overall impression of towering Texas influence to any store opening event.

The first out-of-state store to be opened was in Bal Harbour, Florida. For its opening in January 1971, the facsimile derrick was disassembled and shipped by company truck to the Dade County location, some thirteen hundred miles east and south of Dallas. A hollow Plexiglas tube ran from inside the enclosed base up through the derrick to its very top. Within the base was a pressurized tank containing some twenty-five gallons of what appeared to be orange juice for this first Florida opening. It must be admitted that this was not really freshly squeezed Florida orange juice but rather a color enhanced version of Tang, the artificial commercial product that needed much orange color added to it so that it might even begin to look like the genuine but much too sticky real thing.

The plan was that following the obligatory words of welcome from the manager of the new store, the guest of honor would open a valve to let the "orange juice" surge upward through the tube and thus bring forth a gusher of the liquid, to symbolize the melding of Texas and Florida, or something along those lines.

On this occasion, the guest of honor was none other than Mrs. Herbert Marcus, Sr. Though nearly ninety, Miss Minnie was delighted to turn the wheel that would open the valve and let the juice surge upward. Being somewhat hard of hearing, however, she missed her cue but noticing that all eyes had suddenly and uniformly turned in her direction, she turned to the derrick's base to perform her task. Unfortunately, in her haste she had forgotten her instruction to turn the wheel only to the right. Instead, by rotating the wheel in the opposite direction, she opened the drain of the tank thus allowing several gallons of the orange-colored fluid to flow downward onto her apparently newly purchased white Ferragamo pumps. Fortunately, an alert company executive was standing close by just in case some such mishap might occur. He rushed to her side and gently turned the wheel in the proper direction. With a whooshing sound, the fluid that was left in the hidden tank shot up through the tube and into the air, splattering only a few of the Floridians who had ignored a stanchion erected around the rig to prevent eager onlookers from being sprayed.

Miss Minnie, it should be noted, accepted her suddenly recolored shoe more graciously than some of the locals who expressed concern over their unwanted simulated orange juice shampoo. The rest of the crowd, however, found it all quite humorous and probably thought it all part of the act. The most poignant memory of what came to be known as the "Orange Juice Morning" was the sight of Minnie Marcus, gamely leading the throng of onlookers into the brand new store, leaving behind her a single trail of brightly orange-colored right shoe prints. Fortunately, by the time she reached the store's expensive sand colored carpet, the sticky residue of Tang had been worn away by the concrete on the sidewalk.

As we had hoped, word of the Texas oil well that produced a gusher of Florida orange juice quickly spread throughout the greater Miami area. It was clear that such hijinks could be a key ingredient in attracting the attention of the media and, through it, the customer.

The next store in line to be opened was in Atlanta, Georgia. This new store held a particular place in Stanley's heart because Atlanta had been the site of his parent's decision to turn down the Coca-Cola offer and go back to Dallas. Had they decided to become distributors of the world famous soft drink in Missouri or Kansas, another world famous entity would not have been created on Elm Street in downtown Dallas. As things turned out, Stanley was returning in triumph, bringing his Neiman Marcus to Coca-Cola land.

His first public appearance in the city a year earlier had not been triumphant by any stretch of the imagination. Still flush with the media smash hit of the oil derrick in Miami, I came up with what proved to be a particularly lame-brained idea to have a nationally known fireworks company come to Atlanta to use their pyrotechnic skills to announce the groundbreaking of the new store. As this would be a daytime use of fireworks, the emphasis would necessarily be on very loud explosions with hardly any sky-born rockets and such. This, I reasoned, would tell everyone within a ten-mile radius that something big was coming to their shopping center and that big something could only be, of course, Neiman Marcus.

All the media were notified of the planned event only after an incredulous city manager gave his permission to have the peace of a cool autumn afternoon shattered by some sixty thousand dollars worth of very loud but largely invisible fireworks. The newspapers and the television stations responded just as we had hoped. For days in advance of the event, readers, listeners, and viewers were warned not to panic when they heard massive explosions at 2:00 P.M. on the chosen day. This was in 1971, after all, and while panic would have been less likely then than it might well have been thirty years later, the public did need to know what was going to happen. That same public also needed to know, or so we reasoned, that the long awaited Neiman Marcus store was at last getting underway.

The finale to the repercussions of bombs and mortars was to be the arrival of Stanley in a helicopter, dramatically descending through the smoke created by the thirty minutes of detonations. It was, I thought, a fitting return for the man who had left Atlanta as a toddler only to return as a retailing giant. Curiously, Stanley went along with this whole somewhat addled approach to public relations. If only he had not bought new shoes for the occasion, all might have turned out well, but he had and it didn't.

On the momentous day, he and I sat in the helicopter on the ground about five minutes flying distance from the site where the store was to be constructed. At exactly 2:00 P.M., as planned, the first ear shattering explosion was detonated. The initial blast was powerful enough to cause our helicopter to actually recoil. We looked at each other without saying a word as a series of rapid fire explosions penetrated the sunny Georgia afternoon. Billowing clouds of smoke rose from the construction site as the bomb bursts continued at twenty second intervals for what seemed an eternity. Apparently the city manager's office had somehow failed to notify the police and fire department of our pyrotechnically enhanced ground breaking as in between the explosions came the sound of multiple wailing sirens mounted on numerous fire trucks and police cars.

As this was long before cell phones, and as the firework technicians had serious job related hearing problems anyway, the walkie-talkies were useless and any attempt to stop the festive sound barrage was futile. Having become slaves to our own fevered imagination, we could only go through with the rest of the act.

At the designated time, the still shuddering helicopter lurched skyward and set its course toward the towering columns of smoke at the construction site. Just as the last bomb went off and just before the last of five fire trucks arrived at the scene, the helicopter touched down on the parking lot next to the speaker's platform erected at the site.

It was only then that I noticed that Stanley had found the occasion worthy enough to warrant the purchase of a new pair of very fine Italian shoes. These were excellent shoes for attending a board meeting or going to a reception, but with their very slick and still virtually un-marked soles, they were not at all the best choice for alighting from an aircraft amid shrouds of foul smelling smoke.

The media, fascinated by this madness, had turned out en masse to witness and record what was likely the noisiest event in their city since Union General William Tecumseh Sherman had blazed his way down Peachtree Street a century or so earlier during the Civil War. The cameramen and reporters surged forward toward the aircraft when the copter was just inches from its final touchdown. Apparently thinking the flight was over, Stanley abruptly opened the passenger hatch and stepped out onto the helicopter's skid bar that served as its landing gear. The slick leather of his new Italian shoes could gain no traction on the equally slick steel of the skid bar and for one dreadful moment, he hung suspended in mid air with one elegantly shod foot sliding off the end of the skid and the other vainly seeking anyplace else it might find traction.

As the television cameras whirred and the newspapermen's flashbulbs cast their light through the by now thinning smoke, Stanley Marcus, ex-Atlantan and famed merchant, hit the parking lot with all the grace of a bag of Texas rice. He somehow managed to land on his hands and knees and within a split second, being the trouper that he was, he was on his feet. In the process, however, his fashionable straw hat had come off his head, and caught up in the copter's prop-wash, it was bounding merrily away in the general direction of South Carolina.

I, too, gave serious thought to leaving at once for South Carolina as it seemed likely that I would soon be among the unemployed and the Carolinas were probably nice that time of year. Although I was on the receiving end of one of Stanley's infamously black looks, not a word was said until after his short speech to the still-shell shocked audience who very likely could not hear anything he said anyway because of the continued ringing in their collective ears.

The ceremony over, the fire department placated, the media engorged with fodder, and the helicopter long gone, we rode in a limousine back to our hotel in blessed, yet absolute silence. He was clearly unhurt, his Oxxford suit still neatly pressed, but his pride was severely damaged and his straw hat was probably still airborne. As he opened the car door, he turned to me and said "Well, that is just one hell of a way to break ground."

Apparently, the whole fiasco somehow satisfied his innate appreciation for making headline news. It is doubtful that any ground breaking ceremony in all retail history ever again generated such airtime and ink. He and I did not mention the event for over two years but at last I decided to test the waters. As a Christmas gift in 1974, I presented Stanley with a set of Army Paratrooper Wings encased in a small block of Lucite. The inscription read, "In memory of the second invasion of Atlanta, June 18, 1971." Those silver wings sat on his desk amidst the paper canyons for many years and I, somehow, managed to survive that ill fated invasion for just as long.

To dedicate the opening of the Atlanta store when it was completed some months later, the oil well rig was once again trucked east from Dallas. If orange juice had been determined the liquid of choice for a Florida geyser, then clearly only Coca-Cola would do in Atlanta.

Just as had been the case at the Bal Harbour opening event, throngs watched in amusement as a steady stream of Atlanta's most famous export product rose upward through the oil rig's clear tube to erupt at its top and splash in a sticky spray back to earth. This time, no mishaps occurred such as the one that defiled Miss Minnie's shoes in Florida and the media filmed every moment of the event.

The oil well gag continued to work well for the next few store openings. In St. Louis, the faux well brought in a gusher of Budweiser beer as a tribute to that city's famous liquid product. To launch the new store in Washington, D.C., we departed from the liquid theme to bring in a steady stream of red tape through the by-then-road weary drilling rig. The Mayor of Washington turned the wheels that activated the eruption of the long red tape and his infectious laugh when he unleashed the colorful surprise instantly brought the same reaction from the crowd of soon-to-be customers.

Even though the local witnesses to the oil well trick in each city had only one opportunity to see it, those of us who traveled to the four new store openings then taking place each year began to grow a bit jaded with the gimmick. It was used for the last time for the Beverly Hill store opening in 1979 when movie film blew upward and out of the rig.

By the time the company's magnificent store was ready to open in downtown San Francisco, we had been made well-aware that anything Texan was going to be too much Texas for the sophisticated City by the Bay. The initial relationship between Neiman Marcus and San Francisco had been rocky from the start and had deteriorated appreciably as time passed. There would likely be no warm reception for a Texas oil well spouting a nice little California Bordeaux.

It had all begun when the company had purchased a prime retail site across from Union Square at the very heart of the city. Occupying the site, as it had since long before the famous earthquake of 1907, was a dilapidated old store know lovingly to San Franciscans as the City of Paris.

The store was only marginally in operation when Neiman Marcus bought the property and announced its plan to demolish the building to make way for an all new store rather than attempt the massive remodeling effort that the public apparently desired. Well-orchestrated protests and media campaigns were staged to force the Texas company to renovate the old rather than build a new store altogether.

Extensive engineering studies had proved conclusively that while the old building had withstood the earthquake over seventy years earlier, it had sustained irreparable damage to its foundation and load bearing walls. This discovery only served to further encourage the large local contingent demanding the City of Paris be saved at all costs and granted landmark status to prevent it being razed. The rationale of the preservationists seemed to be that having survived the historic earthquake, the noble, if unattractive old relic certainly should never be allowed to fall before the onslaught of the upstart Texans' hired wrecking ball.

Undaunted, the company hired famed architect Philip Johnson to design the building that would replace the old store and showcase the new. Perhaps predictably, the introduction of an architect with the international stature of New Yorker Johnson inflamed the protesters even more, and since they lived and voted in San Francisco and the invaders from Texas along with their high profile architect clearly did not, city hall soon became the jousting place between the antagonists.

Most public relations experts would probably agree that attempting to start a multi-million dollar business in a community that seemed, for the most part, to be violently opposed to any such plan is far from an ideal situation. Further, having a mayor and the city's board of supervisors indelibly linked through the ballot box to those opposing the store did little to improve the chances for Texas success.

At the time, the local media seemed almost rabidly opposed to permitting the store from Dallas ever opening its doors onto the hallowed ground of Union Square. Herb Caen, the popular columnist for the *San*

Francisco Chronicle, led the attack. When Dallas-based Braniff Airlines once used the catch phrase "Texas Chic" in its promotional copy, Caen proclaimed this to be the penultimate oxymoron. He then went on to write that using fashion in the same breath with Neiman Marcus was even more ridiculous.

Curiously, during lengthy luncheon interviews, Caen was friendly and courteous in asking deceptively mild mannered questions about Neiman Marcus and its plans for Union Square. Upon returning to his office, however, all pretense of cordiality disappeared into a sea of barbed caustic comments about the cowboy culture of Neiman Marcus and its association, by sheer location, with the archconservative political environment that he envisioned permeating the Dallas air. The irony was that Stanley Marcus, the most visible symbol of the store, was very likely more liberal in his political and social views than Herb Caen and the entire editorial staff of the *San Francisco Chronicle* combined.

Building permit applications were routinely rejected or at best deferred by the city's zoning officials who kept one wary eye on the mayor's office and the other eye on the lookout for any Neiman Marcus attorney who might well come knocking on the door with lawsuit documents in hand.

After months of lengthy debate, additional engineering studies, market research focus groups, and the costly entertaining of city officials, the discussions became serious enough to bring the by now semi-retired Stanley Marcus into the lion's den that was the city hall of the great city of San Francisco at the time. With Philip Johnson at his side, Stanley softly but firmly enunciated a surprise proposal. If permitted to tear down the shell of the crumbling old building that both sides in the issue had finally come to agree was unsafe, Neiman Marcus would, at outlandish expense, reconstruct the soaring enclosed rotunda that was the only redeeming architectural feature of the entire building. At the top of the rotunda was a mosaic glass dome that depicted the original City of Paris which it developed, had not been a traditional store at all, but rather a deliberately beached ship from which the founders of the old store had originally sold goods to those lucky enough to have hit pay dirt in the California Gold Rush of 1849.

The rustic floating retail outlet of Gold Rush fame had been successful enough to provide the cash necessary to build the once grand mercantile emporium that Neiman Marcus now wished to destroy. The image of the good ship City of Paris, it seemed, was forever enshrined in mosaic high above the selling floors of its landlocked successor.

When the courtly Stanley offered in his address to the city fathers to take down one by one the tiny mosaics that made up the dome, have each tile refurbished, and painstakingly re-stained to be carefully stored until such time the feature could be reinstalled in the new building, a cheer arose from the preservationists assembled at city hall. Simultaneously, a muted groan could be heard emanating from the store's construction managers who would be ultimately responsible for the tedious undertaking as well as from the company's financial officers who would have to find the extra funds to pay for this undoubtedly brilliant but thoroughly unplanned, completely unexpected, and very expensive decision.

Dazzled by Stanley's ability to strike a dramatic compromise that clearly pleased their supporters, the city council approved the application for the destruction of most of the City of Paris building. For a brief moment in time, it looked as though the war between the Texans and the Golden Gaters was over but unfortunately the battles were to continue for some time to come.

When barricades were erected around the site prior to the removal of the glass dome and certain elements of the rotunda itself, other preservation groups in the city apparently for the first time came to realize that the old facade of the City of Paris building was indeed doomed. Picket lines were organized to prevent men and equipment from gaining access to the site and for several days a stalemate was observed.

On the fourth day of inactivity at the site, save for the strolling mostly elderly ladies who comprised the picket lines, a small platoon of policemen arrived and politely asked the ladies to depart. To everyone's surprise and relief, they complied with the citation issued by the mayor's office and the decrepit old walls soon came tumbling down.

The glass dome, however, carefully disassembled into many thousands of tiny individual tiles, was sent all the way across the nation to a New England firm that specialized in the refurbishing of such rare and historic stained glass. The balustrades that had adorned each floor around the rotunda were also placed in storage and the rest of the building was then destroyed without further incident.

It was not until Phillip Johnson's new design for the Neiman Marcus store was unveiled that serious opposition again arose. Sketches of the building's marble façade was shown to feature large diamond shaped argyle patterns fashioned of contrasting stone, a design much too lively to suit many conservative San Franciscans. The rotunda, with its breathtaking reconditioned dome back in place just as Stanley had promised, was shown on Johnson's renderings of the interior. That kept promise eventually wore down much of the opposition to the large diamonds, but not until even more and often rancorous meetings at city hall took place. On one occasion, a young architectural student had the courage to vigorously attack the Johnson plan with the colorful Mr. Johnson seated not ten feet away. Unfazed, the internationally famed architect continued to read the Sherlock Holmes book he had brought, somewhat disdainfully, to the meeting. His only response to the assault was to briefly lower his book to peer owlishly at his highly vocal critic for no more than five ticks of the clock. Smiling faintly, he returned to his text with nary a word of rebuttal nor even an acknowledgement that his youthful bearded attacker even existed. The meeting continued without further interruption.

Only a few minor hurdles remained before the city could bestow its final blessing on the entire project and in so doing bar any future demonstrations or efforts to block the building of the new store upon the ruins of the old. Then, genuine disaster struck. The mayor and Harvey Milk, a supervisor, were assassinated in their offices by an enraged former fireman and the entire community was plunged into shock and grief. For a time, all functions of the city government seemed to hang in suspended animation with the approved construction of a new store quite rightly very low on the priority list. In time, things returned to something resembling normalcy for San Francisco, and work on the new store proceeded without further interruption.

At long last in late 1982, the new argyle-clad Neiman Marcus on Union Square opened its doors to a glittering society audience at a private pre-opening gala. The least said about Texas on this memorable occasion, it was correctly surmised, the warmer the reception would be.

To underscore the very expensive fact that the rotunda and its beautiful glass dome had been retained and indeed enhanced as promised by Stanley Marcus, a scheme was devised that would instantly attract the attention of all those who entered the store for the opening gala. On each of the floors that encircled the rotunda, violinists in full white tie regalia, were playing lustily as the guests walked in. A hundred musicians filled the vast high ceiling chamber with the soaring full dimensional surround sounds of the works of Vivaldi, Paganini, and Brahms, with an occasional bit of "I Left My Heart in San Francisco" thrown in to amuse and perhaps pacify the locals. Nary was a note of "Deep in the Heart of Texas" heard.

The rotunda served as a giant five floor echo chamber with the music rising to its summit. All eyes went almost involuntarily straight upward, past the circles of violinists, to rest at last upon the sparkling glass tiles and the depiction of the original City of Paris sailing ship of yore, saved from destruction by a casual and apparently unrehearsed remark by Stanley Marcus. It is quite likely that by saving that dome, he also saved the entire project from the short sighted wrath of those who had so fervently protested its inception.

About the time the oilrig had outworn its welcome, Neiman Marcus for the first time launched a line of merchandise that called further attention to the store's deep Texas roots. Given the brand name "Red River" and featuring a stylized Texas Longhorn as its logo, the line eventually proved to be highly successful even in such non-Texas venues as San Francisco.

The line was actually created in response to the countless requests from frustrated visitors to Dallas who expected to find at least something in the store with a Western touch to purchase as gifts to take home. Fortunately, at the time, a cyclical resurgence in what passes for cowboy chic was just returning into vogue, so the company's first full line venture into Western hats, high-heeled boots, red-hot chili, and even long cigarillos could not have been better timed. To the surprise of many, the Texas cowboy-inspired Red River brand proved equally popular on Chicago's Miracle Mile, upstate New York, and in Southern Florida as it did in Dallas, Fort Worth, and Houston.

The store commissioned western artist Melvin C. Warren to create a miniature bronze rendering of Red River, the living trademark. The original casting of one hundred pieces sold out in a matter of months, but the piece bearing the number "one of one" distinction was presented to then Texas Governor William P. Clements in Austin.

Part of the appeal of the broad range of clothing and food items that bore the Red River Brand was the fact that it came exclusively from the same Neiman Marcus that was more famous for its diamonds, minks, and elegant gowns from the world's top couture houses. There is a certain inexplicable warmth generated by the true fashions and traditions of the American West and the presence of the Red River line in juxtaposition with all the accompanying glitter expected in a Neiman Marcus store produced a pleasant almost earthy contrasting sensation that quickly translated into an immense volume of sales.

The multi-million dollar brand had still been in its earliest stages of development when a unique opportunity arose to obtain a living trademark to call attention to the new Wild West adventure taking shape at the store. I was personally involved in the cattle ranching business at the time and as a result, notices of upcoming cattle auctions frequently came my way. One such sales notice showed a photograph of a particularly attractive registered Texas Longhorn steer. He had an impressively wide rack of nicely shaped horns and was, at seven years of age, probably reasonably docile with an appreciable life span ahead of him. Most important, though, was the exciting fact that the steer's actual registered name was "Red River."

After convincing the company's treasurer that purchasing this animal was absolutely crucial, I drew a cashier's check for six thousand dollars which I assumed from having visited many cattle auctions would be far more than the amount needed to buy the first Longhorn steer to ever bear the store's brand. Unfortunately, word of the company's interest in buying the animal preceded my arrival at the auction barn in Fort Worth and, somehow, my reason for wishing to buy Red River had also been leaked to the auctioneer.

When the bidding for what should have been about a three thousand dollar animal began at forty-five hundred dollars, I knew I was in a rigged situation. After a time, and with only one other bidder still in the race when the bid had reached eight thousand five hundred dollars, my opponent, who it later developed was actually a shill, walked away. Red River had become the property of Neiman Marcus, but just barely. I gave the auction clerk my cashier's check which was twenty-seven hundred dollars short of my final bid. After a short discussion with the auction's manager, it was determined that the sale would stand if I promised to get the balance to the animal's owner by the next business day. As all proceeds from the sale were eventually to go to a charity, the payoff rules could easily be relaxed a bit.

The next morning, I obtained a check for the balance due from the store's treasurer, who never fully grasped why a red and white Longhorn steer could possibly be worth nearly nine thousand dollars.

At any rate, the charity had all of the proceeds and Neiman Marcus was in the cattle business for the first and probably the last time.

It did not take long to prove that the living breathing Red River was worth in publicity far more than the money paid for him. Just as Elsie the Cow had made a fortune for Borden's, the steer proved equally valuable to Neiman Marcus. He was both accustomed to traveling by trailer and quite gentle, at least by usual Longhorn standards, so the decision was made to use him as our store opening publicity trick in lieu of the oilrig that had become old news.

Branded with the distinctive RR brand, the real Red River was soon on the road to such exotic places as Westchester County in New York State, Las Vegas, and even Chicago, Illinois. Solely for publicity purposes, the steer's adventuresome spirit proved invaluable. Never content to remain in whatever stable or corral he was given while on the road, Red River frequently escaped to explore backyards, vegetable gardens, and even busy interstates as he traveled to and from new store opening gigs. In Westchester County, for example, he managed to free himself from a corral provided by the sheriff's department to wander by twilight through the manicured yards of upstate New Yorkers who had apparently never seen anything like a "large cow with really big horns," as one caller put it in her frantic phone call to the sheriff. As patrol cars tracked him down, Red River treated himself to some lettuce being nurtured in one garden before casually trampling a bed of roses being lovingly cared for just three backyards away. Fences were, unfortunately, the least of the wandering bovine's concerns.

The steer, probably bored with his freedom, was lassoed and led back to the sheriff's corral where the gate was this time doubly locked behind him. On exhibit in many larger cities, Red River proved to be a delight to children, many of whom had never seen a large farm animal of any kind let alone a big Texas Longhorn.

Stories of his frequent nocturnal escapades generated considerable publicity but surprisingly no lawsuits. Those whose gardens and flower beds had received his unwanted attention seemed pleased to let the matter drop after their local newspapers ran the story, always with a journalistic tongue in cheek. "NM Steer Horns in on Local Gardens" was a typical offering.

In Las Vegas, Red River almost made the front page by nearly goring the governor of the state of Nevada. His Excellency had consented to appear at the opening of the company's new store on the famous Las Vegas Strip where Red River was attracting a large crowd of admirers. Perhaps wishing to share in some of the attraction, the governor opened the gate of the enclosure in which the steer was, at least temporarily, in residence.

The sight of the governor posing next to the large Longhorn on the Las Vegas Strip did indeed make for an unusual photo op, and cameras whirred and flashbulbs flared as the unique event was recorded by amateur and professional photographers alike. Unfortunately, either the blinding flashes of the bulbs or the proximity of an unknown person seemed to unsettle the steer. The politician had entered the enclosure before our wrangler could get to him in time to discourage such a potentially dangerous act since most large farm animals do not care to be close to humans they do not recognize.

Longhorns seem particularly prone to moving either away from an unknown person or in some cases, moving rapidly toward that unknown person with head slightly lowered to permit his horn tips to quickly create the desired breathing room for himself. In the case of the invasive governor, the steer merely eyed him with apparent disdain but then turned his head rapidly so that the tip of his right horn grazed the visitor's coat sleeve just enough to leave a shallow scratch mark across the fabric. The governor rather ungracefully leaped away much to the delight of the crowd, but the smile on his face remained gamely fixed as he hurriedly made his way to the gate, passing the wrangler who was hastening toward his steer in case the capricious animal took a sudden notion to propel the fleeing politician unceremoniously over the top rail of the enclosure.

In the end, no one was hurt, the steer was content to be by himself, the crowd had been given something to talk about later and the governor had his picture taken many times. All in all, it was a good publicity day for Red River and, of course, for Neiman Marcus as well.

Even when the steer did not make the trip, store openings during those years of rapid expansion were often chaotic but still productive. The time honored tradition of making the store a theater, laid down by Stanley Marcus, was followed with gusto by those associates he had trained. Stanley once asked if Red River's numerous escapes were all accidental, but then held up his hand to stifle my response.

Perhaps he was remembering another bovine experience that had generated some questionable media coverage for the store. It had occurred in 1975 during the Italian Fortnight made famous by the appearance of Sophia Loren. To provide photographers to shoot as reference points as they followed the movie star around the store, it was decided to give new life to the old adage ". . . a bull in a china shop." To do this, we arranged to have a yearling bull calf brought up in the freight elevator to the china department on the fourth floor.

The young animal, named Marcello in honor of Miss Loren's frequent co-star, Marcello Mastroianni, was a Chianina, an Italian breed then gaining popularity in America. The calf weighed around three hundred pounds but fortunately proved to be quite docile with no apparent interest in going on a china-shattering rampage.

He endured his elevator ride with considerable poise and it was not until he was being led toward his temporary pen did he begin to have a field day. At least, the newspaper reported that Marcello apparently believed that he was still out in the field somewhere rather than on the selling floor of the elegant Neiman Marcus store. It was not until he was in full sight of the curious customers who had gathered to see the rare sight that nature took its inevitable course to the delight of the media. Completely unabashed by his act, Marcello allowed himself to be led into his pen with its sawdust and canvas flooring. Had he delayed his indiscretion a mere thirty seconds, the photograph of harried store maintenance men arriving on the scene with shovels and mops would have not been possible.

As it developed, the carpet was more or less returned to its pristine condition before Miss Loren arrived at the pen. She and the little bull, both Italians in a strange environment, seemed to bond warmly without further incident.

When animals were not around, a signature piece of each opening gala in the new store was a surprise parade of musicians through the usual thousand or so formally attired revelers. Bagpipers, high school bands, and marching military drum and bugle corps making their way up escalators and past smiling, clapping onlookers gave out the very clear signal that this was not an ordinary store that had come to town. In San Francisco, a large group of Chinese-American musicians were persuaded to play "The Eyes of Texas" as they made their way up the escalator. Surprisingly, no one seemed to be upset at this bit of Texana on the road.

Always staged as a fundraising event for a local charity, the pre-opening day galas attracted the very top tier of the buying market Neiman Marcus hoped to dominate. Individual ticket prices ranged well upward from one hundred dollars per person to gain admission to what proved to be among the premiere social events of the year. Well known musical groups and entertainers such as Bobby Short, Peter Duchin, and Jerry Jeff Walker were among the stellar attractions. Open bars usually seemed to influence guests to make advance purchases of costly items that in theory would not be available until the next day.

Party goers dined on exotic food, downed the finest of champagnes, and the driest of martinis to salute the coming of the legendary Neiman Marcus to their city. The lights of television cameras ensured that those not able to attend the big shindig could vicariously share in the fun and the excitement that many compared to the opening night of a Broadway play. Through that comparison they captured the motive behind it all.

It cannot be said that the opening bashes were always without mishap. Despite a standing policy to anticipate the very worst that could happen in such many faceted events and have contingency plans accordingly in place, things sometimes did go awry.

At the opening of the store at Newport Beach in 1978, for example, plans had been made to stage part of the pre-opening event under a large tent placed in the adjoining parking lot. A canvas canopy large enough to provide cover for at least four hundred people at one time is indeed a sight to behold. Bigger than many circus tents, it is also a challenge to erect properly and for hours before the big event, crews of rope-tugging, pole-raising experts pulled and hammered and strained until finally the huge tent was fully erect, towering nearly as tall as the store itself.

As night fell, store employees looked with pride at the monster canopy that next evening would welcome a throng of well-to-do Southern Californians to the wonder world of Neiman Marcus. That prideful expectation, at least as far as the tent was concerned, was never to be fulfilled. Sometime in the darkness of the night, a capricious but forceful wind blew into the coastal city of Newport Beach from the east with disastrous results. The employees who had left the store the previous night with admiration for the tent returned the next morning to find the tent no longer there. No shred of canvas, no loose ropes, no once towering poles were anywhere to be found. Only the holes where the stakes had been driven gave any hint that a huge temporary structure had but a few hours earlier loomed impressively beside the new store building.

It had been far more temporary than anyone could have imagined, for it was gone long before it was ever used. No report of a mammoth piece of canvas, or even tiny pieces, was ever reported by the Coast

Guard or local pilots. If it went out to sea in one piece, ropes trailing harmlessly in its wake, or up into the mountains in a series of tattered panels will likely never be known. Shopping center security guards reported that no trucks entered the cordoned area where the tent had stood. They did notice a strong gust of wind at one point during the night, but the only visible after effect of that wind throughout the entire region was that one gaily striped tent big enough to please the Ringling Brothers had gone curiously missing never to be seen again.

The show business aspect of the store openings always seemed to please Stanley as they clearly reflected his powerful and lasting influence on the company's way of doing things. If the show business got a bit out of hand on rare occasion, he only smiled and shook his head, I hope, in only mock concern but sincere appreciation.

When the volume of a heavy metal rock band performing at Beverly Hills grew uncomfortably loud for even those with a somewhat diminished hearing capability such as his, Stanley approached me with one of his sly expressions on his face. Acting as though he was going to remove the hearing aid he had found necessary to wear, he proclaimed, "Well, I sure don't need this damned thing around here tonight." Efforts to encourage the so called musical group to turn down their megawatt amplification equipment only resulted in the volume knobs being rotated to an even higher level of thunderous cacophony.

Another famous ensemble playing at the Beverly Hills store later that night somehow had the impression that any merchandise that caught their fancy after their performance was theirs for the taking. Shearling coats for men were very much in vogue at the time and each member of the country and western group saw nothing irregular in selecting one or two for himself from stock and placing it in a fitting room for safe storage until the party was over. The store's security detail, although greatly overtaxed in dealing with freely imbibing celebrity guests, became aware of the shearling stash. Their diligence in action resulted in all the coats being moved to an even safer place unknown to the musicians to be returned to the sales floor the next day.

The opening day stunts continued for many years, even when the company was in a virtual frenzy of expansion. In 1981 alone, three new stores were opened. Four additional units were ready for business over the next two years.

To focus attention on the opening of each new store, all manner of news making activities were utilized. Although Red River became a staple attraction, the oilrig, as noted, was retired for a time in favor of artillery canon fusillades at a Dallas store opening and later, large firework displays almost replicated the excitement created in Atlanta in 1971.

These pyrotechnics consisted of a framework some ten feet in height by twenty feet in length. Looped into the frame was a network of fuse that, when ignited, proceeded to display the name Neiman Marcus letter by letter from the first "N" to the last "S." When the dramatically burning fuse reached that "S," the entire store name then flared even more brightly, thanks to a secondary fuse device. The name continued to burn as customers were admitted into the new store for the first time. The media, having grown universally weary of ribbon cuttings, loved this novel idea without exception.

The device proved to be particularly popular with television crews who liked the visual excitement of the entire procedure. The crew covering the 1980 opening display at White Plains, New York, however, had a field day when things did not quite work out as planned. It seemed the pyrotechnic team that had performed so reliably at other openings had overslept as the result of a strenuous night of partying down in New York City. Arriving at the store with just an hour to spare before the appointed time for lighting the fuse, the somewhat bleary-eyed members of the team attempted to accomplish in less than sixty minutes what regularly required at least twice as long.

In their haste, several key connections were overlooked and when the master fuse was ignited in front of a large crowd, a series of uninspiring fizzles quickly resulted in a sign that brightly spelled out the curious name "man Mar." Neither the missing "Nei" nor "cus," let alone the hyphen then being used was ever set afire. The crowd of onlookers, however, eagerly awaiting the store to open and probably not in the least impressed by the failed fireworks gimmick anyway, surged past the still smoldering "man Mar" display and pushed through the just opened doors into the building.

Great sums of money were invested in the store opening events, including very expensive formal galas, the shipping of a steer, the travels of an oil rig, and the cost of sparkling logotypes that might or might not spell the store name correctly. In retrospect, it is easy to speculate that most of the opening day crowds probably did not much care about such sophomoric hijinks. Those who came when the new store opened its doors for the first time probably did so just for the excitement of the event itself. As we saw it, the hijinks were for the media anyway.

At the opening of the first store outside Texas, in Bal Harbour, Florida, in 1971, the crushing crowds that literally exploded into the building past the oilrig when the doors opened obviously came to collect souvenirs of the event. The company's always colorful shopping bags were torn first from their stands on the selling floor and then from the hands of store personnel hurrying to refill the holders. Over the course of that opening morning, the bags would be literally torn away from their hemp handles which remained dangling from the hands of employees much as voracious piranha might leave only the bones of a hastily consumed prey.

Clearly, Neiman Marcus store openings, with or without fireworks or steers, were exciting events from the bag-snatchers of South Florida to the thwarted coat-robbers of Southern California. Maybe the big expensive publicity events that surrounded the openings from coast to coast during the hectic expansion years were superfluous but probably not. At any rate, expensive or excessive as they may have been, the excitement that each stunt created in every new marketplace was undeniable and told the buying public, through the media, that Neiman Marcus had finally come to town.

Becoming a Legend

Though he was by no means a humble man, it is unlikely that Stanley Marcus ever seriously set out to become a legend. That he actually became one long before he reached the age of fifty is an enduring tribute to his many accomplishments.

By the time he became president of Neiman Marcus, he had already put in place many revolutionary retailing concepts. During the next quarter century, he created a merchandising and marketing entity unlike any other in the world.

There were several primary keys to his success. He was never fully satisfied with the end results of any of his endeavors and innovations. No matter how successful something seemed to others, and particularly to his competitors, he relentlessly pursued ways to make improvement. Each day brought endless opportunities to try something new and to vigorously challenge something long established.

Fresh ideas brought to him by his associates were rejected out of hand only if they lacked imagination enough to stimulate his excitement. Such ideas, under his magic touch and fine tuning frequently became dazzling concepts that far exceeded the original suggestion.

Had Neiman Marcus continued to be a privately held corporation, it is probable that Stanley would have remained at the store's helm indefinitely. However, by 1973, four years after the acquisition of the company by the Carter Hawley Hale Corporation, it began to become apparent to many of his associates that his reign at the store was likely to end.

At the time of the acquisition, it had all seemed benign enough at least on the surface. Given the fine personal characters of the principal executives of the huge Carter Hawley Hale conglomerate, it is possible that the intentions of the merger were every bit as noble as the press releases about it indicated. As is usually the case in such acquisitions, however, the bottom line and the money managers often trump the good intentions.

The new owners of Neiman Marcus had gained success by acquiring and then expanding mid-market department stores known for their vast assortments of general merchandise offering something for everybody at a wide range of prices. By sublimating high quality merchandise and effective customer service in favor of higher margins of profit, the California-based company had fared very well in the retail scheme of things, at least well enough to acquire the prestigious name of Neiman Marcus.

In all fairness, it must be noted that Neiman Marcus was, in a sense, a willing if not overtly aggressive bride in what some analysts at the time delighted in calling a shotgun wedding. Archival documents clearly show that the Dallas company had for years carried on a flirtation with other retailing firms in an effort to attract more operating capital. Mergers were at one time or another considered with such firms as Macy's and Saks Fifth Avenue among others.

Marshall Field and Company, the famed Chicago mercantile giant now so sadly gone from the American retailing scene, was at one time a highly potential suitor. It is not entirely clear from the exchange of correspondence between the two companies as to who would acquire whom. A fascinating "pro" and "con" study on a proposed merger with the Chicago store can be seen in the Marcus Collection. By the late 1960s, however, a number of studies comparing the benefits and downsides of merging with either the Field's store or the California conglomerate persuaded Stanley and his executives to accept the proposal offered by Broadway Hale Company, later better known as Carter Haley Hale.

Even market analysts wearing glasses with the rosiest of lenses could have sensed that even what appeared to be bottomless pools of ready cash soon to be made available to Neiman Marcus were bound to have treacherous snags lurking beneath the surface. When the California company closed the merger deal in 1969, the snags were invisible, but shortly thereafter, that old devil known as greed rose to the surface.

The merger, at least at its outset, was indeed a good deal for Neiman Marcus. Wrapped within the glowing promises that nothing whatever would be changed as a result of the takeover was a $40 million buyout offer that more than doubled the value of Neiman Marcus stock from its previous high. In return for the extremely generous price being paid for the Dallas company, the new owners initially asked only that Stanley and his executives undertake a massive nationwide expansion program. As an article in "D" magazine once put it, "Carter [of Broadway Hale] offered Neiman's the capital it needed to expand, Neiman's offered Carter the most prestigious specialty store in America."

As Stanley put it in his inimitable and colorful way, "Once you decide not to be a virgin, it's just a matter of deciding how far from home you want to sleep." If he had sold his store's virtue to finance expansion truly with no strings attached soon became a burning question in the minds of the store's clientele as well as its competitors.

Immediately after the change from family to California corporate ownership was made public, Stanley began to receive telephone calls from agitated customers eager to report that things were already deteriorating. One distressed caller told him that on the very day of the merger, a store delivery truck driver had caused his vehicle to run over and destroy her son's bicycle. Although he was able to calm the lady's anguish by offering to buy the boy a replacement bike, he had great fun with the alleged incident during a store employee meeting a few days later. "The lady was right on target" he said with heavy irony, "as soon as the merger announcement ran in the paper, I told all of our drivers to go out and destroy as many bicycles as they could."

The new owners, after making those obligatory and perhaps even sincere vows to leave everything at their newly acquired property just as it had traditionally been, began to tinker. They asked why specialty stores such as Neiman Marcus could not generate the same percentages of profit as their department stores could. They wondered why so many salespeople were needed on the selling floor and why marketing costs were so much higher than other stores, and on and on.

Soon, the soft queries became firm directives issued in order to put Neiman Marcus into lock-step performance with the conglomerate's department store operations. The correspondence files of Stanley Marcus are filled with letters and telegrams from him to his new business partners trying to explain why this goal of conformation was neither desirable nor attainable. His letters carried the clear message that the continued success of his store was built on a rock solid foundation of the very highest quality goods, effective and frequently expensive marketing efforts and exemplary customer service. To cut back on the expenses involved in any one of those key factors in order to wring a point or two higher percentage of profit from the sales volume would, in his valid estimation, likely kill the goose that was nevertheless producing a goodly sized golden egg of profit as it was.

As time passed, this inevitable and predictable clash of retailing philosophies became increasingly intense, and, just as predictably, the conglomerate's shareholders began to lose patience with the apparent inability of the parent firm's management to improve the profits at Neiman Marcus and, in the process, increase their stock's dividends. On the surface, the public relationship between Stanley, in Dallas, and the money managers in Los Angeles remained cordial enough, but to no one's particular surprise, his valiant efforts to defend his vaunted principles came to naught.

Nudged without much subtlety from his office as chief executive in 1975, Stanley was nevertheless pleased when his son Richard was named chairman. The parent company, in the course of time, dispatched to Dallas a fast changing slate of young merchants given the title of president in an obvious effort to accomplish their profit objectives and in doing so, likely transform a silk purse into a sow's ear. It was not until Richard Marcus was named chief executive officer that the brief aberrant course was corrected and the company once again set in motion in the original direction. Stanley, in the meantime, was handed the noble, if essentially ineffectual, title of chairman emeritus of Neiman Marcus and executive vice president of Carter Hawley Hale.

In 1976, when some at the California headquarters began to suspect that the still forceful chairman emeritus might be much too active in store policy, it was decided that he be elaborately and publicly retired to be placed in retailing's pantheon of mythical gods whose useful time in stores had come to a noble end.

As a result of this decision, a gala golden anniversary celebratory banquet was arranged in order to salute Stanley's fifty years of phenomenal service to retailing and at the same time let him know that a half-century at the reins was more than long enough and that the time to go fishing or write another book or do whatever had at last arrived.

Never anyone's fool, the cagey old honoree surprised his ostensible well-wishers at the banquet by mounting a masterful counter attack. In his remarks that followed his introduction, he made use of a tale from ancient Greece. In short order, Stanley had his audience firmly in his grasp as he told of an old Grecian warrior who found himself being honored by his contemporaries at what seemed to be the end of his service. In the tale, the Athenian chieftain recounted his many victories and then shouted defiantly that although he was old, he was not weary, and since victory had often come his way so many times before, he flatly refused to lay down his sword and spear just because he was being honored so lavishly.

Those in the Dallas audience who had hoped the honoree would simply acknowledge the evening's accolades and then simply fade away became increasingly restive as Stanley's speech went on. It soon became very clear that he was not in fact speaking of some long-dead Greek who had refused to lay down his sword but rather of a very much alive Dallas Merchant Prince who had not the slightest intention of slipping meekly into obscurity.

Stanley's speech was greeted by a standing ovation by those who clearly realized what had taken place but understandably by tepid applause from those few conspirators at the head table who realized they had been outsmarted. A bit of later research by amused store staffers proved that the noble Greek so vividly described by Stanley had been solely a product of his imagination.

His brilliant banquet ploy ended, at least for a time, the reduction of his power within the company. Eventually, however, his direct hands-on influence began to recede at an increasing rate.

His role as executive vice president of the conglomerate was not to his liking, and he must have found it difficult to suddenly have not one but several bosses for the first time in his life, except for his father fifty years earlier. His visits to the stores became fewer, yet news of his presence in any Neiman Marcus store spread rapidly whenever he appeared. Small groups of longtime employees would soon surround him, perhaps fearing that the man who had made their store so famous might never pass their way again.

As the years rolled on, he kept his chairman emeritus title intact while he formed a one-man consulting firm aided only by a sizeable corps of efficient secretaries. Through a combination of his reputation and proven ability to offer good business advice to a tightly restricted number of satisfied clients, Stanley amassed an enviable clientele list that included a Cadillac dealer, quality clothing manufacturers, shopping malls, and even the Carter Hawley Hale Corporation itself.

Always entertaining, imaginative, and often controversial in his approach to most facets of life, he was much in demand on the lecture circuit both in the United States and abroad. He devised a fee schedule for his speeches that generated a sizeable income from that endeavor, and since all travel expenses were by agreement to be borne by his sponsors, he and his wife were able to travel in grand style and be well-paid for doing so.

Although his records show that he made 199 speeches out of town in just over ten years, it is obvious that he accepted invitations to speak based at least partly on his lifelong fondness of seafood. As a result, he made it a point to be in New York City just as the season for shad came around, in Baltimore in time for crab, and on the West Coast as the abalone harvest commenced.

When he was not on one of his many lecture and gustatory tours at home or abroad, he was frequently the guest of honor at appreciation banquets that saluted his long lifetime of achievement. As the events became more numerous as he neared and then surpassed his ninetieth birthday, he publicly claimed that it was all becoming a bit too much. It was not receiving the glowing tributes that bothered him, he once wryly commented to a newspaper reporter, but he regretted all the inconvenience it created for his many friends who had to don formal attire so frequently to hear him be praised.

He once wrote to a friend that he was becoming a little embarrassed by all the public accolades that were coming his way so frequently. When a customer called him directly to say he was getting sick

and tired of reading about Stanley Marcus, Stanley replied, "I sympa-
thize with you, I am also getting tired of reading about Stanley
Marcus."

In his later years, he emerged as the senior darling of Dallas society. Few editions of the city's newspaper failed to have a photograph
of him at the most prestigious social event of the week. He also developed a new twinkling sort of persona that gave his image in every society page photo a cherubic appearance that those of us who had
worked for him many years before found to be a bit atypical, if not almost unfathomable. Clearly, he was enjoying life immensely as that life
passed its eighty year milestone and moved on beyond the ninetieth.

His continued long and productive life, filled with more honors
than he could count, lent him an ever increasing aura of celebrity that
reached nearly all levels of society. In 1975, for example, the
Northwood Institute conducted an extensive study throughout Texas to
determine what individuals were considered to be the most widely admired.

Topping the list of favorites was Roger Staubach, the popular and
successful quarterback of the Dallas Cowboys. Stanley was sixth on
the list immediately following the inspiring Barbara Jordan but just
above Mork, a television sitcom character. If Stanley was pleased that
he was more admired than the mythical Mork, he was surely delighted
at having received more votes than Ross Perot, Jimmy Carter, and Miss
Piggy, who came in as number fourteen, fifteen and eighteen on the list
respectively. The glamorous lady pig, it might be noted, was seven po-
sitions higher on the list than Richard M. Nixon.

The ninetieth anniversary of the founding of Neiman Marcus in
1997 found Stanley, himself at age ninety-two, in apparent good
health. He made appearances at many of the celebratory events and
entertained a large group of employees at a reunion in the store.

On the occasion of his own ninetieth birthday two years earlier, the
store had mounted an extravagant salute to the man who had made it

famous. Vignette exhibits throughout the Dallas store underscored his countless contributions to the company's success and internationally known fashion leaders joined in a celebration of the legendary figure who took it all in warmly and with his now characteristic twinkle in his eye.

To those of us who saw him only infrequently in the final years of his life, he seemed to visibly age very little. He had become a bit frail, and a broken leg incurred in a fall made the use of a walking stick necessary. When he claimed with a bright smile that his fracture had come about as the result of his careless chasing of a beautiful blonde, it was clear that in that somewhat frail and slow-moving body, the ribald Stanley Marcus of seventy years earlier was still very much in fine fettle.

Newspaper and television reporters sought him out whenever an event in Dallas needed a sage observation from the aging oracle who had seen his city grow many hundredfold larger to become a massive cosmopolitan urban force of nature, now more sophisticated than Herbert and Carrie could have possibly imagined in their fondest dreams. The fact that the oracle they interviewed had done so much to bring about that transformation was not lost on the reading or viewing public.

Stanley had never shied away from controversy during the years when Dallas was growing up and Neiman Marcus was teaching it how to do so with grace. His father had assured him that when he came to work for the store, he would be free to take public stands on any issue that confronted the city, no matter how controversial. His views on all such issues, for all of his adult life, were widely known. Even though he was almost always on the liberal side of the political equation, he spoke out on issues directly from his heart and his conscience. He once described himself to be a "conservative liberal or perhaps the other way around." If he believed a presidential candidate to be the best qualified for the job, he backed the man regardless of political affiliation. The fact that he actively campaigned and raised funds to help elect the Republican candidate Dwight Eisenhower over the famously liberal Adlai Stevenson seems out of character, yet he was, again, responding to his own beliefs.

Many of his public opinions voiced during his long years in command of the store provoked the ire of many of his customers. His decision to stage a French Fortnight despite a popular outcry throughout America over the antics of French President Charles de Gaulle produced many envelopes holding Neiman Marcus credit cards cut in half and taped to nasty notes. One disgruntled former customer even mailed in the wastebasket into which he had hurled his mutilated credit card.

When he supported some students who were expelled from a Dallas school because their hair was too long, angrier reaction came forth because of this perceived assault against school district discipline. A clergyman took him to task for offering to pay the legal costs to get the students' expulsion order revoked, saying that long hair was sinful. Stanley publicly replied that he did not recall ever seeing a picture of Jesus with a crewcut. That remark, he later remembered, cost the store about 450 cancelled charge accounts.

He had fared much better with the clergy when he took a strong civic leadership position following the assassination of President Kennedy in Dallas. Although frequently mentioned as a possible candidate as Kennedy's appointment to be ambassador to France, Stanley was not in the city when the president's motorcade made its fateful turn in front of the Dallas School Book Depository. When word of the assassination reached him in New York City, he felt an instant shock of dismay and horror as did the entire world.

It fell to him, however, to get the city of Dallas back on its feet in the after-shock of the horrendous crime. As other civic leaders seemed to cringe in the brutal glare of the worldwide spotlight of blame and accusation that flooded the city, Stanley alone had the courage to take a stand. In a paid message that appeared in the newspaper soon after the murder, he offered a short essay entitled "What's Right with Dallas." His words earned him the support of nearly every church in the city and the wholehearted gratitude of all but a few narrow minded citizens of the city he so dearly loved.

"We think there's a lot right with Dallas," his essay declared. Without directly mentioning the assassination, he went on to enumerate the many factors that made the city great all the while indicating that, clearly, a climate of political extremism existed that obviously knew no bounds. His clarion call for tolerance and the immediate elimination of such extremism struck a chord that resonated from coast to coast and even far across all the seas.

There was a backlash from some of his customers who challenged his temerity to presume to speak for them. Chopped credit cards came by the hundreds. Letters claimed he had insulted the city and some contained threats against his life. Despite it all, he stood his ground in what was very likely his finest hour.

He remained fearless for the rest of his days. One of his favorite lecture topics was the decline of customer service in many American retail establishments and how this trend would most surely put those most flagrant violators of this once fundamental of retailing principles soon out of business altogether. That he was being handsomely paid to make these dire, if accurate, predictions to audiences at retail meetings did not faze him at all. The more controversial he became, the greater the demand became for his words of wisdom.

For a time, Stanley participated in a series of radio broadcasts which he termed "Narrowcasts" as they focused on very specific subjects that were close to his heart. He spoke about things he liked, such as Sara Lee's cheesecake and things he did not like, such as children on airplanes or ladies with prototypically Texas big hair. Even though his radio time was sponsored, his observations, as usual, remained unstructured, uncensored, and totally unafraid of public reaction.

He wrote four books during his lifetime, an occupation that clearly mirrored his deep affection for the printed page. His autobiography, *Minding the Store* was particularly well-received and its early success afforded him an opportunity to appear on nationwide television shows to promote the work. In the process, he discovered that he was by his own admission something of a ham.

That previously submerged aspect of his multi-faceted personality had first bloomed into full brightness on the occasion of the banquet honoring the store's seventy-fifth anniversary in September 1982. To entertain the thousand or so guests attending the gala event, Stanley had, strictly on his own volition, decided to sing, or actually to voice lyrics in the style of Rex Harrison, all the while accompanied by piano music.

He asked his friend Sammy Cahn to write his script along the lines of the Frank Sinatra anthem, "I Did It My Way." He also asked that I come to the dress rehearsal of his theatrical debut to ascertain if it would play well to the audience that would include his wife, his children, his sole surviving brother, the widows of his other two brothers, and Mrs. Lyndon B. Johnson.

Early in the afternoon, Stanley entered the empty ballroom of the hotel where the black tie event would be held in just a matter of hours. He spoke to his accompanist, took off his jacket, threw it over the piano, and began to rehearse. He was immediately transformed. Although he was seventy-seven years old at the time, one could have mistaken him, or at least his demeanor, for a much younger Bobby Darrin.

At the banquet, confidence in his own ability oozed from every pore as he strutted about the stage as though he was appearing at the M-G-M Grand in Las Vegas. He had memorized both his lyrics and the script that accompanied it, cueing him when to pause for laughs and, if none were forthcoming, how to milk one or two from the audience.

Apparently in love with the spotlight, he began to chant, with at least some faint hit of a melody. "The praise, the cheers/for all the years/I do accept/and in no shy way, I can't disclaim/the family name/I did it *my* way!" The audience seemed at first to be more stunned than amused. They had expected a sober-sided speech from this wizard of retailing fame and not an apparently self-promoting tour de force.

Unabashed, he soldiered onward strutting across the stage with microphone in hand. "The store became/a magic name, shot like a flame/across the skyway, and I'm the man/with the Fortnight plan/I did it *my* way!" His performance was flawless, even though some in the crowd of onlookers began to grow restive, wondering if what they had contributed to the store's success might be recognized in his final verses, but such was not the case.

"For what is a store/what has it got? If not pizz-zazz?/then not a lot! And Neiman Marcus/you'll agree has pure pizz-zazz abundantly/ and in great style/all the while I did it *my* way!"

Just when it seemed to some that perhaps he had gone on a bit too much about his single-handed success, the music stopped for a few beats as he all but skipped to a nearby table and picked up a full glass placed there for him. The music resumed and the chanting continued, but now softly. "And now, I'll kindly ask you all . . . if you will please raise your alcohol . . . please toast the stores! The floors! The shelves! Above all/kindly toast yourselves! For the family . . . for them . . . for me, I thank you . . . *MY WAY!*"

With that, he shouted out, "Bless you all for seventy-five glorious years." The seventy-seven year old Prince turned performer raised the glass on high before draining it dry in one theatrical toast to all who now stood in awe and adoration. The ovation that followed was loud, loving, and long-lasting. As some wept happy tears, he smiled, bowed, and kept smiling as the cheers and waves of applause swept across the huge room to embrace him.

Stanley Marcus was to live on for another almost twenty busy years, but on that memorable night so long ago, the old master show-man hit his peak as he stood in the brilliant circle cast upon him by the solitary spotlight. He had brought a thousand of whom he called his closest friends to their collective feet. He had, perfectly as was al-ways the case, done it *his* way.

SM with LBJ. Stanley's private address book contained the private phone numbers of seven U.S. Presidents, n.d.

Joan Crawford and her husband come to visit Stanley at his store. His address books held the names and numbers of hundreds of famous celebrities, n.d.

235

Brigitte Bardot and Stanley finally find something to share during a lunch in Paris, 1972.
—DeGolyer Library, Southern Methodist University,
Dallas, Texas, A 1933.1869

Lord Mountbatten, then the last surviving Supreme Commander in WWII, introduces his daughter to Mrs. Edward Marshall Boehm, 1973.
—DeGolyer Library, Southern Methodist University,
Dallas, Texas, A 1933.1869

236

John Wayne and his wife Pilar celebrate his successful completion of a well-lubricated flight from Mexico in 1970.

—Author's Collection

Sophia Loren makes an impressive entrance to the Italian Fortnight Gala in 1975. Her se-rious-looking escort has his usual cigar in hand, 1975.

—DeGolyer Library, Southern Methodist University,
Dallas, Texas, A 1933.1869

To open the Italian Fortnight, Miss Loren turns the wheel that activated 186 working water fountains on the store's walls, 1975.

—From the collections of the Texas/Dallas History and Archives Division of the Dallas Public Library

Sophia presides over a crowded but captivated Dallas press conference in 1975.

—From the collections of the Texas/Dallas History and Archives Division of the Dallas Public Library

239

Never timid, the store featured an Italian breed bull in its China Shop for Miss Loren to ad-mire. He was only relatively well-behaved, 1975.

—From the collections of the Texas/Dallas History
and Archives Division of the Dallas Public Library

Jack Benny is met by the author at the Dallas Airport in October 1974. The popular entertainer was fatally stricken before his performance for Neiman Marcus the next day.

—Author's Collection

Thailand's Queen Sirkit arrives at the 6666 Ranch by jet. The welcoming cowboy wrote this book, 1981.
—From the collections of the Texas/Dallas History and Archives Division of the Dallas Public Library

Her Majesty often found it necessary to good naturatedly remind her cowboys about how to hold a queen while dancing, 1981.
—From the collections of the Texas/Dallas History and Archives Division of the Dallas Public Library

241

Britain's HRH Princess Margaret is greeted by the author following her flight from the Caribbean, 1982.

—Author's Collection

"Red River," the only living trademark ever owned by Neiman Marcus, traveled from coast to coast to appear at store openings. © The Advocate, *September 12, 1980.*

—From the collections of the Texas/Dallas History and Archives Division of the Dallas Public Library

San Francisco Chronicle
THE VOICE OF THE WEST
D. 480,233 SAT. 450.227

MAY 3 1 1974

Photos by Dave Randolph

Pickets at the Mark Hopkins came out against discrimination and for the City of Paris building

Double Trouble

Landmark buffs and feminists set up separate picket lines outside the Mark Hopkins Hotel on Nob Hill yesterday, while stockholders of the Broadway-Hale stores met inside.

A handful of protesters from the Victorian Alliance urged Broadway-Hale not to tear down the old City of Paris building on Union Square. The firm plans to replace the store with one of its Neiman-Marcus outlets.

A dozen members of Women's Action, an Oakland group, marched nearby to protest alleged discrimination against women in the credit policy of Capwell's stores.

A spokesman for the Broadway-Hale organization said officials of its Capwell's stores have been meeting with the women and already have agreed to revise the chain's credit application forms.

Inside the Mark Hopkins, stockholders voted to change their corporation's name from Broadway-Hale, Inc. to Carter-Hawley-Hale, Inc. A spokesman said the new name reflects the current top officials of the company, which has expanded in recent years through mergers.

The Chronicle's *article does not fully reflect the ire of the protestors who opposed the store's entry into the San Francisco market.* © San Francisco Chronicle, *May 31, 1974.*

—From the collections of the Texas/Dallas History and Archives Division of the Dallas Public Library

243

When the magnificent rotunda and dome of the otherwise demolished City of Paris store were retained and revitalized in the new Neiman Marcus store, the protestors seemed at least mollified, 1975.

Stanley Marcus, age 95, and the author get together one last time, April 2000.
—Author's Collection

The front page, as well as many other pages in the newspaper revealed the sad truth that not even princes can live forever. © Dallas Morning News, January 23, 2002.
—From the collections of the Texas/Dallas History and Archives Division of the Dallas Public Library

The Dallas Morning News

Texas' Leading Newspaper · Dallas, Texas, Wednesday, January 23, 2002 · DallasNews.com · 50 cents

Prisoner abuse denied

Angry Rumsfeld says charges of mistreatment at base in Cuba are 'just plain false'

By RICHARD WHITTLE
Washington Bureau

WASHINGTON — Al-Qaeda and Taliban prisoners at Guantanamo Bay, Cuba, are being treated well, contrary to protests by human rights groups and others, an indignant Defense Secretary Donald Rumsfeld declared Tuesday.

The allegations that have been made, by many from comfortable distance, that the men and women

Indonesia may be haven for al-Qaeda, 8A

in the U.S. armed forces are somehow not properly treating the detainees under their charge are just plain false," Mr. Rumsfeld said at a Pentagon news briefing.

"The treatment of the detainees in Guantanamo Bay is proper, it's humane, it's appropriate and it is fully consistent with international conventions," he said.

Human rights groups and some European governments have protested that the United States may be depriving the inmates rights by refusing to designate them "prisoners of war," which would entitle them to protections under the Geneva Convention.

U.S. officials refer to the captives as "unlawful combatants."

Mr. Rumsfeld said keeping the detainees "off the streets and not killing people" is the Pentagon's first priority, while their status and future is a question for lawyers.

Some may be charged with crimes and tried in U.S. courts, he said, and some may be tried before military tribunals under an order President Bush signed last year. Others may be returned to their native countries.

Al-Qaeda, the radical Islamic network founded by Osama bin Laden and blamed for the Sept. 11 attacks on New York and Washing-

See DETAINEES Page 11A

STANLEY MARCUS: 1905-2002

He rose to top of retail and took Dallas along

Stanley Marcus transformed Neiman Marcus into an international retailing star — and Dallas basked in the glow.

FILE 1994/Erwin Gaskar

Friends recall a great mind with a spirit to match

By JOHN KIRKPATRICK
Staff Writer

Retailing legend Stanley Marcus died Tuesday at Zale-Lipshy Hospital. He was 96.

"He really died of old age. He just got tired, the third greatly," said daughter Jerrie Smith. Mr. Marcus had been hospitalized since Sunday.

Mr. Marcus was best known for leading the Neiman Marcus chain to international promi-

A gracious legend, 1D

nence.

"I will surely miss him because he has been such a great reverence point for what is the right thing to do," said Ken Hughes, a Dallas developer who had lunch with Mr. Marcus last week.

Mr. Marcus is survived by his wife, Linda Marcus of Dallas; daughters Ms. Smith of Dallas and Wendy Raymont of Washing-

Merchant prince made Neiman's 'The Store'

By MARIA HALKIAS
Staff Writer

Stanley Marcus was a retailing genius who put Dallas on the international fashion map, gave Texans good taste and defined the retail industry's highest standards.

His unparalleled career spanned an amazing six decades, from the fedoras of the

Tuesday at 96.

Stamping his imprint on a Dallas that was far smaller, more similar and less cosmopolitan than the city of today, Mr. Marcus made his homespun a sophisticated shopping destination. Celebrities from Coco Chanel to John Wayne all fell under his spell.

His tour was the specialty

Gramm defends wife on Enron

Wrongdoing as board member denied; couple lost $600,000, he says

By JIM LANDERS

WASHINGTON — Texas Sen. Phil Gramm on Tuesday defended his wife's actions on Enron Corp.'s board of directors and said the couple lost more than $600,000 in the energy company's bankruptcy.

Wendy Gramm, a research scholar on regulatory matters who has a doctorate in economics, has served on the Enron board's audit and compliance committees since 1993. Several Enron shareholder lawsuits alleging securities fraud and insider trading have named her as a defendant.

The lawsuits seek tens of billions of dollars in damages from Enron's board, management and accountants. Arthur Andersen LLP.

"When all the facts are known, people will find she did nothing wrong," Mr. Gramm said. "But this thing's going to be around for a long time."

Mr. Gramm is the senior Republican on the Senate Banking Committee. He said he would stand aside from congressional hearings dealing with the range of Enron's demise because of his wife's seat on the company's board and their personal financial losses.

But, in an interview, the senator said he would participate in any ensuing congressional debates about deregulation, accounting standards and retirement plans.

"I'm still an employee of 260 million people in Texas. I'm going to be involved."

The senator said he was not aware that Enron was in operational financial state in the months leading to the company's Dec. 2 bankruptcy filing because he and his wife do not discuss her business activities.

Dr. Gramm chaired the federal Commodity Futures Trading Commission from 1988 to January 1993, when the commission

Saying Goodbye

ven though Stanley and I spoke occasionally during the first years of the twenty-first century and sent each other inscribed copies of books we had just published, I only saw him once again, in April 2000. A mutual friend had invited my wife and I to Dallas to attend what would prove to be his next to last birthday party. A small group of former associates gathered at a home on the shores of the city's White Rock Lake to partake of Stanley's favorite Fort Worth barbeque and some really cold beer.

It was my good and memorable fortune to spend about a half hour alone with him. He was thin now, at last, his beard snow white, his steps a bit faltering and uncertain, but his mind and his piercing dark eyes were as sharply keen as ever. Just as he had on the ill-fated Atlanta helicopter flight, he had chosen to wear brand new shoes with very slick soles to his birthday party. As we walked down a short flight of tile steps, he slipped and might have fallen had I not grasped his upper arm by way of support. Through the fabric of the shirt he wore,

I could feel nothing but a thin bone no more substantial than that of a cat.

As we sat and reminisced about old times for a while, his thoughts soon turned to the more immediate past and the foreseeable future, which to a man just turned ninety-five must, actuarially at least, be fairly short in range. In one quick observation, he put in focus much of what his long life had witnessed. "Dallas has changed immensely," he said, "and that is a wonderful thing. People have come here by the hundreds of thousands since I was born, and they have each brought something new. Without change, there is no challenge," he mused, "and without challenge there is only the status quo but no progress."

Not many old folks embrace change as wholeheartedly as did this now frail old man, looking at the skyline of his city now emblazoned by the gold of the setting sun. He had accepted challenges and created change throughout his long life, and the end result of all that was the glittering retailing empire that still proudly bore his family name on that April evening.

His legacy endures. Although change and challenge have continued to mold and indeed embellish the mystique that is Neiman Marcus today, the tangible evidence of his guiding hand is still to be seen throughout the stores. The ambiance, the almost palpable feeling of well-being that is inexplicably the aura of every visit is still in place. Those who have held the reins of stewardship of this vast empire since him have done their job well. Time and technology have changed many things at Neiman Marcus during its century-long pursuit of and possession of excellence. The indelible desire to keep the founding principles of the business in place, however, is true to the spirit of the bearded Renaissance Man who sat beside me that night in Dallas. He had diminished in size, to be sure, but he remained a giant in stature as he always will.

When someone has lived for almost a century, it somehow seems possible that he will, by extension, live forever. Stanley Marcus had become, over the years, literally synonymous with Neiman Marcus and to a large extent with Dallas itself. It only seemed reasonable to many then that he might be immortal in some miraculous way and thus destined to be with us always.

When the phone call came telling me so starkly otherwise on January 22, 2002, my initial reaction was not sorrow but one of total disbelief. While recognizing that such denial of inevitability is by no means uncommon, I still found it nearly impossible to accept.

I cannot say that I was truly a close friend of the man although we had shared times both good and not so good over a span of years exceeding thirty-five. We had long since outlived the boss/employee stigma to become, as he smilingly termed it, "colleagues." That was a good way to put it, even though he was, colleague or otherwise, for some curious reason never far from my thoughts in the twenty-five years after I retired from the store.

The city of Dallas, every bit as much his legacy as is the store, was plunged into mourning upon the news of his death. The front page of the *Dallas Morning News*, his frequent adversary in battles long since forgiven, carried almost no other story save that of his passing.

Television screens were filled with his image, shots of the Christmas Books he had created, along with their famous His and Her gifts, footage of international celebrities marveling at his magical Fortnights, and the telling and re-telling the story of the now world-famous store that had been born in Dallas, just as he had been two years before it.

The announcement of the plans for his memorial service was awaited by the thousands who wanted to say goodbye. Even though he had in 1964 specifically requested that there be no ceremony of any kind to mark his passing, with the additional admonition from a true merchant not to close the store for even a moment, plans to the contrary were soon in place.

On January 28, the day of the service at the Myerson Symphony

Hall, thousands of mourners, or perhaps more accurately celebrants of his life, stood in long queues waiting for the doors to open. Despite his innate merchant-like wishes, the downtown store was closed for the day and employees, retired and active alike, crowded into the hall to claim a seat for the service.

There were not seats enough, but a usually strict adherence to fire department crowd size was waived for just this once. Members of his immediate family rose to speak endearingly of him, while a massive photograph of he who was once "the most natural boy" of Forest Avenue High School loomed over their heads, his eyes a'twinkle.

The entire Dallas Symphony assembled to pay homage to one of their greatest benefactors, and his friend New York entertainer Bobby Short, sang and played some of the tunes that he knew Stanley would have asked him to perform.

Almost thirty-five hundred people sat in the darkened hall for nearly an hour, touched and sometimes amused by the words of the speakers. The music was not soulful nor funereal, but instead soaring, reflective of the man for whom they had gathered to bid farewell, a man whose life in some way had touched their own for so many years.

When it was all over, old friends who had spotted each other in the massive throng somehow found one another to hug and to reassure themselves that life would still go on, even without him around to make certain it went on in style.

He had lived a good and stylish long life of his own and all those who remember and revere him to this day have finally come to accept the undeniable fact that he is truly gone. There is also the knowledge that who Stanley Marcus was and what he accomplished in his ninety-six years on this earth has become legend. That legend, and the shining legacy of America's Merchant Prince, will live on forever in the magical name, Neiman Marcus.

The Fortnights

Year	Country	Year	Country
1957	France	1972	France
1958	Great Britain	1973	Great Britain
1959	South America	1974	Japan
1960	Italy	1975	Italy
1961	United States	1976	Ireland
1962	Asian Nations	1977	France
1963	Switzerland	1978	Brazil
1964	Denmark	1979	Great Britain
1965	Austria	1980	Spain
1966	France	1981	Asian Nations
1967	Great Britain	1982	Mediterranean Nations
1968	Italy	1983	Germany
1969	Asian Nations	1984	Great Britain
1970	Ruritania	1985	France
1971	"Fete des Fleurs"	1986	Australia

The Christmas Books

Year	His and Her Gifts/ Fantasy Gifts	Year	His and Her Gifts/ Fantasy Gifts
1960	Beechcraft Airplanes	1991	LTV Hummers
1961	Ermine Bathrobes	1992	Vintage Motorcycles
1962	Chinese Junks	1993	Flarecraft
1963	Submarines	1994	Observation Bubble
1964	Balloons	1995	Name the Plane
1965	Parasails	1996	Airstream Trailers
1966	Bathtubs	1997	Windjets
1967	Camels	1998	Cracker Jack Prizes
1968	Jaguars	1999	Environmental Gifts
1969	Vasarely Art	2000	Rokkaku Kites
1970	Ford Thunderbirds	2001	NYC Fantasy Weekend
1971	Mummy Cases	2002	Action Figures
1972	Mannequins	2003	Life-Size Robots
1973	Greek Kraters	2004	Bowling Center
1974	Hovercraft	2005	Photo Booth
1975	Safaris	2006	Commuter Vehicles
1976	Buffalo Calves	2007	Portrait in Chocolate
1977	Windmills	2008	Life-Size Lego Sculptures
1978	Safe Deposit Boxes	2009	Customized Cupcake Car
1979	Dirigibles	2010	MetroShip Houseboat
1980	Ostriches	2011	"Dream Folly" Yurt
1981	Robots	2012	"Poetic Wish" Watches
1982	Lasertours	2013	Falconry Set
1983	Shar-Pei Puppies	2014	Vilebrequin Quadskis
1984	Wooden Steer/Desk	2015	"World View Exploration" Experience
1985	Diamonds		
1986	Spangled Cats	2016	Cobalt Valkyrie-X Private Plane in Rose Gold
1987	Day at the Circus		
1988	Cloud Hopper	2017	Rolls Royce Limited Edition Dawn Coupes
1989	Quest for the West		
1990	Portraits		

The Neiman Marcus Award
for Distinguished Service
in the Field of Fashion

Recipients

1938

Germaine Monteil
Nettie Rosenstein
Dorothy Liebes
Louise B. Gallagher
Dan Palter
George Miller
Mr. John
Richard Koret

1939

Hattie Carnegie
Clare Potter
Elizabeth Arden
John Cavanagh
Janet May

1940

Elsa Schiaparelli
Sylvan Stroock
Edna Woolman Chase
Lilly Dache

1941

Eleanor LeMaire
Carmel Snow
Anthony Blotta
Omar Kiam
Madame Tobe
Max Meyer

1942

Voris
Betsy Talbot Blackwell
Norman Norell

1943

Adrian

1944

Countess Mara
Brooke Cadwallader
Ben King
Jo Copeland

1945

Vera Marghab
Louis A. Weinberg
Emily Wilkens
Tiny Leser
Mrs. Thea Tewi
Dr. Francis Taylor
Maurice Rentner

1946

Mrs. Howard Hawks
Mr. William Phelps
Adele Simpson
John Gates
Mr. William H. Joyce
Mrs. Faei Joyce

1947

Irene
Christian Dior
Salvatore Ferragamo
Norman Hartnell

1948

Madame Henri Bonnet
Gen. Julius Ochs Adler
Claire McCardell
Antonio Castillo

1949

Alice Cadolle
Mrs. Robert Geissman
David Evins
Jacques Fath

1950

Gloria Swanson
Pauline Trigere
Fleur Meyer
Bonnie Cashin

1951

Michelle Murphy
Mrs. Ernestine Cannon
Jane Derby
Ben Zuckerman
Jacques Lesur

1952

Anne Fogarty
Roger Fare
Vincent Monte Sano
Dolores Del Rio

1953

Marchesa Olga di Gresy
Charles James
Ben Sommers
Gilbert and Helen Orcel

1954

James Galanos
Emilio Pucci
Mr. & Mrs. Herbert Levine

1955

Mrs. Florence Eiseman
Pierre Balmain
Sally Kirkland
Henry Dreyfuss
Vera Maxwell
HSH The Princess Grace of Monaco

1956

Cecil Beaton
Guillana Camerino
Marie-Louis Bousquet

1957

Coco Chanel

1958

Yves Saint Laurent
Jens Quistgaard
Helen Lee

1959

Rosalind Russell
Arnold Scaasi
Piero Fornasetti
Emme

1960

Dinah Shore
Sylvia Pedlar
Edward Burke Smith
Roger Jean-Pierre
Claude Staron

1961

Greer Garson
Harry Rolnick
Count Fernando Sarmi
Roger Vivier
Sydney Wragge

1962

Estee Lauder
James Laver
Sports Illustrated
Jules-Francois Crahey

1963

Georges Braque
Maurice Tumarkin
Margaret Clarke Miller
Bud Kilpatrick

1964-65

Geoffrey Beene
Mr. and Mrs. Arthur Edelman

1966

Madame Helen Lazareff
Jacques Tiffean

Tzaims Luksus

Lucie Ann
Mary Brosnan

1967

Fiamma Ferragama
Valentino
Lydia de Roma
Giancarlo Venturini
The Artisans of Florence

1968

Roland Jourdan
Kenneth Jay Lane
Oscar de la Renta
Armi Ratia

1969

Bernard Kayman
Anne Klein
Bill Blass
Emanuel Ungaro
Gloria Vanderbilt Cooper

1973

Levi Strauss & Company
Hanae Mori
Mr. and Mrs. Ottavio Missoni
Jean Muir
Ralph Lauren

1979

Giorgio Armani
Richard Avedon
Artisans of Baccarat
Perry Ellis
Mary McFadden

1980

Karl Lagerfield
Judith Leiber

1984

Issey Miyake
Jack Lenor Larsen

1995

Stanley Marcus
Miuccia Prada
Jean-Paul Goude
Grace Mirabella

The Stores

Location	Year Opened	Location	Year Opened
Dallas (Original)	1907	Scottsdale, AZ	1991
Dallas (Downtown)	1914	Troy, MI	1993
Dallas (NorthPark)	1965	Short Hills, NJ	1995
Houston (Galleria)	1969	King of Prussia, PA	1996
Bal Harbour, FL	1971	Paramus, NJ	1997
Atlanta	1972	Honolulu	1999
St. Louis, MO	1974	Palm Beach	2001
Northbrook, IL	1976	Plano, TX	2002
Ft. Worth	1977	Tampa Bay	2003
Washington, D.C.	1977	Coral Gables	2003
Newport Beach, CA	1978	Orlando, FL	2003
Beverly Hills	1979	San Antonio	2006
Dallas (Prestonwood)	1979	Boca Raton, FL	2006
White Plains, NY	1980	Charlotte, NC	2007
Las Vegas	1981	Austin	2007
Oakbrook, IL	1981	Georgetown–Cusp	
San Diego	1981	(Washington, D.C.)	2007
Ft. Lauderdale	1982	Water Tower Place–Cusp	
San Francisco	1982	(Chicago)	2007
Houston (Town & Country)	1983	Natick, MA	2008
Chicago (Michigan Ave.)	1983	Topanga (Canoga Park, CA)	2008
Boston	1984	Bellevue, WA	2009
Palo Alto, CA	1985	Walnut Creek, CA	2012
McLean, VA	1989	Chestnut Hill, MA–Cusp	2012
Denver	1990	Roosevelt Field	
Minneapolis	1991	(Garden City, NY)	2016

Stanley Marcus
Biographical Information

Born: April 20, 1905

Died: January 22, 2002

Parents: Herbert Marcus, Sr. and Minnie Lichtenstein Marcus

Married: Mary Cantrell, November 7, 1932 (Deceased, March 10, 1978)
           Linda Cumber Robinson, March 30, 1979

Children: Mrs. Frederick M. (Jerrie) Smith
           Mrs. Henry (Wendy) Raymont
           Richard Cantrell Marcus

Education: Harvard University, B.A., 1925
           Harvard Business School, 1926

Neiman Marcus Affiliation:
    Secretary, Treasurer and Director, 1926
    Merchandise Manager of the Sport Shop, 1928
    Merchandise Manager of all Apparel Divisions, 1928
    Executive Vice President, 1929
    President, 1935-1950
    Chairman of the Board, Chief Executive Officer, 1950-1972
    Chairman of the Executive Committee, 1973-1975
    Chairman Emeritus, 1975-2002

Business and Civic Offices and Affiliations:
    Director, Republic of Texas Corporation, Dallas, Texas
    Director, New York Life Insurance Company, New York
    Director, Jack Lenor Larsen, Inc., New York
    Honorary Director, Carter Hawley Hale Stores, Inc., Los Angeles
    Consultant, Carter Hawley Hale Stores, Inc., Los Angeles
    Stanley Marcus Consultancy Service
    Director, Dallas Symphony Society

Trustee, Southern Methodist University
Member, Board of Publications, Southern Methodist University
Director, North Texas Commission
Member of Visiting Committee of University Resources, Harvard
Honorary Trustee, Committee for Economic Development
Founding Member, Business Committee for the Arts
Governing Board, Common Cause
Harvard College, Committee on University Resources
Executive Committee, National Council for Arts and Education
Liaison Committee, USS *Texas*
Member, Executive Committee, Center for the Book, Library of
    Congress Chairman, International Marketing Committee of North
    Texas Commission
Advisory Director, Fort Worth Art Association
Chairman, Library Advancement Program, Southern Methodist University
Director, Dallas Citizens Council
Research Fellow, Southwestern Legal Foundation
Member, Board of Directors for the Dallas World Trade Center
Chairman, Gulf District Committee of Selection for Rhodes Scholarship
Goals for Dallas Advisory Council
Director, Dallas Council on World Affairs
Director, Southwest Center for Advanced Studies
Member, Texas Fine Arts Commission
Director, The American Arbitration Association
Member, Board of Overseers, Harvard University
Chairman, Board of Trustees, American Retail Federation
President, Dallas Symphony Society
President, Dallas Art Association
Member, Performing Arts Panel, Rockefeller Brothers Fund
Member, Wage and Hour Millinery Committee
Co-Chairman, Dallas, Interracial Council for Business Opportunity
Trustee, Eisenhower Exchange Fellowships
Chief, Clothing Section of Textile, Clothing and Leather Branch of War
    Production Board
Regional Vice President, National Jewish Hospital, Denver, Colorado
Chairman, Aviation Committee, Dallas Chamber of Commerce
Trustee, Texas Research Foundation
Trustee, United States Council of the International Chamber of Commerce
Harvard College, Committee to Visit the Loeb Drama Center
Member, Marshall Scholarship Regional Committee
Board of Governors, U.S.O., Inc.

Director, Slick Airways
Director, Dallas Transit Company
Management Member, Dallas Area Labor-Management Committee for
    Defense Manpower of the U.S. Department of Labor
Counselor, Harvard Fund Council
Governor, Harvard-Yale-Princeton Class of 1925 Association
Member, National Council, National Planning Association
Member, National Committee for the U.S. Art in the U.N. Building
Member, Commission on Race and Housing
Director, Council on Foreign Relations, Inc.
Member, Committee in Charge of Plans, National Community Theater
    Month
President, Dallas Citizens Council
Chairman, Board of Directors, Dallas Council on World Affairs
Chairman of the Executive Committee and Trustee, Hockaday School
    for Girls
Director, Better Business Bureau of Dallas
Member, Board of Directors, Texas Law Enforcement Foundation
Member, National Committee for International Development
Executive Committee, National Citizens Committee for Community
    Relations
Director, A.C.T.I.O.N. (American Council to Improve our
    Neighborhoods)
Executive Committee, American Retail Federation
Member, Blair House Fine Arts Committee
Member, Committee for the National Arts Trust Fund
Member, Advisory Committee for the HemisFair
State Campaign Chairman, Easter Seal Society Drive for Crippled
    Children and Adults of Texas
Member, Advisory Council of Fine Arts Foundation, University of
    Texas, Austin
Social Organization Memberships:
    Harvard Clubs of Dallas and New York
    Grolier Club of New York
    The Club of Odd Volumes, Boston
Honors:
    "The Tobe Award" for Distinguished Service to American Retailing,
        1945
    "Distinguished Salesman of the Year" for 149, Dallas Sales Executive
        Club

"Kudos College" Award of the Dallas Advertising League, 1949

Chevalier of French Legion of Honor, 1949

Honorary Member, Dallas Chapter, American Institute of Architects, 1955

Star of Italian Solidarity" (Italian Government), 1956

Commandeur of Economic Merit (French Government), 1957

"Headliner of the Year," Dallas Press Club, 1958

Grand Camerier, Confrerie des Chevaliers du Tastevin, 1958

Officier of French Legion of Honor, 1958

New York Fashion Designers Annual Award, 1958

Honorary Order of the British Empire, 1959

Chevalier of the Order of Leopold II (Bestowed by His Majesty King Baudouin of Belgium), 1959

Gold Medal, National Retail Merchants Association, 1961

Commendetore al Merito della Republica Italiana (Italian Government), 1961

Ambassador Award for Achievement, London, 1962

Royal Order of Dannebrog (Danish Government), 1965

The Great Cross of Austria, 1965

Honorary Doctor of Humanities Degree, Southern Methodist University, 1965

First Milwaukee Medallion, Metropolitan Milwaukee Association of Commerce, 1968

Honorary Fellow of the American Institute of Architects, 1972

Commander of the French National Order of Merit, 1975

Grand Ufficiale dell' Ordine della Stella della Solidarieta Italiana, Al Signor Stanley Marcus, October 15, 1975

Membership, Texas Institute of Letters, April 1976

"Adam" Award, American Image Award in Category of Business and Commerce Leaders, presented by Men's Fashion Association of America, 1976

The Stanley Marcus Library of Fashion, Southern Methodist University, established December 13, 1976, by Neiman-Marcus Company honoring his fifty years in retailing

Recipient of 1978 B.A.M.B.I. "Flying Colors" Award (Buyers/Apparel Mart—Braniff International) for Outstanding Service to the Apparel Industry, October, 1978

Honorary Member, National Association of Display Industries Visual Merchandising Hall of Fame (NADI), June 3, 1979

The Neiman Marcus Award for Distinguished Service in the Field of Fashion, 1995

Index

CPSIA information can be obtained
at www.ICGtesting.com
Printed in the USA
LVHW05s0015010918
588566LV00014B/35/P